The Future of Educational Entrepreneurship

The Future
of Educational
Entrepreneurship

Possibilities for School Reform

FREDERICK M. HESS
Editor

HARVARD EDUCATION PRESS
CAMBRIDGE, MASSACHUSETTS

Library of Congress Control Number 2008928879

Paperback ISBN 978-1-891792-98-4
Library Edition ISBN 978-1-891792-99-1

Published by Harvard Education Press,
an imprint of the Harvard Education Publishing Group

Harvard Education Press
8 Story Street
Cambridge, MA 02138

Cover Design: Alyssa Morris

The typefaces used in this book are ITC Stone Serif for text and ITC Stone Sans for display.

Contents

Acknowledgments

This book had its genesis in fall 2005 at an American Enterprise Institute research conference that I hosted on educational entrepreneurship. That gathering produced *Educational Entrepreneurship: Realities, Challenges, Possibilities* (Harvard Education Press, 2006), a volume that sought to provide an introduction to relevant ideas and debates that had received little sustained attention. In particular, that earlier effort explored how the notion of entrepreneurship applies to education, just who these entrepreneurs are, how entrepreneurship does (or does not) fit within the culture of K–12 schooling, the case for and against for-profit providers, and how public policy affects entrepreneurial activity. Those analyses, and the subsequent discussion, suggested a dearth of understanding among policymakers, practitioners, philanthropists, and scholars about what it would take to foster socially desirable entrepreneurship at any substantial scale. For me, the point that emerged most clearly from that earlier effort was how rarely we discuss the thorny questions of what it takes for entrepreneurial activity or markets to thrive and deliver beneficial results when it comes to schooling.

This book represents a first stab at that charge; contributors here consider what it would take to nurture a more dynamic and quality-conscious sector. To date, only a handful of organizations, most prominently the NewSchools Venture Fund and Education/Evolving, have addressed these questions at any length. Apart from them, even most advocates of school choice and social entrepreneurship have tended to assume that, if demand exists, the supply of quality providers will take care of itself. Unfortunately, experience both inside and outside education suggests the frailty of that assumption. Markets characterized by insufficient quality-control mechanisms, a lack of transparency, a scarcity of human or investment capital, and harmful regulatory and institutional barriers are more likely to produce mediocrity than effective solutions. That grim context appears to be very much the case in K–12 schooling.

The contributors here examine what we might do to address that state of affairs. They ask how reformers might promote the emergence of more effective schools and service providers today and in years to come. In short, this is a book about the political economy of educational entrepreneurship. Penned by an elite group of cutting-edge scholars, analysts, and entrepreneurs, the following chapters explore what needs to be done to boost human capital, attract investment capital and funding, ensure quality control, improve research and development, and remove the barriers that hinder new providers if entrepreneurship is to make a real difference in the education of America's children.

I am grateful to all of the people who contributed to or helped with the compilation of this book. Specifically, I thank the contributing authors who wrote the conference papers that were presented at the American Enterprise Institute in October 2007. I would also like to express my gratitude to the discussants who participated in that conference and gave invaluable feedback on those early drafts. That impressive collection of public officials, educators, and entrepreneurs included: Morgan Brown, Assistant Deputy Secretary of Education for Innovation and Improvement at the U.S. Department of Education; David Harris, president and CEO of The Mind Trust; Wendy Kopp, CEO and founder of Teach For America; Michelle Rhee, chancellor of the District of Columbia Public Schools; Sharon Robinson, leader of the American Association of Colleges for Teacher Education; Larry Rosenstock, principal and CEO of High Tech High; Elliot Sainer, cofounder and former CEO of the Aspen Education Group; Jon Schnur, CEO and cofounder of New Leaders for New Schools; Don Shalvey, CEO and cofounder of Aspire Public Schools; Jim Shelton, a program director in the Education Initiative at the Bill & Melinda Gates Foundation; Laura Smith, director of the Market Maker for the New York City Department of Education; Nelson Smith, president of the National Alliance for Public Charter Schools; and Chris Whittle, chairman and founder of Edison Schools.

At the American Enterprise Institute, Thomas Gift did a stellar job of assembling, revising, and editing the papers for publication and assisting with the accompanying research and analysis. Morgan Goatley, Rosemary Kendrick, and Juliet Squire also played invaluable roles in producing and editing the volume.

As always, I am indebted to the American Enterprise Institute, and especially to Christopher DeMuth who, as president of AEI, has always given his steadfast support and engendered an atmosphere of collegiality and extraordinary intellectual freedom. The funding for this project was generously provided by the Ewing Marion Kauffman Foundation, and for it, I am most indebted. Finally, I would like to thank my publisher, Doug Clayton, and production manager, Dody Riggs, for the terrific work they did in translating the manuscript into the volume that you now hold in your hands.

The Supply Side of School Reform

Frederick M. Hess

The one constant in K–12 education is dissatisfaction with the status quo. In 2007, the National Assessment of Educational Progress scored 38 percent of America's fourth graders and 31 percent of eighth graders proficient in math and just 31 percent of fourth graders and 29 percent of eighth graders proficient in reading.[1] In a 2006 comparison of fifty-seven industrialized countries, the Program for International Student Assessment ranked the United States twenty-ninth in science and thirty-fifth in math.[2] Nearly a third of the nation's students do not complete high school, and many urban school systems fail to graduate even half of their students.[3]

Representative George Miller, Democratic chair of the U.S. House Education and Labor Committee, declares, "We aren't doing enough to prepare all students—especially poor and minority students—for 21st-century workplaces. The question is what to do about it."[4] U.S. Secretary of Education Margaret Spellings says, "Even at the elite level we are losing ground. But our biggest problem remains at the most basic level: We're getting only half of our minority kids out of high school on time."[5] Michelle Rhee, chancellor of the District of Columbia Public Schools, laments, "For far too long, the schools in our nation's capital have been failing our kids . . . [while] crippled by a growing and non-responsive bureaucracy. Calls and e-mails are ignored. Employees are not paid. Parents take time off of work to fill out forms only to have them lost."[6] Microsoft chairman Bill Gates warns, "When I compare our high schools to what I see when I'm traveling abroad, I am terrified for our workforce of tomorrow."[7]

1

Frustration prevails despite decades of well-intentioned reforms. Once-popular proposals to reform schools and systems by adopting site-based management or reconfiguring the school day have fallen from favor, only to be replaced by a new rash of remedies. When they have worked, systemic reform and accountability measures have yielded only incremental progress. The question is whether we can find a more promising path to follow. This volume is about answering that charge by cultivating a supply of new school and service providers capable of yielding dramatically better teaching and learning.

The challenge is particularly salient given technological advances and workforce changes that create opportunities to pioneer imaginative, more effective solutions. The emergence of near-universal computing and wireless communications, a large college-educated workforce marked by professional mobility, and information technology and accountability tools that make feasible niche services and multisite operations have radically altered the landscape. Yet schools and school districts have remained largely impervious to these advancements, breeding frustration.

Against this backdrop, the promising work of bold ventures like the KIPP Academies, Green Dot Public Schools, High Tech High, Uncommon Schools, Citizen Schools, the National Heritage Academies, Teach For America, New Leaders for New Schools, and The New Teacher Project have drawn notice. Yet even these marquee efforts have been hindered by difficulties raising funds, finding talent, and securing operational support, as well as unreliable quality control and an inadequate commitment to research and development.

Moreover, such honor rolls can be deceptive. Because observers tend to focus on the handfuls of thriving ventures in one or two dozen districts where they have an active presence, they give the impression that education already boasts a robust supply of dynamic organizations tackling stubborn problems. The reality is that the scope of existing activity pales beside the larger American education enterprise. The 57 schools operated by KIPP, the 4,800 teachers recruited each year by The New Teacher Project, and the 150 principals produced annually by New Leaders for New Schools are dwarfed by a national education system that encompasses 15,000 school districts, 90,000 schools, 50 million students, three million teachers, and more than $500 billion in annual spending. In any given year, it is a safe bet that competitors in industries like breakfast cereal and television programming are investing more heavily in new ideas and product development than the entire K–12 sector.

THE SUPPLY SIDE: THE MISSING DIMENSION OF REFORM

This volume examines what it will take to help entrepreneurial problem-solvers fulfill their potential, whether in nontraditional (or new sector) ventures like KIPP or The New Teacher Project, in districts like New York City, New Orleans, and Indianapolis, or in the nexus between traditional systems and new sector ventures. What obstacles hamper the emergence and growth of successful new providers? What might be done about these barriers while ensuring that new ventures are held accountable for performance? What promising initiatives or proposals deserve consideration?

Broadly speaking, would-be reformers of K–12 education can be sorted into two general camps. One camp, the capacity builders, typically emphasizes improving schools and systems with tools such as professional development, mentoring, more rigorous curricula, and formative assessment. Other capacity builders take a slightly different tack, emphasizing the role of formal accountability systems, standards, and incentives in driving systemic change and the adoption of best practices. A second camp emphasizes choice-based reform, especially charter schooling and school vouchers, as necessary to bypass dysfunctional systems or as the only means for bringing sufficient pressure to force meaningful reform of existing districts. (Of course, this broad characterization obscures much nuance and can be misleading if carried too far or interpreted too literally—but it will prove useful for our purposes here.)

Cultivating new, dynamic providers has received scant attention from policymakers, scholars, and foundations focused on capacity building. For those concentrating on systemic reform, accountability, or professional development, nontraditional ventures operating at the edges of the system can be casually dismissed as peripheral or even distracting. Leading voices in teacher education, for instance, have long argued that loosened licensure restrictions and alternative certification programs represent threats to teacher professionalism and a diversion from the most important tasks of raising teacher pay, promoting professional development, and strengthening preparation in schools of education.

The most passionate and visible advocates of school choice have generally focused on the ends of social justice and opportunity while overlooking the complexities of deregulation and market liberalization. In practice, dynamic markets depend on institutions, regulation, social and financial capital, the availability of talent, research and development, and the utilization of technology. Insufficient regard for these considerations invites disappointment and may help explain the uneven results of charter schooling and the failure of existing voucher programs to stimulate noticeable growth in the supply of high-quality schools.[8] The tendency to subsume educational innovation under the rubric of school choice has further obscured that many new ventures offer products and services primarily to traditional school districts. For instance, The New Teacher Project and Wireless Generation devote most of their time and effort to providing personnel, tools, and services intended to make a difference for conventional schools.

In practice, each camp has stumbled because of a failure to engage seriously with the role that the supply side can and must play in delivering on the promise of best practices or choice-based reform.

THE LIMITS OF CONVENTIONAL REFORM

Efforts to improve familiar schools and systems with best practices, accountability, curricular alignment, and professional development are frequently termed "capacity building" (that is, they seek to improve the capacity of schools to educate effectively). Richard Elmore, professor at the Harvard Graduate School of Education and author of *School Reform from the Inside Out,* defines capacity building by its focus on enhancing the resources, knowledge, and skills that teachers and schools bring to the classroom.[9] Capacity building presumes that best practices are either already known or will present themselves in due course, with the major challenge being to identify and then systematically implement these through instructional leadership, coaching, professional development, assessment, and curricula and pedagogy.[10]

Some capacity builders concede the need to rethink district practices, infrastructure, or leadership, but the examples they highlight and the strategies they propose take for granted that schools and districts are capable of making the necessary adjustments with the right guidance and resources. For instance, while those who champion test-based accountability and merit pay believe it is necessary to alter incentive structures, many go on to accept implicitly the supposition that if these structures were changed, today's teachers, schools, and school systems will then have (or can themselves readily create) the tools to deliver dramatically improved results.

Such a perspective tends to ignore, or even dismiss, the difficulty of changing troubled organizations from the inside and the resulting importance of entrepreneurial activity. In an elegant admonition that can too easily be interpreted as implying that just about any school system can execute as effectively as a few best-practice districts, Elmore cautions against excessive faith in the "magic of markets" and instead proposes that schools "focus leadership on instructional improvement, and define everything else as instrumental to it."[11] This dismissal of supply-side approaches reflects a questionable premise—namely, that robust improvement will occur without remaking the personnel, leadership, tools, or design of the schools or districts in question. One consequence is that a handful of districts which have enjoyed seeming success with this approach are held up as models that other school systems can emulate.

When other school systems pursue reform but do not achieve similar results, the failures are inevitably chalked up to leadership style—this superintendent was "too confrontational" and that one was "too slow"—rather than as a signal that even the handful of recognized successes are cases where leadership has successfully threaded the needle due to a combination of skill, luck, and context. In fact, most capacity-building efforts are plagued by inefficient human resource systems, a dearth of effective school leaders, and the need for more effective information technology and assessment tools. Considerations like professional development and curricular quality are critical—these *are* schools after all—but their impact depends on organizational muscle tone that is sorely lacking in most cases. The same problems have hampered accountability programs and given lie to early hopes that holding educators accountable for results would be enough to encourage (and enable) them to devise ways to deliver dramatically superior results.

Experience offers scant reason to believe that traditional districts, colleges of education, textbook publishers, and familiar providers are likely to generate breakthrough improvements. It is hard to think of any sector in which such gains have been the product of widespread improvement in quality across hundreds or thousands of distinct organizations. More typically, radical and disruptive improvement is the result of new entrants devising a product or formula that works for them and managing to devise an organization and culture that provides for fidelity to the innovation at increasing scale.

School districts struggle with asphyxiating bureaucracy, a culture of timidity and risk-aversion, restrictive regulations and collective bargaining agreements, and anachronistic technology and human resource setups. It would be surprising if this system allowed mavericks much leeway or yielded many leaders equipped to drive substantial and sustained change. Even when conditions permit them to do so, district officials and school-level personnel have shown little inclination to aggressively employ new accountability systems, exploit flexible provisions in collective bargaining agreements, or take advantage of opportunities to have teacher pay reflect quality.[12]

One complicating factor in all this has been the "distraction of decentralization," in which the nation's wealth of schools and districts is imagined to yield a culture of dynamic problem-solving and meaningful innovation. There is, in fact, a lot of innovation and change—but it is shallow, prone to faddism, and constrained by rules and norms that prevent it from upending incentives, arrangements, delivery models, or staffing in any fundamental way. It is not hard to find schools and districts leaping from one curriculum or instructional approach to another; but it is enormously difficult to find those that have retooled their operations or hiring processes in far-reaching ways. Not even a handful of the nation's 15,000 school districts, for instance, have experimented with annually culling their weakest teachers or focusing on instruction by farming out operations to subcontractors. In contrast, effective organizations outside K–12 education remain focused and disciplined in their core tasks—avoiding faddism and change for their own sake—even as they adapt to changing environments and reengineer their operations and structures.

Given disappointing experiences and the inability of even the champions of accountability to claim more than grudging progress in the No Child Left Behind era, one increasingly popular stratagem has been that of pledging to turn around troubled schools. The hope is that the obstacles impeding radical improvement can be identified, addressed, and surmounted in a systematic fashion. It is an appealing notion and one that has a valuable, if inevitably limited, role to play.

Unfortunately, the hope that we can systematically turn around all troubled schools—or even a majority of them—is at odds with much of what we know from turnaround efforts outside education. Despite the passion, money, and expertise thrown into organizational change, most efforts fail to deliver. Consulting firms Arthur D. Little and McKinsey & Co. have studied moves to implement Total Quality Management at hundreds of companies and have determined that about two-thirds fall short of their hoped-for results.[13] Leaders of the corporate reengineering movement have reported that the success rate for Fortune 1000 companies is possibly as low as 20 percent.[14] Even in the private sector, where management enjoys many more degrees of freedom and competition can lend a sense of profound urgency, turnarounds are an iffy proposition. Peter Senge, director of the Center for Organizational Learning at the MIT Sloan School of Management, has observed, "Failure to sustain significant change recurs again and again despite substantial resources committed to the change effort (many are bankrolled by top management), talented and committed people 'driving the change,' and high stakes."[15]

This highlights the role that supply-side activity has to play in supporting turnaround strategies. Turnarounds are not a one-size-fits-all proposition but require personnel, programs, and providers sufficient to address their needs. This is where new recruitment and training programs and more effective instructional tools can play a key role. Ultimately, though, the research suggests that turnaround efforts—even when undertaken by corporate leadership committed to the strategy and operating with the flexibility afforded by the private sector—are successful less than half the time. Turnaround strategies will work in some places some of the time and are an important tool in promoting radical educational improvement, but the reality is that many schools and districts will prove stubbornly resistant to such efforts.

The Difficulty of Reinventing Established Organizations

In sector after sector, solving new problems—or more effectively addressing old ones—has been the province of new entrants. There is a reason that IBM, for all its resources and muscle in the 1980s, was not able to provide access to personal computing in the way that Apple, Microsoft, and Dell would. An IBM sales force built around selling giant machines to corporations with hands-on customer service was not positioned to compete with Michael Dell selling hand-assembled personal computers through the mail. There is also a reason that Microsoft, for all its manpower and might in the 1990s, could not "become" Google or Amazon when it came to leveraging the new Internet. And there is a reason that legacy airlines like United, U.S. Airways, and Pan Am, with their gilded service, pricey jets, and top-heavy workforce, floundered while upstarts like Southwest and JetBlue adapted to the new demands of the flying public.

There is a reason that the composition of the Dow Jones Industrial Average looks so different from one generation to the next. Just thirty years ago, for instance, now-ubiquitous brands like Wal-Mart and McDonald's were still hungry young companies, dwarfed by such august titans as American Tobacco B and the Aluminum Company of America. In fact, only a single company, General Electric, has remained on the Dow since its inception in 1896. Other giants of the day—including the likes of Amalgamated Copper and American Smelting and Refining—eventually gave way, despite their success and talent, to upstart competitors better able to negotiate the new economy.

For all their resources, these organizations had to cope with the handicaps imposed by their success. Size, habit, and an established position rendered them stodgy and heavy-footed. They built their processes, metrics, and hiring and compensation systems around the familiar—the things they were good at. This made them well-suited to keep doing the same things but left them stumbling when technologies, management practices, or consumer demands changed. Meanwhile, new organizations—freed from a rigid mentality about how things "should" be done—cropped up, more easily took advantage of new opportunities, and more nimbly tackled looming challenges.

The lesson here is not new. This tendency of successful firms to become hidebound is a key component of what Harvard Business School professor Clayton Christensen has termed the "innovator's dilemma."[16] The fundamental insight is piercingly simple: established firms do well by sticking to what works and continuously providing incrementally improved versions of the same product. This focus makes them lousy at developing new products and services, reaching out to different segments of the market, or harnessing new technologies. Doing so would require executives and managers to consciously steer energy away from what is safe and profitable in order to launch experimental efforts that are likely to be unsuccessful. It is no great surprise that incentives and temperament discourage such efforts.

As famed organizational sociologist Arthur Stinchcombe explained decades ago, organizations tend to be shaped by the era in which they are launched. In more technical terms, he argued: "The organizational inventions that can be made at a particular time in history depend on the social technology available at the time. Organizations which have purposes that can be efficiently reached with the socially possible organizational forms tend to be founded during the period in which they become possible. Then, both because they can function effectively with those organizational forms, and because the forms tend to become institutionalized, the basic structure of the organization tends to remain relatively stable."[17] When opportunities, challenges, and the larger world change sufficiently, it can be difficult for muscle-bound behemoths to keep pace with nimble new entrants attuned to new circumstances, able to create new cultures and routines, and free to hire with an eye toward new circumstances. In the public sector, professional incentives, bureaucratic routine, and a civil service system shaped by seniority further complicate matters and make officials especially reluctant to rock the boat.[18]

Perversely, it is the agile and successful organizations of one era that are most likely to become the entrenched and hidebound institutions of the next. The upside of success is that it yields stability and resources; the downside is a tendency to be cautious and to hold tight to old practices and familiar routines. The longer organizations exist and the more they thrive, the more difficult it can be to step away from established best practices and adapt to changed circumstances. This is why it is so frequently new entrants that seize on improved technologies, changes in the labor market, or shifting consumer demands to devise radically new ways of providing products or services. In the public sector, the absence of new entrants can make for long periods of lethargy during which frustrated public officials struggle through elephantine bureaucracies in the face of new legislative demands, regulatory codes, political resistance, deeply etched practices, and established cultures. This state of affairs may be unavoidable in the U.S. Department of Defense or the Central Intelligence Agency, where it is hard to imagine new providers springing up to complement or displace the old. In education, however, supply-side activity offers an alluring alternative to corralling intransigent bureaucracies.

Ultimately, new entrants are eventually bedeviled by the same sorts of problems that once made them necessary. When that happens, progress depends on yet another set of new ventures. This is why no generation of educational schools or providers should ever be regarded as the ultimate solution. In education, the aim should not simply be to devise a new generation of best-practice providers that will be more effective today but to create a dynamic sector in which this self-replenishing process becomes part of the fabric of the nation's school system. The bottom line is that most districts, schools, textbook publishers, test companies, and colleges of education lack the tools, incentives, opportunities, and personnel to survey the changing educational world and reimagine themselves in a profoundly more effective fashion.

THE LIMITS OF SCHOOL CHOICE

Skeptics of internal reforms and those dubious of more aggressive tactics to turn around schools naturally look outside conventional districts for solutions. Typically, this camp argues for choice-based reforms—like school vouchers or charter schooling—that will permit families to seek out better schools, enable the emergence of more effective alternatives, and allow competition to press districts to improve. Seeing little evidence that existing schools and districts have the incentive or ability to fundamentally reinvent themselves, choice-based reformers look outside traditional institutions. As political scientists John Chubb and Terry Moe famously concluded in *Politics, Markets, and America's Schools*, "Choice is a self-contained reform with its own rationale and justification. It has the capacity all by itself to bring about the kind of transformation that, for years, reformers have been seeking to engineer in myriad other ways."[19]

Suggestions that choice can serve as a self-contained remedy, however, overlook that choice is only half of the supply-and-demand market equation. Proposals that increase parental choice may create or unleash demand but typically do not address the supply of quality options available. The implicit assumption is that creating charter school laws or voucher programs will be enough to spur the creation of new schools and programs. For instance, *Education and Capitalism* authors Herbert Walberg and Joseph Bast assert that choice schools will be free from the lack of competition, labor unions, political interference, lax standards, and centralized control that hamper existing schools and districts.[20]

Such claims are misleading. In truth, in a variety of sectors, many relatively "free" markets are still plagued by these challenges. School choice is no elixir. Most proposals to promote school choice have done little to eliminate the hindrances posed by licensure requirements or state reporting systems and have paid little attention to ensuring that choice systems are underpinned by efficient support services, effective quality control, or a stable political and regulatory environment. Ed Kirby points out in chapter 9 how often regulation, bureaucracy, teachers unions, and politics have continued to play a critical role in stifling new entrants even after the passage of charter school legislation. The expectation that the simple adoption of charter schooling or voucher plans will prompt the emergence of a raft of promising competitors is not borne out by theory or experience.

While there has been enormous effort among advocates to make the moral case for parental choice, to design saleable programs, and to demonstrate that choice can serve both students and the larger democratic community, these efforts have been marked by lax attention to the other half of the market equation—the supply side. After all, in fields like foreign policy and economics, it is taken for granted that vacuums will not naturally or automatically be filled by effective or virtuous actors. Whether dealing with nascent democracy in Iraq in the 2000s or nascent markets in Eastern Europe in the 1990s, reformers have struggled to establish the institutions, norms, and practices that foster the emergence of healthy markets. Proponents of choice programs have too rarely paid attention to such considerations or the infrastructure that will encourage the emergence of effective providers.

Dynamic Sectors Require More Than "Choice"

If capacity-builders place too much faith in sluggish institutions, choice-based reformers place too much faith in the presumption that simply permitting families to choose their child's school will foster a dynamic sector. The more optimistic accounts overlook that the entrepreneurial education sector lacks the wealth of venture capital, human capital, internal quality control, and accompanying networks and infrastructure that characterize dynamic sectors across the economy. As Matt Candler makes clear in chapter 6, those counting on new schools to consistently deliver quality, on middling schools to improve on their own, or on lousy schools to shut down have found the process much less automatic than they might have hoped.

This point should not be overstated. Just as some capacity-building efforts are effective, just as accountability can help, and just as some turnaround attempts are successful, so has choice opened the doors for a number of promising providers. Yet it is also true that, after more than fifteen years, charter schools enroll fewer than two percent of the nation's students—and only a fraction of those attend schools that are clearly outstanding.

Nearly two decades of choice have delivered only limited evidence of quality providers. Moreover, most of those exemplary organizations are consciously and aggressively "old school" in their orientation. Schools like KIPP, Achievement First, YesPrep, and SEED are driven more by their dazzling success at setting expectations, establishing cultures, and attracting bright and hard-working teachers than by any particular innovations of educational delivery. A supply-side perspective suggests that this may be because even the most entrepreneurial thinkers have been limited by statutes, inadequate resources and personnel, and a lack of research and development—and that helping new ventures build on the shoulders of such pioneers requires attention to these precise considerations.

The challenge in education is not simply to loosen regulation on an established competitive marketplace but to summon new competitors to build from the ground up. We have learned that much can be done in such circumstances to stack the odds either for or against success. In *The Competition Solution,* a bracing defense of deregulation, former Clinton administration official Paul London writes, "The Founders had recognized that setting rules for markets was a function of government."[21] Market economies and entrepreneurial environments stem from multiple forces: law and regulation, talent, social networks, and investment capital. In this sense, markets are the product of human design, and their efficacy is dependent on both the formal and informal foundations upon which they rest.

Ultimately, just as school improvement does not simply or miraculously happen without attention to instruction, curriculum, and school leadership, so a rule-laden, risk-averse sector dominated by bureaucracy, industrial-style collective bargaining agreements, colleges of education, and public funding will not casually become a fount of dynamic problem-solving. Removing the barriers and burdens that prevent such efforts is a critical start—but it is only a start. This volume is ultimately about the steps that come next.

THE POLITICAL ECONOMY OF THE SUPPLY SIDE

Some environments are more hospitable to a robust supply side than others, and in K–12 schooling, it is in our power to terraform accordingly. Deregulation is not as simple as educational debates about choice suggest. Creating a vibrant market is not simply a matter of eliminating regulations; markets depend critically on transparency, predictability, human talent, financial resources, and opportunities for entrants to succeed.

Inattention to these topics in the case of choice-based school reform is puzzling because leading students and advocates of "the market" are the first to make this point.[22] As Nobel Laureate Milton Friedman observed, "In some ways, referring to 'the market' puts the discussion on the wrong basis. The market is not a cow to be milked; neither is it a sure-fire cure for all ills." Creating a "market economy" is not about producing a vacuum that all manner of things might fill but about crafting a certain set of arrangements. Friedman elaborated, "The market is a mechanism that may be mobilized for any number of purposes. Depending on the way it is used, the market may contribute to social and economic development or it may inhibit such development."[23] Deregulation is no panacea; experience has shown that, depending on how it is handled, deregulation and the creation of markets can deliver happy results as well as disheartening ones.

Efforts to spur vibrant supply-side activity in formerly state-run economies are instructive. China's heralded, gradual introduction of a market economy within a single-party, communist state illustrates how a vibrant supply side can emerge even under seemingly prohibitive conditions—and offers a useful example for efforts to nurture entrepreneurial activity in America's state dominated, heavily regulated K–12 sector. Since the 1980s, China's totalitarian regime has enjoyed enormous success in liberalizing its economy, nurturing entrepreneurial activity, and fostering growth even as it has maintained repressive political and social policies. It has done so in large part because of its focus on cultivating human capital, encouraging foreign investment, fostering a more responsive banking system, and boosting investment in technology and research and development.[24]

In their book *The Emergence of China*, economist Robert Devlin and his colleagues report that the government also streamlined the state workforce, shuttered tens of thousands of inefficient state-owned enterprises, and pushed to "enhance the efficiency, competitiveness, and effectiveness of state enterprise through consolidation and public listing in equity markets, restructuring, sell-offs of majority stakes, [and] the demonopolization of certain public services."[25] China's transition featured careful attention to market design. Major programs were tested as pilots, tweaked, and then slowly expanded. World Bank economist Shahid Javed Burki noted that this approach "created space for economic innovation while minimizing the political risks that make the Chinese reticent to embrace far-reaching or dramatic reforms."[26]

Eastern Europe also provides something of a laboratory into how institutions, culture, and context matter. Some post-Soviet countries enjoyed substantial success in shifting to market economies, while others fared worse. Poland, widely seen as achieving one of the most effective transitions, employed a "shock therapy" approach, which featured aggressive and immediate changes addressing liberalization, privatization, a social safety net, and the need for international assistance.[27] The Czech Republic, inspired by Poland's success, carried out a similarly successful shock therapy transition. Christopher Hartwell, an economist and consultant for the U.S. Treasury, has observed, "Once the communist regime ended in 1989, the Czechoslovak Federal Republic (CSFR) attempted an ambitious set of reforms modeled on Poland's example [of] austere fiscal and monetary policies, including devaluation, institution of a fixed exchange rate, current-account convertibility, and a mass privatization scheme based on voucher distribution."[28] These successful efforts consistently recognized that creating healthy and dynamic markets requires careful attention to conditions, infrastructure, and policies. A cautionary tale about the risks of poorly conceived transitions is offered by other post-Soviet economies, such as Slovakia and Bulgaria, where a failure to emulate Poland or the Czech Republic yielded corruption and stagnation.

Domestic airline deregulation in the late 1970s illustrates the complexities of cultivating a dynamic marketplace where bureaucracy and regulation once ruled. After the Airline Deregulation Act of 1978, the emergence of new supply was constrained by the fact that major airports could only handle so many takeoffs and landings per hour. Moreover, exclusive gate leases that airlines had previously been awarded remained in effect after deregulation. When attempting to sublet these exclusive gates, newer carriers found themselves paying higher prices and restricted to off-peak times. Policies and arrangements that may have been innocuous in an earlier era served to restrict the size, nature, and extent of the supply-side response to deregulation.[29] Moreover, despite nominal federal deregulation, airlines still confronted state regulations, interest group pressures, and constraining contracts. Meanwhile, flight availability and performance suffered due to an air traffic control system plagued by bottlenecks like outdated technology, limited runway capacity, and federal regulations governing pricing and work rules. The lesson is that those skeptical of capacity building cannot simply embrace choice or competition but must understand that a robust supply side begins with careful attention to market design.[30]

MAKING SUPPLY-SIDE REFORM WORK

Dramatic improvement in schooling will require the emergence of new problem-solvers, and the number, scope, and success of these ventures will depend on the larger political economy of K–12 education. In particular, this volume focuses on four elements that will help determine the incidence and promise of entrepreneurial ventures in education: human capital, financial capital and related infrastructure, barriers to entry, and mechanisms for quality control.

Human Capital and Talent Development

The presence of entrepreneurs able to take advantage of new opportunities is key to any dynamic sector. Research on start-ups shows that about 80 percent of successful firms are launched by individuals with experience in or adjacent to the relevant sector.[31] In education, however, there is a dearth of individuals inclined or prepared to thrive as entrepreneurs. Consequently, truly innovative ventures in education are rare. The majority of new entrants are not growth-oriented; they are instead mom-and-pop charter school operations or the result of large testing firms and publishers simply adding one more line of business.

Entrepreneurship requires a wealth of talented, motivated innovators tackling problems in a variety of ways. In an array of sectors, breakthroughs in quality and efficiency have required the emergence of coherent new business models. While efforts like Teach For America, Indianapolis's The Mind Trust, and related efforts profiled by Bryan Hassel in chapter 2 may be attracting individuals with a more entrepreneurial bent, there is no guarantee that even a few will be prepared to navigate the rigors of entrepreneurship, which requires a mixture of seasoning and experience on one hand, and energy and a fresh perspective on the other.

In the most vibrant sectors, this pipeline of human capital is filled by college graduates whose paths generally progress like this: gain some experience, change jobs, gain new experience, join a new venture, watch it fail, try again, try to launch one's own, and so on. This process—with an array of providers, willing investors, and dense networks spanning academe, industry, and finance—ensures a constant stream of talented, seasoned individuals. Today, little machinery exists to cultivate would-be educational entrepreneurs or to allow them to grow. Young teachers work alone in their classrooms, have little non-classroom responsibility, develop networks restricted to fellow teachers, and gain limited insight into team management or how to build a new enterprise. In other entrepreneurial fields, twenty- and thirty-somethings move easily among ventures, gaining experience and developing networks of mentors and peers.

What kinds of career opportunities might better equip young, problem-solving educators to become successful entrepreneurs? What kinds of investments could help expand the human capital pipeline and then maximize the likelihood that more of these individuals will fulfill their potential? What lessons or practices might be drawn from other sectors?

Venture Capital and the Attendant Infrastructure

A second consideration is the availability of financial capital and a support system that can direct those resources to promising ventures. New companies can neither launch nor grow without money. To date, as Joseph Keeney and Daniel Pianko note in chapter 3, little attention has been paid to this challenge in the education sector. Money is mostly invested in the dominant publishers and testing firms, which generally return higher profits. Little private capital is directed at start-ups; there is almost no infrastructure to help interested investors and entrepreneurs locate one another; and there is no support system to cultivate or nurture new entrants.

Meanwhile, the public dollars that comprise more than 90 percent of all K–12 spending rarely support entrepreneurial problem-solving. This means that philanthropic giving, which accounts for a fraction of 1 percent of education spending, has played an outsized role in the launch of ventures like the KIPP Academies, Aspire Public Schools, New Leaders for New Schools, and Teach For America. Because K–12 education is dominated by government spending, and because this money is consumed in salaries and operations, precious little is invested in research and development or new ventures. Outside of the limited funding for charter school facilities and start-up costs, almost none of it supports entrepreneurial activity.

In the private sector, the torrent of venture capital is accompanied by an ecosystem of institutions and actors that provide quality control, support new ventures, and selectively target resources. In education, especially when it comes to directing philanthropic dollars, such infrastructure is sparse. The venture-capital communities that have sprung up in corridors like Silicon Valley and Route 128 in Boston are not plugged into K–12 education and equivalents do not exist in the world of schooling.

How can public or philanthropic dollars be more effectively used to support entrepreneurial activity? What strategies, institutions, and arrangements exist in the venture-capital sector that might be imported or replicated in education?

Barriers to Entry

Barriers to entry are the laws, rules, and practices that make it harder or more costly to launch a new venture. These range from regulations hindering the opening of a charter school to textbook approval systems so onerous that only the largest publishers are able to compete. Barriers deserving particular attention are those that put obstacles in the path of new providers or impose constraints on how they can operate.

The ways in which existing arrangements prohibit or impede entrepreneurial providers are routinely overlooked in the heated disputes over choice-based reform. Proposals for choice could help address the rules, regulations, facilities issues, and funding formulas that limit the entry of new providers, but even ambitious school voucher proposals do not necessarily address barriers to entry of new textbook publishers, test manufacturers, and teacher recruiting agencies. In fact, some entrepreneurs note that school choice can make their work more difficult—as they find it more manageable and cost-effective to negotiate with large districts than with a slew of independent operations. More generally, there is a need to explore how procurement policies, personnel rules, and organizational routines may stifle the emergence of effective new providers.

What are the barriers that restrict providers? What steps might help reduce these barriers, and what are the consequences, good and ill, of doing so? How does the latticework of regulation and statute affect entrepreneurial efforts to reinvent school systems as high-performing organizations?

Quality Control and R&D

Given that K–12 education has been designed to operate bureaucratically, it is no surprise that its mechanisms for monitoring and policing quality have historically focused on metrics like attendance, teacher credentials, textbook provisions, and tracking expenditures. It is only since the late 1990s that metrics beyond those that monitor spending and enrollment have been widely employed as management tools. For the most part, innovation in quality control has entailed collecting test-score data for students in reading and math and then using those to compute value-added measures of teachers or schools. Nowhere has there been discussion of whether the available metrics are useful or appropriate ways to judge the panoply of new educational ventures or what kinds of measures would be most useful for judging the performance of organizations that recruit new staff, provide diagnostic services for particular grades, deliver Web-based instruction, or offer tutoring in advanced subjects.

Meanwhile, the practical challenges of quality control have also received little attention. Charter schooling, for instance, is nothing more than an opportunity for new providers to emerge. The challenges of aggressively weeding out weak performers, supporting strong operators, and nurturing promising providers have been largely ignored amid public debates that seem to presume that the quality of what emerges from the marketplace is a natural phenomenon beyond our capacity to control.

Are there promising ways that other sectors monitor and police the quality of providers? Are there lessons to be drawn from experience to date in charter schooling? Is it possible to craft metrics sensitive to the heterogeneity and specialization of new providers without giving up on transparency or the possibility of sensible regulation and throwing ourselves to the mercy of the market?

Finally, an essential component of quality control is cultivating a base of substantial, applied knowledge that can support the emergence of effective schools and service providers. Absent such a resource, new ventures will be a dicier proposition and less likely to attract investors and entrepreneurs who may be more likely to look to sectors where there exists the intellectual capital needed to drive breakthrough advances. Today, the kind of extensive research and development capability that characterizes biotechnology is simply absent in education. What would it take to develop that capability? What roles would public and private actors need to play in making that a reality?

OVERVIEW OF THE VOLUME

In the 2006 volume *Educational Entrepreneurship*, I sought to explain the arguments, actors, and activity that characterize entrepreneurial activity in education. This volume is intended to pick up where that effort left off, as contributors consider the measures that might help nurture a robust, quality-conscious entrepreneurial sector in K–12 education. Drawing from experiences both inside and outside education, they take particular care to explain how policymakers, funders, and educators might help educational entrepreneurship deliver on its potential and identify concerns deserving of attention.

The volume begins with two chapters that take up the critical question of human capital—the challenges of finding and cultivating individuals with the knowledge, skills, and makeup to reinvent schooling. In chapter 1, Christopher Gergen and Gregg Vanourek, founding partners of New Mountain Ventures, explore the issue of talent attraction, development, and retention outside of K–12 education. They first map the contemporary talent landscape and identify key trends in this area. They then describe how forward-thinking organizations outside education have addressed the challenges associated with talent development. Finally, they close by recommending several key talent recruitment and development strategies worth using in K–12 schooling, with concrete suggestions for how they might be imported.

In chapter 2, Bryan Hassel, codirector of Public Impact, starts from the premise that a thriving entrepreneurial sector will require an influx of entrepreneurial individuals capable of launching and leading promising ventures. In profiling efforts like The Mind Trust, the Charter School Growth Fund, and Building Excellent Schools, he considers the kinds of people who could fuel entrepreneurship in K–12, potential sources of that talent, and the range of constraints that restrict the flow of enterprising people into education. Taking note of a number of initiatives across the country that could, directly or indirectly, bring fresh talent into the sector, he considers the preliminary lessons of those efforts and suggests ways in which funders, policymakers, and entrepreneurial organizations could more effectively attract talent to education.

Chapters 3 and 4 turn from the question of human capital to that of financial capital. In chapter 3, Joseph Keeney, founder and CEO of 4th Sector Solutions, Inc., and Daniel Pianko, a principal of Knowledge Investment Partners, look outside the sector for promising ideas on how to make the education space more hospitable for entrepreneurial investment. They begin by noting that the K–12 industry has not attracted significant private investment relative to its size, then provide an overview of the private capital investment markets, and conclude by considering different ways to catalyze private investment in educational entrepreneurship. Specifically, the authors outline the differences between K–12 and postsecondary education from an investor's perspective and offer three models to promote investment: a prize model to attract investment to meet a defined need, the establishment of an investment portal to facilitate and promote angel investing, and a traditional venture-capital coinvestment model.

In chapter 4, Kim Smith, cofounder of the NewSchools Venture Fund, and Julie Petersen, communications director of NewSchools, consider how foundations and social capital might better support entrepreneurial reform. Like entrepreneurs in any other sector, educational entrepreneurs must rely on a variety of resources in their quest for the money, people, and ideas that they need to turn their vision into reality. One of the most challenging is financial capital—particularly for social entrepreneurs in education who seek to improve school access, equity, and outcomes. Smith and Peterson focus on the "social purpose capital markets" that help to fund entrepreneurs, describing the types of investors who comprise these complicated markets, how they operate, the flaws in their structure, and the ways these limitations could be remedied.

In chapter 5, Larry Berger, CEO of Wireless Generation, and his associate David Stevenson, examine the barriers to entry that stifle entrepreneurial efforts to deliver more effective tools, services, and support for teaching and learning. While K–12 schooling is a $500 billion market with massive unmet needs in exactly the areas that Wireless Generation targets its efforts, the educational marketplace often fails to attract entrepreneurs and encourage them to develop or disseminate better solutions. From their perspectives as practicing entrepreneurs, Berger and Stevenson explore the barriers that stifle innovative activity and the practices that give established firms an advantage over new providers. They touch on questions like the role of minimal investment in research and development, the publishing oligopoly, the lack of a return-on-investment mindset, and limited start-up capital. They close by offering recommendations that could help mitigate these barriers and make entrepreneurship a more potent force for educational improvement.

Efforts to unleash entrepreneurial energy are all well and good, but skeptics quickly turn to the issue of quality control. In chapters 6 and 7, two authors tackle the imposing question of how quality can be monitored or policed in an entrepreneurial environment. In chapter 6, Matt Candler, CEO of New Schools for New Orleans, shares lessons learned at KIPP in New York City and in New Orleans. He addresses the particular challenges of quality control as well as broader efforts to implement supply-side reforms on the ground. He argues that active management of the quality of schools—both before and after they open—is key to achieving scale with quality, and it is best done in tandem between charter school authorizers and independent organizations. In offering lessons from personal experience, Candler reflects on the need to shut down poor schools and to both support and demand more from middling schools. In closing, he highlights the importance of human capital in classrooms and leadership roles when it comes to making any supply-side reform effort work.

In chapter 7, Chester Finn, president of the Thomas B. Fordham Foundation, offers a broader and more theoretical take on quality control in the entrepreneurial sector. Finn urges reformers to be as attentive to rethinking quality control and the relevant metrics as to issues of school redesign or teacher quality. The entry into K–12 education of entrepreneurial providers delivering a diverse array of goods, services, and personnel creates the need for quality-control mechanisms very different from the traditional model that relies on regulations and monitoring inputs. Absent such a shift, Finn fears that promising new providers will find themselves tangled in red tape and have difficulty demonstrating their value. Moreover, because children and public dollars are involved, simply "trusting the marketplace" is not a credible response. Rather, as in the case of industries ranging from restaurants to automobiles to pharmaceuticals, he sees the need for careful attention to market-friendly quality-control mechanisms. Given the changing characteristics and needs of providers and students, as well as the availability of new data, Finn calls for new-style quality-control approaches that will be flexible and adaptive. He closes by offering a provocative framework to guide the necessary innovation and experimentation on this front.

Finally, in chapters 8 and 9, authors tackle two issues central to any vibrant supply-side response: developing a substantial research and development capability and the role of politics in supporting entrepreneurial reform. In chapter 8, Anthony Bryk, president of the Carnegie Foundation for the Advancement of Teaching, and Louis Gomez, the Aon Professor of Learning Sciences at Northwestern University, argue that it inconceivable that reformers will successfully produce dramatic changes in the efficiency or effectiveness of education without a serious transformation of the research and development infrastructure for school improvement. They contend that current arrangements in public education—in which the work of schools, universities, and commercial ventures are disjointed and marked by inattention to building a coherent body of professional knowledge—lead to market failure and a dearth of useful educational innovation. Consequently, Bryk and Gomez call for efforts to catalyze and nurture a new design-engineering-development enterprise in education, whereby practitioners, researchers, and commercial ventures collaborate in the creation and rigorous evaluation of new advances.

In chapter 9, Ed Kirby, who manages the Walton Family Foundation's work in the U.S. school choice movement, contends that entrepreneurs involved in the supply side of education reform must build powerful advocacy operations to advance and protect their work. Dramatic changes in the regulatory environment are necessary to enable new supply-side initiatives to attain both scale and performance. Kirby argues that efforts to create opportunities for entrepreneurial reform have been reluctant to engage in bare-knuckle politics and advocacy. Pointing to the density of the regulatory environment and the formidable barriers that it presents to reform, he urges a strategy that employs a full range of advocacy tools—from the "501(c)(3)" research and policy efforts that entrepreneur-friendly foundations have found most comfortable, to an increased investment in "501(c)(4)" entities that engage in legislative advocacy and direct political action.

The contributions to come are distinctive because advocates and researchers tend to be so professionally and personally invested in seemingly safe solutions like best practices or school choice that it is difficult to garner interest for supply-side efforts guided by the twin catechisms that there are no sure things and that the path to improvement is necessarily uncertain. In the private sector, those crucial admonitions are delivered naturally and invisibly by market forces. The question is whether it is possible to approximate their ability to check hubris in K–12 schooling when faced with the dictates of public policy and a public taste for ostensible guarantees.

Conscious that fevered reform efforts have had only limited success in catalyzing a new supply of effective problem-solvers, the contributors ask what we can do differently. Charter schooling, alternative teacher licensure, virtual schools, choice programs, and other innovative policies have opened the door a crack, but such policies are not solutions—they merely create opportunities for educators and service providers to devise ways to more effectively tackle thorny problems. The challenge is to take the next step, open that door wide, give entrepreneurs the tools and support they need, and then nurture the successes and police against failures.

Yet, to date, no one—not the school choice community, not foundations, and certainly not colleges of education or professional educators—has devoted much attention to the machinery that can help bring promising ideas to the surface and maximize the chance that innovators will have an opportunity to make a difference. In short, no one has focused on the supply side of school reform in a deep and sustained way. That is the task the contributors tackle in the pages ahead.

CHAPTER 1

Talent Development

Looking Outside the Education Sector

Christopher Gergen and Gregg Vanourek

Only by attracting the best people will you accomplish great deeds.
—*Colin Powell*

At the turn of the millennium, venerated management consulting firm McKinsey & Company sounded the alarm bell that there was a "war for talent" in its landmark study of almost 13,000 executives in 120 large U.S. companies across a wide range of industries.[1] "Talent" in this context has been defined as "smart, sophisticated businesspeople who are technologically literate, globally astute, and operationally agile."[2] The war for talent is still raging, and many argue that it is more intense than ever.

According to the authors of that pathbreaking study, "At a time when the need for superior talent is increasing, big U.S. companies are finding it difficult to attract and retain good people. Executives and experts point to a severe and growing shortage of the people needed to run divisions and manage critical functions, let alone lead companies."[3] Meanwhile, a link was being made between talent and organizational performance. In an update to the original study, the authors write, "The companies doing the best job of managing their talent deliver far better results for shareholders. Companies scoring in the top quintile of talent-management practices outperform their industry's mean return to shareholders by a remarkable 22 percentage points. Talent management is not the only driver of such performance, but it is clearly a powerful one."[4]

Do such analyses have anything to contribute to the field of K–12 education? Some might suggest that schooling is a specialized endeavor with utterly exceptional and nontransferable talent dynamics. Others might propose that the motivations and rewards that attract people to teaching and other education jobs are unlike those in other industries and sectors. While recognizing numerous important differences, we submit that a fair review yields more similarities than differences—and that education professionals have much to learn from their colleagues outside the sector. In a talent-starved sector, it is shortsighted to overlook approaches that are bearing fruit elsewhere.

Examples of cross-sector talent approaches abound. Some might be surprised to learn that West Point consistently generates impressively successful cohorts of leaders suited not only for military roles but also for business, government, education, and other fields. The nine hundred men and women who graduate each year are commissioned as second lieutenants in the U.S. Army and soon sent to places like Germany, Kosovo, Afghanistan, and Iraq. Most just 22 years of age, they are entrusted with waging war, keeping peace, and deploying the world's most powerful arsenal. In a telling example, a lieutenant colonel at West Point took his young charges to an elementary school playground with the simple mission of overseeing seven minutes of recess.

The lesson? Command-and-control approaches do not always work, and sometimes the best way to influence complex, chaotic systems is simply to set the starting conditions and boundaries and then manage on the fly.[5] If the U.S. military can draw leadership lessons from the world of education, why can education not do the same from other sectors? Too often, educational leadership is addressed absent the larger context of what we know broadly about talent development and effective leadership. According to a 2004 review of 496 education administration programs, leading business leadership thinkers such as Jim Collins (*Good to Great*), Michael Porter (Harvard Business School), Clayton Christensen (*The Innovator's Dilemma*), and Tom Peters (*In Search of Excellence*) were entirely absent from the courses in the study sample.[6]

Though leaders from fields as disparate as the military, business, government, and sports frequently emphasize the importance of talent, we must be careful not to overstate the case. Observers from best-selling author Malcolm Gladwell to late management guru Peter Drucker have emphasized the importance not of talent but of the systems in which people work. Drucker writes, "No institution can possibly survive if it needs geniuses or supermen to manage it. It must be organized in such a way as to be able to get along under a leadership composed of average human beings."[7] We do not seek to resolve this longstanding debate, except to posit that quality talent and smart systems are two sides of the same coin, utterly lacking value without their "other half."

In a quest to "win the war," forward-thinking organizations are recognizing the critical importance of talent and investing in bold initiatives to attract, develop, and retain the best and brightest. Talent has become widely accepted as a critical driver of organizational performance and competitive advantage. One of the most important points in Jim Collins's best-seller *Good to Great* is that every great company profiled had "level 5 leadership" during its pivotal transition from being a good company to a great one: people who, through a paradoxical blend of personal humility and professional will, built a culture of greatness in their organizations by defining and measuring success, hiring and retaining the best talent ("getting the right people on the bus"), demanding focus and discipline (the "hedgehog concept"), and getting the "flywheel" spinning in the right direction—thereby attracting more exceptional talent and building momentum toward great performance.[8]

Building a culture in which exceptional leaders can grow and shine is famously difficult. There is much to learn from organizations that have cracked this code. In this chapter, we tease out these lessons from three vantage points. First, we map the talent landscape, including seven leading trends that are shaping its contours. Second, we address the question of how forward-looking organizations outside the education sector have successfully addressed these trends and challenges. Third, we identify several key talent strategies worth deploying in the K–12 education sector (pertaining especially to education leaders and entrepreneurs but also relevant to some degree to teachers), with concrete suggestions for how they can be imported.

For a host of reasons, the K–12 sector must compete for talent in a way that it traditionally has not had to. Globalization, shifting demographics, and increasing demands on the workforce have put human-resource strains on education institutions and organizations. Of course, the days of the sector enjoying a quasi-monopoly on professional women flocking to teaching are long gone. As a consequence, it is essential that schools, districts, and other K–12 organizations understand talent practices being deployed elsewhere— and that they respond vigorously to the challenges with fresh thinking and bold approaches.

MAPPING THE TALENT LANDSCAPE

As we surveyed the talent landscape outside the education sector, we spotted seven leading trends. The first is a growth in the the arsenal of weapons deployed by organizations across sectors and industries in the war for talent itself. Although there has been some debate about the size and extent of the battlefront, the war for talent is now almost universally accepted and has led to dramatic responses from leading organizations worldwide.[9] Examples include creative recruiting tactics, robust investments in development and empowerment programs, and sophisticated tracking systems and retention efforts. This has been driven by greater recognition of the importance of talent and its correlation with performance, leading to a significant shift in the balance of power from employers to employees.

Second, the rise of "knowledge workers" that Peter Drucker identified in the 1960s has gained momentum in the wake of the Internet boom, profoundly affecting the U.S. economy and this balance of power. In the 1930s, information workers comprised a third of the workforce. Today, estimates put them between two-thirds and four-fifths.[10] Furthermore, the performance differential between a talented knowledge worker and an unexceptional one is significant. As a result, the demand for the most talented performers is exceptionally intense.

Third, just as demand for skilled knowledge workers is growing, we are witnessing dramatic increases in job mobility—with corresponding decreases in organizational loyalty. According to the Bureau of Labor Statistics, the median tenure for employed wage and salary workers is just four years, and 23 percent of them have been with their current employer for twelve months or less.

Fourth, workers are experiencing the flattening of the global economy, with its propensity for outsourcing, offshoring, and other disruptive competitive practices. In this environment, there is increasing commoditization of certain services (call centers, for example), which is ratcheting up the need for innovation and entrepreneurial activity. This in turn fuels the talent wars and challenges organizations to provide their talent with room to collaborate, experiment, and innovate across boundaries.

Fifth, we are witnessing a boom in entrepreneurship and related phenomena of "intrapreneurship," self-employment, and free agency. For evidence, we need only look at the darlings of the new economy: the founders of Google, YouTube, Facebook, Skype, MySpace, and other examples of enterprising energy. "At any given time," according to Carl Schramm, president of the Ewing Marion Kauffman Foundation, "15 percent of the [U.S.] population is running their own companies. . . . These entrepreneurs, people who now create more than half the new jobs in America, are defining the new economy not just here but around the world. . . . We now live in the most entrepreneurial time in history."[11] Today, nearly half a million new

TABLE 1.1: Relative Priority Placed on Work versus Family across Generations

Relative Priority Placed on Work vs. Family	Gen-Y (under 23) N=250	Gen-X (23-37) N=855	Boomer (38-57) N=404	Mature (58+) N=276
Work-centric (percentage placing higher priority work than family)	13	13	22	12
Dual-centric (percentage placing equal priority work and family)	37	35	37	54
Family-centric (percentage placing higher priority family than work)	50	52	41	34

Source: Families and Work Institute, *Generations and Gender in the Workplace* (New York: American Business Collaboration, 2004).

Note: It is possible—and perhaps likely—for members of Generations X and Y to "age into" new values.

businesses are created each month in the United States; the creation of a new firm is now more widespread than the creation of a new household or the birth of a baby; and more than a third of U.S. households include someone who has founded, tried to start, or helped fund a small business.[12]

Sixth, we are on the cusp of a tectonic demographic shift. As the demand for skilled knowledge workers is increasing, the supply of foot soldiers is shrinking. In the United States, eight to ten thousand baby boomers (born between 1946 and 1964) turn sixty every day. By 2010, the number of what are called "prime-age workers"—between the ages of 35 and 45, from whom organizations draw most of their midlevel managers—will decrease by 10 percent. As boomers retire, this puts a double-bind on the talent markets. According to one recent estimate, for every two experienced workers leaving the workforce, only one (relatively inexperienced) worker joins it.[13] The education industry is, of course, not immune to these demographic trends.

Seventh, we are experiencing profound changes in societal values and perceptions of work. This shows up in two ways. First, there is a louder call for "work/life balance" among rising generations of leaders. As seen in table 1.1, younger generations have different priorities than their older counterparts when it comes to work and family.

Beyond seeking more flexibility and balance in their lives, new generations of leaders also appear more inclined to seek work of significance and impact, as reflected in increasing interest in socially responsible business and the triple bottom line of people, profits, and planet. There is a surge of volunteerism and social consciousness among rising generations, especially Generation Y (born between 1978 and 1994). These shifting values can also be found among what Richard Florida has called "the creative class," a rapidly growing, highly educated, and well-paid segment of society that values creativity, individuality, difference, and merit. According to Florida, the creative class includes 38 million Americans, nearly a third of the workforce (up from just 10 percent at the turn of the twentieth century).[14] In short, rising generations of leaders are being more selective about where they work. Many are starting their own organizations and creating further demand for talent.

In education, the war is on, and it knows no boundaries. The problem is how to win it.

Recognizing these trends, forward-thinking organizations are prioritizing talent management—focusing on talent attraction, development, retention, and measurement. The best of them weave all of this together into a dynamic entrepreneurial leadership culture in their organizations with exceptional results.

A "TALENT MINDSET"

Too often, organizations are caught up with putting out fires and chasing short-term results that are more public-relations flash than substantive victory. In these cases, talent recruitment and management are relegated to human resources checklists, and managers make do with the talent they inherit. In high-performing organizations, by contrast, talent management is a top priority throughout the organization. McKinsey & Company calls this a "talent mindset—the passionate belief that to achieve your aspirations for the business, you must have great talent."[15] This mindset is captured in table 1.2.

This talent mindset must be championed by the top leadership. When Larry Bossidy became CEO of global conglomerate Allied Signal in 1991, he quickly recognized that he had to improve the quality of his manufacturing leaders. After defining what an exceptional leader looked like, his executive team then used this "gold standard" to evaluate each of the company's four hundred manufacturing managers. Those who met the standard were given additional responsibilities. Those who showed promise were coached and evaluated to see if they could reach the standard. Others were counseled out. Meanwhile, the company went into talent recruitment overdrive, replacing half of its managers within two years. The resulting talent upgrade contributed significantly to Allied Signal's remarkable turnaround. According to Bossidy, finding and developing great leaders is "the job no CEO should delegate."[16]

TABLE 1.2: New Ways of Thinking about Talent

	The Old Way	The New Way
Talent Mindset	HR is responsible for people management.	All managers—starting with the CEO—are accountable for strengthening their talent pool.
Employee Value Proposition	We provide good pay and benefits.	We shape our company, even our strategy, to appeal to talented people.
Recruiting	Recruiting is like purchasing.	Recruiting is like marketing.
Growing Leaders	We think development happens in training programs.	We fuel development through stretch jobs, coaching, and mentoring.
Differentiation	We treat everyone the same and like to think that everyone is equally capable.	We affirm all our people, but invest differentially in our A, B, and C players.

Source: McKinsey & Company, "New Ways of Thinking," n.d. www.mckinsey.com/clientservice/organizationleadership/warfortalent/newways.asp (accessed January 4, 2008).

TALENT ATTRACTION

In a 2000 McKinsey & Company survey, 99 percent of corporate officers said that their management talent pools needed to be much stronger, and only 20 percent believed that they had enough talent to pursue most of their business opportunities.[17] What have organizations done to attract the talent they need?

The first step is determining what talent is needed and then being smart about where and how to find it. Many organizations deploy traditional recruitment tactics such as on-campus recruiting at colleges and universities, where they offer attractive financial incentives and multifaceted compensation packages that address salary, bonus, relocation, stock options, cost of living, and more. Organizations utilize executive search firms and "headhunters" particularly for their tougher searches. (Since 1992, the executive recruiting industry has enjoyed twelve years of double-digit revenue growth and only two years of losses.[18])

As such approaches become commonplace, however, organizations are being forced to dig deeper to attract talent. Many are now appealing to the heartstrings and values of their top recruits. This has alternately been called creating an "employee value proposition" and "branding for talent." According to a recent report: "Traditional recruiting focuses on functional employment benefits such as job security, opportunities for creativity and individual growth, and compensation. But an employer's intangible, emotional associations—'it is fun to work at this company,' 'we have a passionate and intelligent culture,' 'there is a strong team feeling here'—are just as important to recruits."[19]

To be successful, twenty-first-century organizations must differentiate themselves. Many do this by communicating what makes their firm unique through a so-called signature experience—a clear message to potential recruits about the unique values of the organization and what it is like to work there.[20] An example is Clif Bar, a leading producer of organic nutrition bars. Its leaders developed "five aspirations" for the company, centered on sustaining their brands, business, people, community, and planet. They offer profit-sharing for employees, sabbaticals, and a remarkable wellness program, including an in-house gym, three full-time trainers, and twenty fitness classes per week—during working hours. Employees take a three-day weekend every other week through a creative form of flex-time and are invited to weekly jam sessions in the company theater. Clif Bar also has a robust community service program, including a goal of over twenty paid hours of community volunteer work per person per year, and it donates one percent of its annual sales to charities. Furthermore, the company appeals to its California-based workforce by being "green," with a robust sustainability initiative led by a staff ecologist.[21] These initiatives serve as a powerful enticement for potential recruits—and a strong glue for retaining them.

One of the biggest attractors of talent into an organization (or sector) is the prevalence of talent already there. Talent begets talent, and so it is with mediocrity. In any organization, there are "A players" (exceptional performers who inspire others), "B players" (solid performers who show potential), and "C players" (who underperform and undermine teamwork).[22] A players should be promoted, B players should be developed, and C players should be weeded out. Once an organization earns a reputation for rewarding excellence and rejecting mediocrity, it will become a magnet for talent.

Take Google, for example. Through a massive recruitment campaign, it has been able to nab the crème de la crème of the math and science community, including an award-winning physician, an Internet pioneer, and top executives and engineers from Microsoft, Apple, eBay, and Amazon.[23] The company's highly selective hiring process has been called "grueling." One of Google's core principles is that "great just isn't good enough." It values not only intelligence and aptitude but nonconformity as well, with preference given to recruits with unconventional experiences and worldviews. Each year, the company hands out multi-million-dollar Founders' Awards to honor teams that have made extraordinary contributions to the company.[24] Together, these approaches have sealed the company's reputation as the place to work for today's tech-savvy creative class.

TALENT DEVELOPMENT

Once talented people are on board, they must be developed. Executives are increasingly realizing that training and leadership development programs must be more than an afterthought. General Electric, for instance, invests over $1 billion a year (out of $163 billion in annual sales) into training and developing its employees. At the center of this investment is the John F. Welch Leadership Center at Crotonville (recently renamed for legendary former CEO Jack Welch). Crotonville sprawls across fifty-three acres in New York's Hudson Valley and trains and connects thousands of managers every year. It promotes GE's talent development mission to "create, identify, and transfer organizational learning to enhance GE growth and competitiveness worldwide" by offering leadership development courses and creating opportunities for collaboration and shared learning.[25]

While few organizations have these kinds of training resources, forward-looking ones are placing similar emphasis on leadership development, knowledge-sharing, cross-functional team development, creativity, and network creation. Trilogy Software, a high-growth technology company based in Austin, Texas, has created a three-month boot camp for new employees overseen by the company's CEO. In the first month, teams of twenty participate in fast-paced creative exercises coached by an experienced executive. In the second month, smaller breakthrough teams are created and charged with developing new product and service ideas, creating business models, building prototypes, and developing marketing plans. In the third month, personal initiative is fostered, allowing employees to continue working in breakthrough teams or to find a company sponsor to support a new project that they will lead. At the end of the boot camp, each employee receives a comprehensive performance evaluation, including rigorous feedback from colleagues, section leaders, and senior management. The results are impressive. To date, more than $100 million in new business has been generated as a result of the recruits' projects. The company also credits the program with intangible benefits such as enhanced camaraderie and motivation among new recruits and better insight into their strengths, weaknesses, and developmental needs.[26]

At the Container Store, the retail company specializing in storage and organization products and services, all new hires (whether full-time or seasonal) go through Foundation Week, an intensive orientation and training program that often leads into apprenticing with high-performers. All employees receive at least 235 hours of formal training in their first year (versus an industry average of about 7 hours). Employees work in different functional areas, a process designed to enhance their overall effectiveness and customer-service sensibilities. (Here we pause to note that a container retailer devotes far more time to employee talent development in the first year than does almost any school or district of which we know, even though schools are in the knowledge business.) The results of this systematic approach include employee turnover rates significantly lower than the industry average and high rates of new employees sourced through internal recommendations, a significant cost-saver.[27]

These organizations have learned that talent development requires talent empowerment. Leadership experts James O'Toole and Edward Lawler III point to "the existence of high-involvement, high-wage, high-profit companies in almost every industry"—from Southwest Airlines to Harley-Davidson to UPS to Costco: "Because these companies involve their workers in decision-making, reward them fairly for their efforts, and provide them with good training and career opportunities, their employees reciprocate the favor in terms of much higher productivity."[28] In addition, talent-minded organizations are increasingly sending emerging leaders on dynamic retreats and are hiring leadership development firms or coaches to work with both established and emerging leaders. In 2002, there were an estimated 10,000 executive coaches worldwide, a number expected to rise to 50,000 within five years.[29]

These investments should be made within a clear blueprint for talent development. Organizations that provide thoughtful and engaging career paths for their team members, with specifically delineated advancement opportunities and milestones for qualifying, are likely to fare better in the talent wars. Forward-thinking employers invest in helping employees achieve these goals, in part by giving young talent exposure to multiple functional areas and different managers. Job rotation—in which employees alternate through different functional areas on a structured basis to gain exposure—can provide not only clarity and motivation but also a breadth of experience that ultimately boosts performance.

At global financial services firm HSBC, individuals seeking to reach the upper echelons of management must work in at least two very different cultural environments within the corporation. To promote this, the firm offers attractive transfers into "stretch" jobs in other parts of the world. As HSBC chairman Stephen Green acknowledges, this approach is more expensive than filling positions locally, but it is critical to achieving the firm's goals. Additionally, it facilitates knowledge transfers across regions, provides growth opportunities for employees, and boosts cross-border collaboration.[30]

At Google, there is a companywide rule allowing developers to devote 20 percent of their time—essentially a day a week—to any project that they choose. This policy has the twin benefits of letting talented people push their limits while also creating a robust pipeline of innovative products and services. Recently, more than half of Google's new products could trace their origins to 20 percent–rule projects.[31] This practice is becoming increasingly common, and Google was not the first to try it; other companies that use some version of this approach include 3M, Intuit, and Linden Lab.[32]

Another example of a company that prioritizes empowerment is the natural foods grocery store chain Whole Foods. Each department in each store is comprised of a small, decentralized team whose members decide who joins the group—with new hires being considered in four-week trial periods. High-performing teams are then rewarded through profit-sharing. The firm's core values of decentralization and collaboration have placed it on *Fortune*'s list of "the 100 best companies to work for" nine years in a row.[33]

The larger point here is that talent development cannot remain merely a function of an active human resources department or a pet project. For talent to thrive, talent development must be an explicit priority across the board, and the organizational culture, structures, systems, and investments must be aligned with leadership growth plans. These lessons are not relegated to specific sectors but can be adopted in creative ways by innovative organizations across sectors, including education.

TALENT RETENTION

Proactive organizations are recognizing the importance not only of getting talent in the door but also of keeping it through effective retention efforts. Done right, retention can help build and sustain an organization's culture, enhance its chances for long-term success, and yield significant savings. It has been estimated that attrition costs companies eighteen months worth of salary for each manager or professional who leaves and six months pay for hourly employees.[34] Of course, there is no magic formula for maximizing retention. Much of what keeps people in jobs has to do with best practices in leadership, governance, and organizational systems, including a healthy focus on developing people and creating a dynamic culture and workplace.

When Internet advertising firm DoubleClick was started in 1996, the founders invested in all the dot-com accoutrements, including an espresso bar in the lobby and free salsa lessons for employees. Most important, though, is the opportunity that the company provides all employees to shape their own careers. Employees are encouraged to switch jobs internally, learn new skills, and take risks. Workers are given a high degree of autonomy and account-ability, with performance-based bonuses. Says CEO Kevin Ryan, "I judge my people on two people leadership questions: Are the people in their group happy working for them? And do they bring in great people? If managers cannot help us attract and retain the best people, they are not doing a good job."[35] This approach has served DoubleClick well. In the wake of the dot-com crash in 2000, the company did not lose any of its top hundred people, even after its stock price dropped 80 percent, helping it to rebound and posi-tion itself for a $3.1 billion acquisition by Google in 2007.

Many organizations offer benefits, such as flex-time and telecommuting, that address hectic schedules and stressed-out workers. In 2004, 28 percent of the full-time wage and salary workforce (excluding self-employed persons) worked on a flexible schedule, and 15 percent of the U.S. workforce worked at home at least once per week as part of their primary job, according to the U.S. Department of Commerce. Today, 9.5 million Americans work from home.[36] According to a recent Families and Work Institute survey, 31 percent of organizations allow employees to work from home or off-site on a regular basis, and 73 percent allow extended career breaks for family responsibilities. By January 2005, 19 percent of the federal government workforce telecom-muted—almost double the 2001 number.[37]

Other enterprises offer job-sharing, in which two or more part-time work-ers can share a full-time job to manage family or other obligations. Firms such as The Business Talent Group and Mindfarm are helping organizations find talented executives not interested in full-time employment. Mean-while, sabbaticals are becoming increasingly common outside of academia. According to a recent Society for Human Resource Management survey, 18 percent of corporate respondents offer unpaid sabbaticals and 5 percent offer paid sabbaticals.[38] Again, these trends are not confined to a few mav-erick organizations in certain sectors; they are being embraced by leadership teams across sectors that are serious about talent—and measuring their progress along the way.

TALENT MEASUREMENT

Having a sophisticated approach toward talent attraction, development, and retention requires that talent be measured systematically, reflecting the old business adage that "you don't get what you don't measure." The best talent shops develop a sophisticated array of metrics, including employee performance, satisfaction, retention, and more, and they deploy smart technology systems to track these measures.

An interesting example comes from the world of baseball. In *Moneyball: The Art of Winning an Unfair Game,* author Michael Lewis documented how the Oakland Athletics upended the conventional wisdom about which baseball players to recruit to help teams win. He draws a distinction between big-market teams that have ample funds to pay hefty salaries to free agents and small-market teams with tight payrolls. Despite being one of the poorest teams in baseball, the A's won their division and made the playoffs regularly even as their bigger-name talent fled to wealthier teams. Their secret was a form of statistical analysis that led to a better sense of which types and mix of players lead to winning games. They discovered that it is not the traditional measures of batting average, home runs, runs batted in, stolen bases, and the like that win games but rather on-base percentage (including walks) and total bases.[39] Once they figured this out, they started winning—a lot.

A talent development strategy is incomplete without the accountability made possible by measurement. This brings us to a weakness in the education sector: our limited ability to gather, analyze, synthesize, and report data in consistent, helpful ways. What we have is a collection of mostly crude output or growth measures that reveal only part of the story. Schools, districts, and providers generally lack the metrics, systems, investments, processes, and expertise necessary for excellence in talent development and measurement, forcing them to "wing it" when they could be methodically improving their practices based on hard data about what works.

GETTING TALENT RIGHT

Across our economy, there are organizations that have defined themselves not only through innovation and bottom-line results but also by their continuous cohorts of effective leaders. These all-star "talent factories" are worthy of further study.

One example of this approach is consumer-products giant Procter & Gamble. Its approach to attracting, developing, and retaining talent is as comprehensive as it is legendary.[40] The company has instituted a global talent review in which various business locations are rigorously assessed for their capacity to find, attract, engage, develop, and retain great people—and all leaders are held accountable for this. With a commitment to hire at the entry level and build talent from within, Procter & Gamble begins with a robust college internship program (led by senior managers) that allows new recruits to assume significant responsibility on important projects—often multimillion-dollar initiatives that are presented to the company's top leadership. Not surprisingly, the company converts interns into employees at rates well above those of its competition. And 90 percent of its entry-level managers come straight from universities, including CEO A. G. Lafley.

Procter & Gamble managers help new recruits plot professional moves to build their career development currency, which engages employees in sophisticated career development paths. The company's leadership helps high-potential employees develop "destination jobs" early in their career that are attainable only if they continue to perform and capitalize on their potential. Procter & Gamble also offers robust training and development programs, both in-house and outsourced. Lafley joins personally with other senior executives to sponsor and teach all the leadership development courses for the company's most senior three hundred leaders. How many superintendents, principals, or heads of education organizations can be found making a comparable investment of time and resources?

Procter & Gamble deploys a talent management system that tracks its more than 135,000 employees, with a special focus on 13,000 management employees. The system captures information about individual capabilities, educational background, community affiliations, developmental needs, diversity, career histories, and succession planning. It makes in-house talent visible to company leaders worldwide. Procter & Gamble also systematically evaluates the success rate of the people that it promotes, using longitudinally a series of qualitative and quantitative measures. All this has allowed it to maintain a low attrition rate of 7.5 percent (including retirements) and create twenty-three different billion-dollar brands.[41] Procter & Gamble is a talent factory not because of some inherent competitive advantage but rather because it has invested strategically in talent.

FIGURE 1.1: The Components of a Comprehensive Talent Strategy

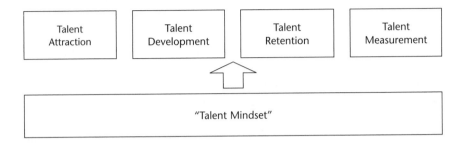

As we look at this array of talent practices outside the education sector—from organizations like Procter & Gamble, GE, Google, Whole Foods, Clif Bar, and others—we see how the combination of talent attraction, development, retention, and measurement infused with a pervasive talent mindset can be a tremendous driver of excellence. Figure 1.1 summarizes the components of a comprehensive talent strategy.

IMPORTING TALENT STRATEGIES INTO THE EDUCATION SECTOR

Great schools have great leaders. . . . Yet finding effective leaders is not easy. As with many things, when it comes to principals, the central issue isn't quantity, it's quality. . . . Leadership matters—a lot. Simply stated, it takes an effective principal to make a successful school.

> —U.S. Department of Education,
> Innovative Pathways to School Leadership, 2004

Our review of promising talent approaches outside the K–12 education sector naturally begs the question: Which ones can be imported into education, and how exactly would they work? Answering that, of course, requires understanding the context of the challenge. K–12 education comprises 6 million employees, including 3 million public school teachers and 250,000 administrators, not to mention all the people working for education service providers, professional development shops, online learning providers, textbook companies, assessment firms, research and policy organizations, foundations, consulting firms, and freelancers.

Within this construct, the kind of talent needed in education has changed, as have the realities of recruiting talent in the sector. Workers have more choices. Organizational and industry loyalty are down. Schools and education organizations cannot sit back and wait for talent to come their way, nor can they count on retaining their best people without getting creative. Indeed, they must become more aggressive about creating magnetic and engaging work environments. Yes, the talent challenges in K–12 education are acute. An estimated 200,000 teachers are hired each year. According to a 2005 report, more than 40 percent of U.S. principals—and an even higher percentage of superintendents—are expected to leave their jobs over the next decade.[42]

Fortunately, the education sector enjoys a powerful secret weapon in the talent war. Education organizations begin with an inherent advantage: the mission of education is closely aligned with the values of rising generations of professionals and emerging leaders eager to engage in meaningful work and make a difference. In that sense, talent recruitment teams in education are beginning on the fifty-yard line; evidence of this is abundant. Teach For America, which has recruited 17,000 teachers since 1990, ranked in the top ten of *BusinessWeek*'s 2007 "Best Places to Launch a Career" rankings (ahead of Goldman Sachs) and on *Fortune*'s 2007 list of "Twenty Great Employers for New Grads," and it has become so popular that it accepted fewer than one in six applicants this year. New Leaders for New Schools has earned a prestigious Fast Company/Monitor Group Social Capitalist Award three years in a row and accepted only about 7 percent of its applicants in 2007. The New Teacher Project, which has recruited 13,000 teachers since 1997, has been selected as one of the nation's best organizations for college graduates to launch their careers according to the Princeton Review. The list goes on. (Notice, though, that the above examples are rising entrepreneurial stars, not old-style textbook companies or standard school districts.)

STEPS TO IMPROVE THE TALENT PIPELINE

Though helpful, education's inherent advantage is insufficient. To carry the ball further downfield, sector leaders must adopt a talent mindset and deploy a comprehensive array of attraction, development, retention, and measurement approaches. Below we outline several recommendations for doing just that.

In terms of talent attraction, there is currently a gaping void. According to an Institute for Educational Leadership report, "recruitment is uneven, spotty, and poorly organized in many places. . . . In a 1998 survey, only 27 percent of school districts reported having a program to recruit or prepare aspiring principals."[43] To fill that gap, sector leaders should create a major new talent recruitment engine focused on aggressively courting the "best and brightest" from all sectors and segments of our society. Imagine a national (or regional) initiative with targeted recruitment zones selected for their potential entrepreneurial talent yield (think Silicon Valley, Route 128, and the North Carolina Research Triangle) or for their potential to be "proof of concept" cities because they have a critical mass of dynamic reform efforts (such as New Orleans, Dayton, Milwaukee, Indianapolis, Albany, Washington, D.C., Chicago, New York, and Los Angeles).

Strong local partnerships and the enthusiastic support of top brass would be critical success factors, and the talent attraction campaigns would have to be well designed, amply resourced, and smartly staffed. Taking a page out of Teach For America's playbook, this initiative could entail partnerships between leading universities and employers, and it could be staffed by "campus coordinators"—young ambassadors who evangelize the industry and spread the word about exciting opportunities. Of course, this effort should leverage the strengths of the industry, highlighting the opportunities for positive social impact. These campaigns should also appeal to recruits' pocketbooks by offering competitive, multifaceted compensation packages that include signing bonuses, salary premiums, performance bonuses, and an array of flexible benefits that can be negotiated to meet individual needs. When that is not possible, attractive and prestigious fellowships and internships can serve as cost-effective substitutes, not to mention incubation funds for aspiring entrepreneurs. (The Mind Trust in Indianapolis currently offers both fellowships and incubation support for education entrepreneurs.)

In terms of talent development, we need a radical overhaul. What we have now has recently been called a "scattershot approach," with change only "at the margins."[44] According to a Public Agenda report, 96 percent of principals indicated that their colleagues were more helpful than their graduate studies in preparing them for the job, and two-thirds reported that "leadership programs in graduate schools of education are out of touch" with what they need to know. A separate study by Arthur Levine, former president of Columbia University's Teachers College, concluded that "the majority of [educational administration] programs range from inadequate to appalling, even at some of the country's leading universities."[45] High-quality leadership training programs, fellowships, and internships that combine rigor and depth with practicality and prestige are all too rare in K–12 education.

To fill the void, education needs its own Crotonville—a world-class training institution for emerging leaders or, better yet, a national educational leader training hub with regional spokes. These could be stand-alone entities or programs at existing institutions. (This leadership development initiative could be married to the recruitment initiative outlined above. A coalition of organizations in the Midwest led by the Thomas B. Fordham Foundation is currently considering such an approach.)

The education sector also needs a leadership apprenticeship track closer to the teaching-hospital model. This would contain five components. First, it would maintain high standards and selective criteria, seeking candidates with a broad array of skill sets and capabilities. Second, it would focus heavily on practice, including on-the-job-training and real-world case studies. Third, it would provide intensive supports, including mentoring and coaching by successful practitioners from inside and outside the field. Fourth, it would provide opportunities for close collaboration and networking among peers. Finally, it would systematically track the performance of its cohorts of leaders. We have some examples of promising approaches, including New Leaders for New Schools, the Knowledge Is Power Program (KIPP) Fellows, and The Broad Foundation's Urban Superintendents Academy, but they are drops in a bucket full of need.

An interesting model is the "corporate university," defined as a centralized hub for the education and development of employees, which often addresses job skills, leadership, and organizational culture. In 2001, such universities existed in two thousand companies, up from four hundred in 1993, with projections of more than thirty-seven hundred by 2010.[46] Examples are legion. Southwest Airlines operates what it calls the "University for the People," a structured training program staffed with thirty-two employees that includes new-employee orientation, leadership, technology, and customer service for up to fifteen thousand employees per year.[47] Other examples include Motorola University (a global pioneer in deploying virtual reality in manufacturing training), Boeing's Leadership Center (focused on executive learning, including performance management, organizational structure, and core leadership courses), the University of Disneyland, Federal Express Quality University, Oracle University, FORDSTAR, Dell University, and more. In education, such endeavors might be cost-prohibitive for a typical school district or education service provider but could be developed by a consortium of districts or providers in collaboration with universities or companies.

The K–12 sector could also benefit from a dramatic change in its leadership paradigm, with full-fledged empowerment and results-based accountability replacing today's dominant mode of top-down, bureaucratic hierarchy. According to an Institute for Educational Leadership report, "the principalship generally is constructed as a position not so much for leadership . . . as for middle management," and micromanagement is as common in the sector as it is deadening—from school boards debating garbage cleanup after Friday night football to lunchroom duties and fundraisers that are carefully scripted by district policy.[48]

Principals and their administrative teams should be treated as the leaders that they are, with wide-ranging autonomy for how things get done (process) and accountability for ensuring that things do in fact get done (outcomes). A significant example of this is being championed by New York City Schools chancellor Joel Klein. In fall 2007, Klein gave all principals in the Big Apple a choice of either converting their school to an "empowerment school" (gaining increased autonomy in exchange for heightened accountability, much like charter schools) or selecting from a dozen school-support organizations on a competitive basis, rather than using a central office with an automatic monopoly.[49]

Similarly, governing boards and their organization's senior leaders— whether a district superintendent or a nonprofit executive director—need a clearer understanding of the "division of labor" across their respective roles, both in terms of where their purviews differ and where they converge. Furthermore, devising more explicit career paths for potential and emerging leaders would give people, including teachers, a sense of what is possible if they hone their skills and advance. (A promising example is the Teacher Advancement Program, which provides multiple career paths, market-driven compensation, performance-based accountability, and ongoing professional growth opportunities.) And there is no reason that policies like Google's 20 percent rule cannot be imported into education to foster autonomy and innovation. If forward-thinking online content houses, education service providers, and assessment firms adopted this practice, schools and districts might find ways to follow suit.

In terms of talent retention, what the sector needs most is a healthy infusion of best practices in leadership, including the creation of high-performing teams and a culture of success. That tends to follow from clear expectations, freedom to innovate, opportunities to take substantial risks, and rewards for performance. It is estimated that half of salaried employees nationwide work in jobs with some performance pay, but the education sector lags woefully behind on this front.[50]

Flexible work arrangements can go a long way toward both retention and attraction of talent otherwise deemed unavailable. For example, long-time educational entrepreneur Stacey Boyd recently launched Savvy Source for Parents, an information hub and network for parents looking for high-quality early childhood education options. Stacey built a "virtual" company comprised of a hundred part-time working moms across the country, with all employees and contractors working from home. Together, they created a Web-based guide to nearly all the preschools in the United States and are now expanding into providing consumer ratings for camps, educational games, learning activities, and more. According to Boyd, "I would say 95 percent of our work is done in the morning before the kids wake up, in the afternoon when they take naps, and at night when they go to bed. . . . Everything gets done faster and better. It's extraordinary."[51]

CREATING A PLACE WHERE TALENT CAN THRIVE

There is no doubt that we need an operating environment in K–12 that is more conducive to fostering talent. Specifically, the sector should have compelling incentives to entice exceptional entrepreneurs to enter the field—or at least a violent dismantling of today's daunting barriers to entry. Too often, budding entrepreneurs spend countless hours and precious resources navigating Byzantine bureaucracies, abiding by layers of regulations and procedures, and suffering through political skirmishes when they could be doing the real work of educating schoolchildren. What they need are policy environments dramatically more conducive to innovation and excellence, including meaningful standards, an embrace of choice and competition, full funding for charter schools and other innovative models, astute deregulation, and results-based accountability. On the last front, public policy could be much more aggressive in promulgating standards for information exchange and transparency and commonality of data across school systems. This must be accompanied by public-private funds that provide seed and early-stage capital to entrepreneurs with promising ideas, not to mention a dramatically more robust support infrastructure for educational enterprise.

In addition, sector leaders need to change policies that prevent the inflow of talent and the outflow of mediocrity. The kinds of protections that some education workers enjoy are unheard of in many other industries. While designed with good intentions and serving some useful purposes, they result too often in bizarre inefficiencies that are terribly frustrating to well-intentioned people trying to work within the system. Consider, for example, collectively bargained transfer, seniority, and "excess teacher" rules that regulate the movement of teachers among schools and cause painful hiring delays. Think also of the complex array of credentialing requirements that vary across states and conflate paper-based certification with qualification and talent. Education professionals are regularly confronted with these challenges and dilemmas, which frequently lead them to exit the field altogether or resign themselves to just "getting by"—not exactly a formula for excellence.

Absent sweeping state-level legislation and regulatory change to remove these barriers, which have so far remained elusive, what is needed is a local holding environment that creates an opportunity space for risk-taking and substantive change. Too many well-meaning superintendents face firing squads of board of education members tied into the interest group politics of union muscling. Without political capital and cover and operational breathing room, they are bound to suffer the same ill fate as their equally well-intentioned predecessors. This speaks to the importance of the political talent pipeline that reformers too often neglect.

Of course, there is much else that could be done. But we believe that these recommendations address the fundamental talent issues prevalent in the sector. In education today, there is no shortage of innovative ideas and reform prescriptions. We are also graced with examples of high-performing schools and dynamic education enterprises. Too often missing, however, is a supply of dynamic, talented, and effective leaders and professionals who can embrace and implement those ideas and lead schools and organizations to excellence.

The larger picture is that we are now in a period of profound transformation, including significant economic, technological, demographic, and social shifts. This presents a major opportunity for the education sector. Unfortunately, it appears as though much of the education sector is content to turn a blind eye to the war for talent—falling back on outmoded practices that have yielded millions of students not achieving proficiency in core academic subjects, alarming test-score gaps, and declining international competitiveness. If we have any hope of offering an education worthy of our children and their full range of possibilities, we must dramatically increase the supply of quality talent in the sector.

CHAPTER 2

Attracting Entrepreneurs to K–12

Bryan C. Hassel

Talk of "human capital" in education typically focuses on the flow of teachers, school leaders, and central office administrators available to the nation's school systems. But as more focus turns to entrepreneurship as part of education reform, it makes sense to devote more attention as well to the pipeline of entrepreneurial people entering K–12 education.[1] Whether entrepreneurship thrives in K–12 education will depend in large part on the amount and quality of enterprising talent flowing into the sector over time.

This chapter begins by defining the need for entrepreneurial people in public education. What kind of people would fuel entrepreneurship in education, and what are some potential sources of that talent? The following section turns to barriers. What constraints currently restrict the flow of enterprising people into the sector? The chapter then analyzes a number of initiatives underway across the country that could, directly or indirectly, bring more entrepreneurial people into education. The final section examines promising actions that funders, policymakers, and entrepreneurial organizations themselves could take to bring more high-quality entrepreneurial individuals into public education.

THE NEED FOR ENTREPRENEURS

Many people contribute to the success of a typical entrepreneurial venture. At its heart is the founder or founding team, the individual or small group of people who initiate and drive the development of the new organization. But the enterprise may also have a board of directors, a senior team of managers, and a host of line managers and employees (or contractors) to carry out the venture's core, day-to-day work. [2] For example, in the case of a charter management organization running schools, the venture needs building principals, teachers, counselors, and other school-level support staff, as well as individuals to staff central office functions such as financial operations and data management.

While the focus of this chapter is on the first category—entrepreneurs themselves—the other pipelines are also critical to the future of educational entrepreneurship, for three reasons. First, enterprise founders cannot simply do their work at scale alone. Second, the pipeline of people available to serve in these other roles is likely to affect prospective entrepreneurs' decisions about whether to apply their talents in the education sector. Entrepreneurs are unlikely to launch ventures in education unless they believe that they will be able to assemble the boards and teams they need. Finally, these secondary pipelines are important because of their potential to feed the founder pipeline of the future. For all of these reasons, a full treatment of the human capital challenge in educational entrepreneurship needs to also consider the supply of these supporting players.

The Entrepreneurial Profile

A wide-ranging literature exists on the determinants of successful entrepreneurship.[3] Several generalizations emerge from this literature about what sets entrepreneurs apart from others. As with any such list, this one carries the caveat that these are general tendencies rather than complete descriptions of all individual entrepreneurs:

- *Need for Achievement.* Entrepreneurs are highly motivated to set high goals and drive toward results, regardless of barriers, with clear metrics that quantify their success.
- *Relentless Problem-Solving.* Entrepreneurs tirelessly search for solutions to problems that arise, trying and discarding strategies with an extraordinary sense of urgency.
- *Internal Locus of Control.* Entrepreneurs see themselves as responsible for the outcomes of their own actions; they are unwilling to make excuses for failing to achieve results.
- *Tolerance for Ambiguity.* Entrepreneurs generally have a high tolerance for ambiguity and perceive such situations as desirable.

- *Strategic Influencing.* Though they may have strong interpersonal skills, they use influence less to foster long-term relationships than to induce immediate actions to advance the organization.
- *Bias for Action through Organization-Building.* As Kim Smith and Julie Petersen note, "their sense of urgency and drive to achieve leads them to take action by creating new organizations that will make their vision a reality."[4]

Of course, many individuals working within existing K–12 institutions possess some, or even all, of these qualities. Indeed, some of today's most successful educational entrepreneurs arose from within the ranks of teachers, school leaders, and other within-system roles. But these are not the qualities that underlie the institutions' daily efforts at recruitment, selection, and professional development. Teachers, in particular, are not selected based on their propensity to conceive of radically new ideas and build organizations to realize their visions; this is not the work teachers are expected to do. And the situation is much the same for leaders of schools and school systems who, by and large, are selected with an eye toward serving as stewards of long-standing and relatively stable organizations rather than as initiators of new endeavors and institutions.

The implication is straightforward: If there is going to be an increase in the supply of entrepreneurs in education, it will need to derive from one of two sources. Either more entrepreneurial people who are currently working outside of education will need to be induced to enter the sector laterally, or a new generation of people will need to be recruited into school teaching and leading roles in the hope that they will eventually found entrepreneurial ventures within the sector.

Potential Sources of Entrepreneurial Talent

These possibilities suggest two pools of talent worth cultivating for future educational entrepreneurship. Both are, in fact, well-represented by the current generation of educational entrepreneurs already at work. Many of the more prominent education ventures today were launched by individuals who came, in one way or another, from the ranks of teachers and school administrators. These people can loosely be grouped into two categories. One is a set of individuals who early in their teaching careers became educational entrepreneurs. A quintessential example is the duo of Michael Feinberg and David Levin, members of Houston's Teach For America (TFA) corps who launched the Knowledge Is Power Program (KIPP) initially as a program within a mid-

dle school, then as a full middle school, and then as a major initiative to seed
KIPP schools all over the United States. Another TFA corps member, Michelle
Rhee, founded The New Teacher Project, which has recruited approximately
23,000 mid-career professionals and recent college graduates to teach in public schools.[5]

Among the young-teachers-as-entrepreneurs, it is not a coincidence that
the two examples are drawn from the ranks of TFA corps members. TFA
recruits top college graduates to assume teaching posts in low-income communities. In 2007–08, approximately 5,000 corps members taught in twenty-six urban and rural regions nationwide, a number that is likely to increase
over time as TFA expands geographically. The number of new corps members in fall 2007 (2,900) is 20 percent larger than last year's crop of recruits.
Although some TFA teachers remain in the classroom beyond the requisite
two years, the vast majority move into other roles in education and beyond;
the organization's goal is not to recruit career teachers but to enlist the next
generation of leaders in a "movement to end education inequity" through
their initial teaching service and a lifetime of engagement in the issue.

As a result, TFA corps members appear much more likely to launch entrepreneurial ventures than the typical teacher. The organization does not currently maintain a full list of entrepreneurial ventures launched by corps
alumni, but it does provide a set of examples that, beyond Feinberg and Levin,
includes the founders of Generation Schools (Furman Brown), Idea Schools
(Tom Torkelson), YesPrep Public Schools (Chris Barbic), the afterschool soccer
program America Scores (Julie Kennedy), and several other ventures with an
educational component.[6] While this is a significant list, it is still a small portion of TFA's pipeline, which has included some seventeen thousand people
over the organization's history. And since TFA's corps is specifically selected
to have leadership potential, the fact that careers in educational entrepreneurship are the extreme exception within TFA suggests that they will be
exceedingly rare among the broader public school teaching ranks.

The other group of educators becoming entrepreneurs is seasoned school
personnel who strike out to form entrepreneurial ventures later in their
careers. One example is Don Shalvey who, in classic public education style,
served as classroom teacher, counselor, assistant superintendent, and superintendent before founding the charter management organization Aspire Public Schools. Another is Larry Rosenstock, founder of High Tech High and the
High Tech High school development organization that is opening schools
across California. Rosenstock's career is more of a hybrid, with stints in
higher education, the U.S. government, and the nonprofit sector—but also

with substantial experience as a classroom teacher and school administrator prior to his launch of High Tech High.

Many of today's educational entrepreneurs came from diverse sources other than the existing ranks of educators and schools administrators. Commonly, individuals developed a track record outside of education before launching their entrepreneurial ventures—whether in government (for example, Jon Schnur of New Leaders for New Schools, who served in the Clinton administration and the U.S. Department of Education), business (for example, Larry Berger of Wireless Generation, formerly president of a web solutions company), or social services (for example, J. B. Schramm of College Summit, who ran a teen learning center). Less common is the path followed by Wendy Kopp, who entered the field much earlier in her career, conceiving of Teach For America while in college and founding the organization right after graduation. With such a set of idiosyncratic career paths, it is difficult to generalize about routes into educational entrepreneurship from outside of K–12.

BARRIERS TO THE FLOW OF ENTREPRENEURS

Why are there not more individuals interested in launching entrepreneurial ventures in the K–12 sector? There are a number of general barriers and constraints that apply across all of these sources of potential supply, though the way these barriers play out differs in some cases from one source to the next.

Policy and Political Barriers

In the literature on entrepreneurship, one of the central determinants of the level of entrepreneurial activity is the regulatory framework that governs the start-up and management of such organizations. Some of the constraints can be absolute, such as prohibitions on certain kinds of entrepreneurial activity. Examples from education are the absence of charter school legislation in ten states, state charter laws that prohibit schools managed by for-profit companies, or textbook adoption policies that prevent new providers from entering the market. Of more interest in this discussion, however, are restrictions that, while they do not flatly prohibit entrepreneurial activity, make it more difficult and, therefore, make education a relatively unattractive sector for individuals interested in entrepreneurship.

These are a subset of the litany of charges that have been leveled at the U.S. K–12 system over the years, and discussing all of them is certainly beyond the scope of this chapter. Two of the most significant include

- *Unmanageability.* Public education is notorious for the web of constraints that make it difficult for managers to take the kinds of actions that are taken for granted in entrepreneurial organizations, such as assembling a team, making ongoing personnel decisions, allocating resources, and real-locating dollars over time to new approaches and strategies. A wide range of federal, state, and district policies, coupled with contractual restrictions negotiated with teacher unions and other employee organizations, make this kind of management activity difficult or impossible. Such an environment is not likely to be attractive to entrepreneurs who have other opportunities that will allow them to manage in a more flexible fashion.
- *Paradox of stasis and "spinning wheels."* Analysts such as John Chubb and Terry Moe have characterized public education as an ossifying system in which competing interests layer on debilitating constraints over years of political conflict—constraints that, for a variety of reasons inherent in American political institutions, are difficult or impossible to change.[7] Frederick M. Hess's work, by contrast, portrays a world of constant, even frenetic change that he calls "spinning wheels."[8] While seemingly at odds, these two accounts appear to coexist within a system that is constantly changing in some respects—most of which have little impact on what happens in classrooms—and that is highly resistant to change in others. Both features are inimical to entrepreneurs. Stasis makes it difficult for entrepreneurs to break in, since old arrangements are unlikely to change in the near-term. Spinning wheels, by contrast, mean that the reform du jour, which may be very hospitable to a certain segment of entrepreneurs, may not last beyond the current superintendent's tenure or state election. In either context, it makes little sense for entrepreneurs to invest in capacity to serve the education market.

One area of policy—charter schooling—is especially important to the attractiveness of the education sector for entrepreneurs, for a couple of reasons. First, when states make it possible for individuals and groups to start charter schools, they open up a direct channel for entrepreneurial activity via launching one of these independently operated public schools. With the added possibility of building up networks of schools as part of a charter management organization or some other enterprise, the prospects for scale-oriented entrepreneurs are even stronger. Second, because they are a new and growing segment of the education sector, charter schools (and networks) are in the process of spawning, through their demand, a range of other entrepreneurial ventures that are not themselves charter schools. Civic Builders, for example, is a New York City–based nonprofit that develops and leases facilities for charter schools. Other examples include the bevy of back-office service providers like Delaware's Innovative Schools Development Corporation that carry out accounting, payroll, and other ancillary functions for charter schools. All of these organizations have been able to form and grow chiefly because of the demand for their services created by charter schools.

If charter policy in a state is relatively open, this state of affairs doubly improves the climate for educational entrepreneurship. If charter policy is restrictive, it discourages talented people from starting charter schools, scaling charter networks, and developing services to support the charter sector. And many states do in fact impose significant growth-limiting restrictions on charter schools. The most obvious is actual caps on the number of charter schools, the number of charter school students, or the charter school market share, currently in force in some form in twenty-five states and the District of Columbia.[9] Sixteen states limit chartering by requiring local school boards to approve new charters; boards that (with some notable exceptions) usually oppose charter schools and are unlikely to approve many of them.[10] States also place restrictions on charter schools by imposing various legal and regulatory constraints on them (for example, requiring them to abide by class size restrictions or restrictions that limit how different sources of funds may be used). Finally, state policy affects charter school growth by limiting the amount of funding available to charter schools. Only seventeen states grant them any kind of facilities funding.[11] And in one study of sixteen states and the District of Columbia, which at the time enrolled 84 percent of the nation's charter students, states were found to provide 22 percent less funding to charter schools, on average, than district schools.[12]

Financial Barriers

Various aspects of the financial scene in K–12 make it a relatively unattractive destination for entrepreneurs. To begin with, as Kim Smith and Julie Petersen discuss in chapter 4, there is not a sufficient flow of venture capital available to launch new enterprises within the education sector. Would-be entrepreneurs face a great deal of uncertainty about whether they will be able to raise the necessary start-up funding. At the same time, they face a great deal of certainty that they will need to devote significant energy year after year to raising funds.

Some entrepreneurial ventures, of course, have the potential to generate sufficient revenue over time to cover costs and therefore do not require ongoing philanthropic infusions. Still, as Larry Berger and David Stevenson illustrate in chapter 5 of this volume, organizations that plan to rely on fee revenue still face a relatively unattractive market of potential customers. Their best bets for winning large contracts are school districts, but most large districts are highly constrained by regulations and political forces in how they allocate resources. The vast bulk of a school district's revenues is spoken for through various grant restrictions, state-imposed line items, and contractual obligations. A more nimble set of customers is the growing segment of charter management organizations, which have much more flexibility than districts. These entities, however, are still a small slice of the education-funding pie and, as a result, are not as attractive as customers.

Finally, it is often said that education is a less appealing venue for entrepreneurship because no one is likely to get rich serving the education market. With tight public education budgets and a culture that recoils at the idea of profiting on children, it is arguably unlikely that many ventures in the education space will generate the kind of riches that many assume are necessary to recruit entrepreneurial people into an industry. This conventional story, however, may overstate matters. Entrepreneurs flock to many other venues, such as retail stores and restaurants, in which most business owners do not get rich. In one comprehensive survey, the 2002 median earnings level of small-business owners was $65,000—higher but not dramatically higher than the median for wage and salaried employees ($52,635). And yet many people (8.4 percent of the survey's sample) still apparently found small-business ownership attractive.[13] And there is certainly some fraction of people with an entrepreneurial bent who are motivated more by the potential for social impact than by the potential for wealth. So the degree to which the lack of a likely financial upside puts a throttle on the supply of entrepreneurs is unknown.

Cultural and Structural Barriers

Two unique aspects of the culture of education are also worth noting as constraints on the flow of entrepreneurial talent into the field—one that affects "outsiders" and one that affects "insiders." Outsiders face the fact that public education's hiring patterns favor people who have worked their way up the system in the conventional fashion—namely, by becoming a teacher and then an assistant principal and/or principal, and so on. According to a RAND study, for example, 99 percent of school principals had been teachers. Fully 90 percent of school superintendents had been teachers.[14] This pattern means that individuals seeking to break into the education industry from other sectors are working against convention.

The typical career path within K–12 education also affects the likelihood that insiders will go on to become entrepreneurs later in their careers. The most important culprit is the way teachers' jobs and careers are typically constructed. As Frederick M. Hess and I put it, "Although some individuals with considerable entrepreneurial potential certainly do enter K–12 as teachers, the teaching job offers few opportunities for them to develop their entrepreneurial skills."[15] Most teachers carry a full teaching load, allowing them little time to participate significantly in developing or managing initiatives that might prepare them for entrepreneurship or signal to others that they have entrepreneurial capabilities. The exceptions are those who have moved into coaching or other support roles, but those functions also largely fill up their holders' time with day-to-day activities, not opportunities to be enterprising. And promotion within education means moving into an assistant principalship or principalship, neither of which, again, is an entrepreneurial position. As a result, people with an entrepreneurial bent are likely to be frustrated as teachers and seek out other ways to flex their enterprising muscles, or they will simply avoid teaching altogether.

INITIATIVES TO INCREASE ENTERPRISING TALENT

In recent years, several initiatives have launched that are designed to increase the flow of talent into public education. Some aim to recruit entrepreneurs to start new education ventures. Others indirectly fuel the entrepreneurial pipeline by attracting talented and, potentially enterprising people who may go on to become entrepreneurs. This section profiles several of these initiatives in those two categories.

Recruiting Entrepreneurs to Launch Education Ventures

Several initiatives exist to recruit entrepreneurial leaders for a wide range of education ventures, and others aim to entice people to launch specific kinds of enterprises—namely, charter school management organizations or individual charter schools.[16] In the first group, here are some of the leading examples.

NewSchools Venture Fund. This California-based nonprofit was founded in 1998 by Kim Smith and two venture capitalists, John Doerr and Brook Byers. New-Schools raises money from philanthropic sources and then invests in entrepreneurial ventures across a wide swath of the education sector. NewSchools's website lists twenty-eight current members in its portfolio. The majority are charter management organizations, collectively operating nearly a hundred schools that together serve twenty-six thousand students. The other ventures fall into three categories: school support organizations, which provide facilities and other support for charter schools; human capital ventures, which recruit people into teaching or leadership and provide professional development; and accountability and performance tools, a catch-all for a diverse set of additional investments.

A number of features of the NewSchools approach are worth noting. First, like a for-profit venture-capital fund, NewSchools is proactive, both in seeking out potential entrepreneurs to address high-priority needs and in supporting the organizations in which it invests in a hands-on fashion, typically taking a seat on an enterprise's board. The predominance of charter management organizations (CMOs) within the portfolio, for example, arose from a strategic decision to focus its investment on this kind of organization, beginning in 2002. Second, building a network of educational entrepreneurs is a priority for NewSchools. NewSchools develops communities of practice in which ventures have the chance to interact with one another in live meetings and through an online knowledge management system. It also runs an annual gathering of educational entrepreneurs in Aspen and an ongoing Entrepreneurial Leaders in Public Education program for cohorts of educational entrepreneurs. Finally, while "recruiting educational entrepreneurs" does not appear on any official list of NewSchools's activities, the organization plays this role to a substantial degree. NewSchools offers funding and support as carrots to entice entrepreneurs to enter the space, but its staff is also out shaking the trees to find people who can launch, staff, or serve on the boards of the ventures that they support.

Teach For America Social Entrepreneurship Initiative. This initiative, launched in 2007, surveys TFA alumni to gauge their interest in social entrepreneurship, the barriers that they perceive, and the support that they hope for. Based in part on that input, TFA will design an array of supports for people at different levels of readiness and interest, from those for whom a social venture is just the seed of an idea to those well on their way to developing an enterprise. This support may be provided in some cases by TFA directly, but its aim is also to cultivate partnerships with existing organizations that already have something to offer would-be social entrepreneurs. TFA hopes that before 2010 the initiative will help spawn as many as ten new social enterprises that have achieved some metrics of scale, recognition, or impact.

The Mind Trust. While the first two initiatives have a national scope, The Mind Trust is a new nonprofit specifically focused on the city of Indianapolis. The Mind Trust's core program to recruit talented entrepreneurs is its Education Entrepreneurship Fellowship, which it launched in fall 2007. The idea of the fellowship is to offer two years of relatively high salary ($90,000), full benefits, office space, and an array of customized support to highly capable people seeking to start new education ventures. The Mind Trust awarded its first fellowship in spring 2008, and it expects to name a cohort of up to four people each year. Their ventures could be new schools, new networks of schools, or organizations that support schools in some way, but they need to have some kind of transformative potential for public education in Indianapolis or elsewhere. The Mind Trust grew out of former mayor Bart Peterson's charter school initiative, in which the mayor and his charter advisor David Harris determined that they needed to do more to create a pipeline of people who could found charter schools and other education start-ups. Harris left the mayor's office to form the nonprofit, whose board included Peterson (as chair), the superintendent of Indianapolis Public Schools, and other civic leaders. In addition to the fellowship, the organization also operates a venture fund that has successfully attracted some existing entrepreneurial organizations—including Teach For America, The New Teacher Project, and College Summit—to set up shop in Indianapolis. Between the fellowship and the fund, the idea is to create a strong network of enterprising talent and energy in a single city, magnifying the potential impact of entrepreneurship.

The next set of initiatives are also aimed at recruiting entrepreneurs but not to found charter management organizations or charter schools specifically. Rather, they are focused on the wider category of educational entrepreneurs. These include:

Charter School Growth Fund. Funded by some of the leading foundations in the charter world, the Charter School Growth Fund is "a philanthropic venture fund founded to significantly increase the capacity of proven educational entrepreneurs to develop and grow networks of high-quality charter schools." The organization invites existing successful charter operators to apply to become part of its business planning cohort program, in which they receive substantial help, feedback, and, if they meet the fund's milestones, grant and loan funding to cover much or all of the central office that the operator will need to develop a network of schools. Participants also have access to the fund's facilities financing program, which addresses one of the critical constraints on charter school growth. As of September 2007, the organization's website listed twelve grantees that have received a combined $30 million from the fund. Like NewSchools, while the Charter School Growth Fund's most visible activity is providing money, cultivating talent is a central focus as well. To start with, a key part of the due diligence process on prospective ventures is the capability of the founding team; feedback and support often centers on filling out that team and shoring up weak areas. In addition, the Fund has just launched a new "C Program" that will convene eighteen people in each of four geographic markets, a combination of people already involved in C-level jobs (for example, CEO, COO, etc.) in charter networks and other talented professionals working in other spheres but with an interest in the charter market. Bringing people together in semimonthly programs, unstructured mentorships, and an annual conference, the program's objective is to expose outside professionals to the sector in the hope that some will end up serving on network boards or even taking C-level jobs in the enterprises.

Building Excellent Schools. Founded by longtime charter school supporter and advocate Linda Brown, Building Excellent Schools (BES) offers a yearlong fellowship to aspiring charter school founders. Fellows receive $80,000 stipends; approximately a hundred days of intense training, including visits to top-performing charter schools; an extended residency in a high-performing urban charter school; and ongoing coaching and support around board and charter application development. BES is based in Boston but enrolls fellows interested in starting charter schools in any of 14 other cities across the country. As of fall 2007, 27 fellow-founded charter schools were open or on their way to opening, the result of five classes of fellows proceeding through the BES program.

New Schools for New Orleans. In every state with charter schools and in some large cities, there are nonprofit organizations that exist to provide support for the charter sector. In some respects, all of these organizations could be considered initiatives designed to recruit founders of charter schools, but in practice their focus on this supply question is often limited. Much more of their time and resources go into supporting existing schools and advocating for the sector as a whole in the policy arena. New Schools for New Orleans (NSNO) is one exception to this generalization, a natural departure in light of the extreme need for supply faced by New Orleans as it seeks to reopen its post-Katrina school system largely by starting charter schools. Central to NSNO's effort is its incubation program, which beginning in 2007–08 will provide $10,000 per month to founders of charter schools or charter management organizations. In addition to payment, NSNO will also offer leadership training, legal and operational assistance, teacher recruitment services, board development help, charter application review, exposure to existing excellent schools, and links to potential community partners. The incubator is too new to assess, but its relatively high pay and high level of services make it a standout among organizations seeking to foster charter supply.

Indirectly Fueling the Pipeline

While these initiatives directly aim to recruit entrepreneurs, several others are designed to entice talented people into other roles within the education system, such as teachers, school principals, or district or CMO managers. Some of them are potentially important to the entrepreneurial pipeline because their existence could make the sector more attractive to entrepreneurs and because some of their graduates may go on to become entrepreneurs.

It is important to point out that within the broad range of programs designed to recruit and prepare people for roles in the educational system, only a handful appear designed specifically with the potential to cultivate a significant number of entrepreneurial leaders. Generally speaking, existing programs (which tend to be university-based principal- and teacher-preparation programs) are not set up to attract entrepreneurially minded people or equip them with entrepreneurial skill sets. In recent years, researchers have raised significant questions about whether most school leader preparation programs are even equipping students well for non-entrepreneurial management roles. Arthur Levine's *Educating School Leaders* study, for example, reached scathing conclusions about how poor most school administration degree programs are.[17] Frederick M. Hess and Andrew Kelly's analysis of administration program syllabi revealed that critical topics for today's school leaders, such as managing for results and using data, received scant attention in core courses across different types of institutions.[18] Another Hess and Kelly review found that even some highly touted new leadership programs were, in fact, fairly traditional.[19] No doubt, there is a great deal of ferment in the field of leader and teacher preparation. Several urban districts, such as New York City and Boston, have developed leadership academies to try to better prepare school leaders. But even these more cutting-edge efforts seem largely designed to equip administrators for conventional principalships, not entrepreneurial roles.

As a consequence, the focus here is on a subset of pipeline programs that have more emphasis in their selection criteria and/or programmatic content on entrepreneurial leadership. Some examples include:

The Broad Residency in Urban Education. Sponsored by The Broad Foundation, the residency provides "graduates from business, public policy, and law schools who have at least four years of work experience in the private or public sector" with "immediate placement into full-time management positions in urban school districts and CMOs, while providing two years of professional development and access to a nationwide network of education leaders."[20] Residents report directly to their hosts' top executives, and the program seeks to have them assigned to major special projects during their tenure. The program pays starting salaries of $80,000 to $90,000. According to the residency website, over 110 residents have been employed by more than 35 school districts and CMOs, and 94 percent remain in the education sector.

New Leaders for New Schools. New Leaders for New Schools (NLNS) is a national effort to attract, prepare, and support outstanding leaders for our nation's urban public schools.[21] The organization recruits candidates nationally, conducts a competitive selection process, and then offers those it selects a five-week Summer Foundations training, paid residency in schools with mentor principals, help finding principalships, and ongoing support after they become principals. From 2001 to 2007, NLNS trained or placed more than 431 principals in cities like Baltimore, Chicago, Memphis, New York, Oakland, Washington, D.C., San Francisco, Milwaukee, and New Orleans. In each city, NLNS develops an elaborate partnership with the school district, local funders, and others to establish its program. In addition to finding placements for its recruits as residents and then principals, it also asks districts to give its graduates sufficient autonomy to lead their schools.

Teach For America. TFA recruits top college graduates to teach for two years in high-poverty urban and rural schools. Over 16 years, 17,000 corps members joined TFA, which now works in 26 communities nationally. In 2007, over 18,000 people applied to TFA, and it selected about 2,900 corps members (16 percent acceptance rate). At some elite colleges, a high percentage of graduating seniors applied to become corps members, according to a TFA press release: "11 percent of the senior classes at Amherst and Spelman; 10 percent of those at University of Chicago and Duke; and more than eight percent of the graduating seniors at Notre Dame, Princeton and Wellesley" applied for the corps.[22] A critical part of TFA's "theory of change" is that its alumni, based in part on the experience that they have as corps members, will go on to some kind of lifelong commitment to educational equality— whether they remain in education, tackle some related social challenge, or influence policy or opinion in some other way. The organization now cultivates its alumni network through means such as the social entrepreneurship initiative described above.

The New Teacher Project. Like TFA, The New Teacher Project (TNTP) recruits talented people to become teachers, though with more of a slant toward mid-career professionals and recent college graduates.[23] As of fall 2007, the organization had "recruited, prepared and/or certified approximately 23,000" teachers in several cities, including four of the five largest school districts nationally. Fully a quarter of New York City's math teachers were hired through TNTP's NYC Teaching Fellows program. In 2007, some 84 percent of recruited teachers filled "critical shortage area subjects such as math, science, and special education."[24] Also like TFA, TNTP seeks to run a selective admissions process, accepting about 14 percent of applicants as fellows, with an average college GPA of 3.3. Unlike TFA, which signs up corps members for a two-year commitment, TNTP explicitly aims to achieve a high retention rate over time.

High Tech High. As of fall 2007, High Tech High (HTH) operated a network of eight charter schools. HTH enters the pipeline discussion because of its unique effort to move upstream in the teacher pipeline, taking control of functions that school-management organizations typically leave to higher education. In 2004, HTH gained authority from the California Commission on Teacher Credentialing to certify teachers for its own schools and others. Interns can now earn their teacher credentials by serving as full-time, salaried teachers in charter school classrooms. More remarkably, in 2007, HTH opened its own Graduate School of Education, which will offer master's degrees in teacher leadership and, in the future, school leadership. In the teacher program, candidates continue to work full-time as teachers, typically within the HTH network. They attend summer classes for a month and have four one-week residencies at HTH schools over the course of a year, working with a mentor throughout that time. Unlike traditional higher-education–based credentialing and degree programs, which tend to prepare teachers generically to teach in many kinds of schools, HTH initiatives explicitly aim to prepare teachers for schools like those in the HTH network (that is, schools that engage in project-based learning with an emphasis on real world application). HTH is one of a relatively small number of charter school networks that has moved into the teacher preparation business. Another example is a teaching institute launched in New York by a partnership between KIPP, Achievement First, and Uncommon Schools, though in contrast to HTH's stand-alone entity, the institute will be linked to an existing higher education institution, Hunter College.

Academy for Urban School Leadership. A final teacher pipeline initiative worth mentioning here is the Chicago-based Academy for Urban School Leadership (AUSL), which has taken an approach substantially different from those of programs discussed above. Each year, AUSL recruits forty to fifty mid-career professionals or recent college graduates to enter a medicine-style residency, working full-time in the classroom of a mentor-teacher and earning a master's degree. Residents make a five-year commitment as a condition for participating, and AUSL helps place and support them over time. Both the intensity of the preparation (an entire year prior to assuming full teaching responsibilities) and the expectation of retention set AUSL's program apart. Also interesting is the organization's decision in 2005 to go beyond its teacher preparation work and assume the management of turnaround schools in Chicago, where it fills a percentage of their classrooms with its own participants.

MAKING BUILDING HUMAN CAPITAL SOMEONE'S JOB

Perhaps what is most important about these initiatives is that they create groups of people whose everyday job it is to attract enterprising individuals into K–12 education. This increases the number of brains focused on the barriers to that pipeline and on their potential solutions. It also makes it more likely that potential educational entrepreneurs will hear the message that public education is a viable sector for them. The more organizations are at job fairs, advertising in the media, speaking at professional schools, and activating professional networks, the more likely enterprising individuals are to consider the sector.

Still, the number (and thus volume and reach) of these voices is still relatively small. TFA currently brings about 3,000 teachers per year into a system projected to need about 90,000 per year in the foreseeable future. Less than a hundred school leaders enter per year under these programs. And the initiatives designed specifically to attract entrepreneurs are likely to support—collectively—no more than a few dozen of them in a given year. It would be a mistake to think that, because of the existence of these initiatives, domains such as teacher, leader, and entrepreneur recruitment are now taken care of.

Funders and other advocates of increased educational entrepreneurship need to do more work in this arena, expanding the number of people whose job it is to recruit entrepreneurial people into public education. They could pursue this expansion through two routes: inducing the existing initiatives profiled above (and others like them) to expand or creating new initiatives with similar objectives.

THE IMPORTANCE OF NETWORKS

One of the central findings of literature on entrepreneurship is the importance of networks of enterprising people.[25] Networks can be formal, in which some organization makes a deliberate effort to convene people in person or electronically and to facilitate interactions. Or they can be informal, arising naturally as individuals engaged in entrepreneurship meet, forge relationships, and begin to exchange information and otherwise help each other. It is within these networks that entrepreneurs make connections to sources of capital, find talented team members, discover business opportunities with one another, benchmark against each other regarding key areas of practice, and share critical information. This network effect is one of the factors that accounts for thriving geographical centers of entrepreneurial activity, most famously Silicon Valley.

Many of the initiatives profiled here have sought to play exactly this sort of network function. NewSchools Venture Fund's various networks, mentioned above, convene entrepreneurs several times a year to discuss common challenges, share tools and resources, and engage in joint learning with experts. Through a variety of formats (among them panel and group discussions, team exercises, presentations from experts or practitioners from other sectors), entrepreneurs have a chance to acquire new information and insights and get to know one another. Charter School Growth Fund's "C Program" connects top CMO leaders with each other and with people currently playing managerial or professional roles in the business world who may someday become CMO board or team members. A central component of the Mind Trust will be forging networks among the people that they recruit. These will likely have benefits for their members, but their value potentially extends one more step: Their existence may make the field more attractive to (and more likely to be discovered by) the next group of prospective entrepreneurs who will know that they can join a vibrant group of like-minded people if they enter.

ADDRESSING THE INFORMATION GAP

These steps will have the effect of informing more people about the possibilities for entrepreneurship available within education. But what other strategies could spread the word even more widely? First, organizations that support educational entrepreneurship might seek funds for high-profile campaigns likely to reach potential entrepreneurs with information about what is happening currently in educational entrepreneurship, how effective some entrepreneurial ventures have been, and what opportunities exist. The Broad Residency's marketing materials represent a potential model, starting as they do with a pitch to talented people that education is a field in which they can apply their considerable capabilities and make a difference. "Are you looking for a management career that allows you to have a major impact on society— improving the lives of thousands of young people?" begins the residency's website, which also features alarming statistics about the state of urban public education as well as stories about current and previous residents designed to convince visitors that they can make a positive difference by pursuing the management jobs offered by the Broad Residency. The materials also express the importance of management skills in education—making clear that the capabilities their target audience members have built in their careers are relevant, indeed sorely needed, in K–12 education. This combination of appeals to individuals' social consciousness and their desire to apply their management competencies appears well-calculated to convince emerging business leaders to take a closer look at the opportunity Broad is offering.

Another strategy is the creation of widely publicized competitions for business plans in educational entrepreneurship—or working with existing business plan competitions to encourage educational submissions. The University of Texas's McCombs School of Business, for example, operates the long-running Moot Corp Competition for plans submitted by teams of MBA students worldwide.[26] These competitions not only have the effect of bringing strong existing proposals to the fore, they also, if publicized well, can have the effect of informing a wider audience of the possibility of entrepreneurship within K–12 education.

LIMITS OF RECRUITMENT PROGRAMS

Some of the most interesting developments in the education talent pipeline are not specifically designed to recruit entrepreneurs. Instead, their aim is to bring highly talented people into teaching or school/district administration. These may have the side benefit of enticing people who will later go on to found transformative entrepreneurial ventures. For a couple of reasons, however, this kind of spillover effect is likely to be limited. First, these programs are not generally geared toward recruiting entrepreneurial people per se. They are seeking talent, drive, commitment, and a range of other qualities that would serve entrepreneurs well, though not the specific constellation of qualities that separate successful entrepreneurs from successful professionals or managers in general—such as the former's particular penchant for risk-taking and organization-building. This is not a flaw in these programs; it is perfectly appropriate that they select people for the jobs they will fill. As a result, however, only small fractions of people entering education even through these routes are likely to become educational entrepreneurs. TFA's social enterprise initiative, for example, has a goal of spawning ten successful entrepreneurial ventures by 2010, out of what will by then approach 20,000 current and former corps members.

Second, these initiatives may face incentives that limit their ability to encourage even their more enterprising participants from embarking on entrepreneurial ventures. For example, efforts like TNTP often sign contracts with districts under which their performance will be assessed based in part on their retention of program participants as classroom teachers. Unless these incentives change, these programs cannot be expected to encourage their participants to become entrepreneurs, because every teacher who leaves the classroom to become an entrepreneur (or anything else) counts against them as districts calculate their retention results. Initiatives aimed directly at enticing entrepreneurs, therefore, remain vital.

Perhaps a more promising way to draw more entrepreneurs from the ranks of teachers specifically is to persuade more existing school organizations to envision and create differentiated career paths for teachers that allow entrepreneurial talent to emerge. As Frederick M. Hess and I illuminate, such paths could allow enterprising people

> to continue to work part-time as classroom teachers, while building skill sets and gaining experience in non-classroom contexts. This would permit educators to explore alternatives and gain diverse experiences while reducing the pressure on energetic and highly capable young teachers to decide at a young age whether to become an administrator or leave education. Such positions would allow potential entrepreneurs to undergo some seasoning, connect them with like-minded individuals and potential mentors, and get a taste of an alternate career path within K–12—all standard issue opportunities in thriving entrepreneurial sectors.[27]

HUMAN CAPITAL AND POLICY CHANGE

In general, the initiatives discussed here are designed to improve the flow of talent into K–12 education in spite of the considerable policy barriers described above. One charge that could be leveled against them, accordingly, is that their efforts are merely quixotic windmill tilts or, worse, a rearranging of the deck chairs on a certain well-known ocean liner. However, it may be that these initiatives (to shift metaphors) contain the seeds of policy change even as they aim to grow within education's currently unfertile soil.

Though calls for making public education more dynamic, less bureaucratic, and more manageable have been sounded for decades, the rise of these various human-capital–seeking initiatives presents the possibility of a different dynamic going forward. These organizations have a strong concentrated interest in certain policy changes that would increase the likelihood that their work would turn out more successfully. New Leaders for New Schools, for example, is in a position to have communities vie for the organization to make it the next NLNS expansion site. This competition could potentially give NLNS the leverage it needs to ensure that the principals it places in those communities have the power to lead their schools effectively. Whatever the impact, this appears more potent than that of another white paper on the importance of principal autonomy.

In this way, such nascent initiatives might help reverse a vicious cycle in education. Currently, the industry is, on the whole, not a hospitable place for entrepreneurial activity; as a result, too few talented, enterprising people select education from among all of their many opportunities; and as a result of that, education remains a relatively unenterprising sector, further discouraging the next generation of talent, and so on. Reversing that cycle by changing the sector's culture overnight is not a feasible starting point for advocates of change. Breaking it by recruiting talent against the odds, however, holds much more promise.

Still, advocates for more entrepreneurial activity in education need to attend to policy questions, given their ultimate influence on the pipeline of entrepreneurial talent. Initiatives that would expand the potential to open high-quality charter schools, give school leaders more authority over critical management levers, open the teaching and school leadership professions to talented people without conventional preparation, and create flexibilities in school funding that make it easier for schools and systems to spend money on or even invest in entrepreneurial ventures all help progress on the policy front make a significant difference for the supply of entrepreneurial people flowing into K–12 education.

CHAPTER 3

Catalyzing Capital Investment

Lessons from Outside Education

Joseph Keeney and Daniel Pianko

> *Revenues of for-profit education companies account for only 10% of the $780 billion spent on education. And the total market capitalization of education stocks makes up less than 1% of U.S. capital markets. But as the millennium dawns, the private sector is poised to play a much larger role. . . . This revolution is being fueled by an explosion in the money available to education startups.*
>
> —BusinessWeek, *January 10, 2000*

BusinessWeek's prognostication did not prove to be prescient—especially in K–12 education. With the exception of a few niche postsecondary education companies, as of 2008, the market capitalization of all education companies is still not much more than it was in 2000. Meanwhile, venture capital and private equity have expanded rapidly into other sectors, with the success of well-known venture-backed companies like Google and MySpace.

BusinessWeek's optimism was based on trends in the knowledge economy, dissatisfaction with the performance of public schools, and education's potential to be the internet's next "killer app." But seven years later, one prominent venture-capital investor—who has made several very successful investments in K–12 companies—laments that she would prefer never to invest in K–12 again:

> Successful venture investors look for opportunities to leverage intellectual capital in situations where an industry is going through a transformative event—that is, an event that wrecks the economics of big industry players.

65

For example in computers and communications, there were many opportunities for creative destruction. In K–12, the things that make the system more effective are not in interests of the system. There are too many obstacles against transformation. K–12 is not a free market. It is regulated, unionized, bureaucratic, and highly fragmented despite its $400 billion size.[1]

The purpose of this chapter is to explain the role that private equity and venture-capital firms play in catalyzing changes within industry structures. For example, while the government provided the research dollars to fund the basic research that became the Internet, private investors took the next step to invest in companies like Google and Amgen (a pharmaceutical biotech firm). Without private capital markets, the basic research dollars that government spends would much less efficiently create broad economic benefits. America's innovation economy relies heavily on private capital investors to do this job; the government generally does not invest directly in companies, and very few philanthropists have the mission or capability of playing that role.

Contrary to *BusinessWeek*'s dawn-of-the-millennium optimism, institutional investors by and large have not discovered large segments of the education industry, leaving a vacuum into which private investment dollars could flow to fund the organizations that would greatly benefit the education industry landscape. While it is not the government's role to invest in companies, policy changes have played a significant role in developing the legal and regulatory structures that created venture-capital financing—and which led to America's leadership position in areas like technology and pharmaceuticals.

This chapter focuses on how the venture-capital investment process works outside the education sector as a way to demonstrate how it could work better within it. The first section provides an introduction to how the government helped create the venture-capital industry. It presents an overview of how venture-capital industry participants operate and provides a summary of some common misperceptions about venture investing. It also describes the equally large, but less documented, angel market for private capital.

The second section compares investment in postsecondary education to that in K–12. It summarizes some of the key differences between these two segments to explain the substantial difference in investment history and opportunity. It also identifies those characteristics that, if employed in K–12, could attract investment capital. While there are substantial differences between K–12 and postsecondary education, advocates of supply-side reform could leverage the experience of postsecondary education investment to germinate a crop of innovative companies in K–12.

The third section explores whether there are concrete models from outside education that could be employed by government or philanthropies to attract and leverage private investment in K–12. Specifically, we present three examples, in increasing order of formality: a prize (or pay for performance) model that is increasingly being used in philanthropy; an angel portal model like the Department of Defense's Defense Venture Catalyst Initiative ("DeVenCI"); and a traditional venture-capital coinvestment model like the Central Intelligence Agency's In-Q-Tel.

Philanthropists and governments rarely invest capital in for-profit businesses. Even venture philanthropists, often funded by the fruits of for-profit enterprises, seldom invest in for-profit entities. Instead, profit-motivated entrepreneurs rely on capital markets to raise debt and equity investment dollars. Capital market investments are typically in the form of securities, like bonds or stocks. Equity capital represents ownership in companies by governments, public or private shareholders, company founders, or some or all of the above. Public companies like Coca-Cola have many shareholders, and anyone can buy or sell publicly traded shares on a regulated exchange like the New York Stock Exchange or NASDAQ. Private companies are owned by founders and private investors who cannot trade their shares on a public exchange but may sell them in private transactions. This chapter is mainly concerned with the private equity market—and within that market, the market for risk capital that can be invested in start-ups and young, rapidly growing companies not yet big or stable enough to have their shares sold to the public in initial public offerings (IPO).

HISTORICAL PERSPECTIVE

American Research and Development (ARD) was the first modern venture-capital firm. It was founded in 1946 to commercialize applications of technologies developed during World War II. Under General George Doriot's thirty-year leadership, its core values were not to "make money," but rather to finance "noble ideas."[2] ARD created today's venture-capital paradigm with its 1957 financing of Digital Equipment Corporation (DEC); its $77,000 investment grew to a worth of $355 million over fourteen years.[3]

Before 1957, most venture-capital firms were based in the Northeast. In that year, Arthur Rock traveled from New York to California to help secure financing for Eugene Kleiner and other employees of Shockley Laboratories. Rock's trail led to Sherman Fairchild (IBM's largest shareholder at the time), who invested $1.5 million to form Fairchild Semiconductor. In 1961, he moved to California and started venture-capital funds that invested in future industry leaders such as Intel, Teledyne, and Apple.[4]

In 1958, the federal government created the Small Business Administration to promote the creation and development of small businesses by chartering new small business investment companies (SBICs) that would provide early stage financing to companies. In less than ten years, seven hundred SBICs dominated the U.S. market for risk capital and accounted for 75 percent of venture-capital financing. There were some inherent flaws with the SBIC model. For example, SBIC managers tended not to be industry experts, and they evaluated investments mainly on the basis of loan repayment. But the biggest problem emerged when the government tried to lever the SBIC investments by guaranteeing four dollars for every one dollar of equity capital. Since the government subsidized debt, SBICs tended to invest in more risky enterprises—ones with less certain cash flows—with more debt than equity capital. Therefore, the government guarantees created perverse incentives, encouraging investment managers to use the wrong form of capital for start-up and growth companies. During the subsequent economic downturn, high debt levels forced many SBIC companies into bankruptcy and the SBIC community shrank. By 1978, only 250 SBICs were active, and by 1988, they accounted for only 7 percent of venture-capital financing.[5]

Two legislative changes drove a surge of venture-capital investing in the 1980s. First, the tax rate on capital gains was reduced from 49.5 percent to 28 percent in 1978.[6] Second, and with a much greater impact, was the 1979 change in the "prudent man" rule—a restriction under the Employee Retirement Income Security Act of 1974 that a professional investor must adopt the perspective of a prudent person seeking reasonable income and preservation of capital to allow pension funds to invest in venture capital. Venture-capital funds now had a huge new source of investment capital. In 1987, pension funds accounted for 15 percent of the $216 million in commitments to venture-capital funds; by 1998, they accounted for almost half of the $19.7 billion venture-capital commitments. Over that period, the share of commitments made by individuals decreased from 32 percent to 11 percent.

While there has been a degree of feast-or-famine cyclicality to the pattern of venture-capital funding (there were significant declines after the oil embargo and again after the stock market crash of 1987), the pumping up and bursting of the internet bubble from 1999 to 2001 was on a completely different scale. During that three-year period, $200 billion of venture investments were made. Excepting those three years, however, the level of venture-capital investments between 1998 and 2006 was relatively stable, at $20 billion to $26 billion per year. And from 2002 to 2006, the share of those investments that were made in start-up, seed, and early-stage companies was consistently 20 percent.[7]

HOW DOES VENTURE INVESTING WORK?

The typical venture-capital firm raises money into a specific investment fund, say Strategic Academic Opportunities 1. If the initial fund is successful, the firm may raise follow-on funds, numbered 2, 3, et cetera.[8] The venture-capital firm's principals serve as general partners (GPs) of the fund, and they raise money from outside investors who are the limited partners (LPs). The partnership agreement among the GPs and LPs specifies the lifespan of the fund (typically ten years) and the management fee structure. The typical management fee structure is "two and twenty"—that is, 2 percent per year of the total capital raised, plus 20 percent of the profits after the LPs have recovered 100 percent of their invested capital at the end of the fund's life. Because of the cumulative effect of management fees, a $500 million fund with a 2 percent annual management fee for ten years would only have $400 million to invest.

Over that ten-year horizon, venture-capital firms typically go through a process of fundraising, identifying and structuring investments, managing portfolios, and exiting (selling) investments. Firms that establish a track record have a much easier time raising additional capital. Most new venture-capital investments are made by follow-on funds of established firms, which typically tend to outperform the initial funds.

Within the capital-markets universe, venture capital is about the most expensive money there is. In evaluating investments, venture firms typically seek a 38 percent annual rate of return on their investment on a particular deal; at that compounded rate, the investment would return 500 percent over five years. In other words, the venture firm would expect a $5 million investment to be worth $25 million within five years. The rate of return required is directly correlated with the investor's risk. Venture firms fully expect to write off 30 to 50 percent of all the companies they invest in, so the winners have to experience outsized returns. By contrast, private equity-buyout funds typically target returns in the mid-20 percents but can afford this lower rate of return because they experience relatively few bankruptcies. Because of its even lower risk of failure, the cost of public equity capital tends to be in the teens, and the cost of debt tends to be in the single digits.

TABLE 3.1: Venture-Capital Investments by Industry (2006)

Industry	Total Investments 2006 (in millions)
Software	$ 5,114
Biotechnology	4,633
Medical Devices and Equipment	2,660
Telecommunications	2,598
Semiconductors	2,050
Industrial/Energy	1,887
Media and Entertainment	1,671
Networking and Equipment	1,075
IT Services	1,025
Electronics/Instrumentation	712
Business Products and Services	637
Consumer Products and Services	516
Computers and Peripherals	430
Financial Services	428
Healthcare Services	416
Retailing/Distribution	220
Undisclosed/Other	20
Grand Total	$ 26,090

Source: PricewaterhouseCoopers, "MoneyTree Report," n.d., https://www.pwcmoneytree.com/MTPublic/ns/nav.jsp?page=notice&iden=B (accessed August 4, 2007).

To achieve high levels of returns despite potential bankruptcies, venture-capital firms seek to invest only in companies that have the potential for home-run returns (in the thousands of percent), such as those realized by the venture investors Yahoo! or Google. Such growth potential is most likely to exist in a big industry in which there are significant opportunities for radical innovation. In fact, as shown in table 3.1, the majority of venture funding has been focused on only a handful of industries, especially information technology and healthcare.

While the education industry is far larger than many of the sectors on the list, education does not even appear on the table. Venture investors are virtually ignoring it, most likely because of the limited potential for radical innovation in the sector.

SOME COMMON VENTURE-CAPITAL MYTHS

The formal venture-capital market has characteristics that are sometimes misperceived and should be understood in the context of policy prescriptions aimed at promoting targeted education industry investment.

Venture-Capital Investors Invest Equity Like Company Founders

Venture-capital investors typically invest the riskiest money, and they usually ensure that their investment is paid back before that of the company founders. They typically structure their investments as convertible preferred stock or convertible debt. These are paid back before common stock, which is held by company founders. "Convertible" means that investments can be converted into common stock once the initial preferred investment is paid back—that is, usually once the founder's equity is worth more than the preferred stock. These structures have several advantages for the venture investor:

- Founders only receive a return on their equity if returns are high, thereby allowing venture investors to ensure that the entrepreneur truly believes in his or her aggressive business-plan projections for revenue and profit growth.
- Preferred shares usually have a dividend so that the venture firm receives some income while retaining the ability to convert to common equity if the investment dramatically increases in value.
- Preferred stock can have a preferred dividend and a liquidation preference so that the venture investors get paid first in the event of a sale or bankruptcy.

A Great Plan Means You Will Get Funded

As a general rule, only 10 percent of business plans received by venture capitalists warrant any response at all, and only 1 percent ever get funded. Business plans coming in over the transom are the least likely to get funded; most venture investors rely on their own network of friends and business contacts to provide investment opportunities.

The Opportunity and Strategy Are the Most Important Parts of the Business Plan

The first page that most prospective investors flip to in any business plan is the people page, which describes who the founders and managers are, what they have done in the past, and who they know that can give a trusted personal reference.

Many Companies Receive Venture Funding

Only about a thousand companies each year receive first-sequence funding. That is about 0.1 percent of the approximately 1 million new businesses started every year in the United States.

Location Does Not Matter

Over a third of venture-capital investments in 2006 were made in California's Silicon Valley. Adding Los Angeles, Orange County, and San Diego accounts for about half of all investments. Route 128 outside Boston, New York City, and Metro Washington, D.C., account for another 25 percent.[9] In other words, about three-fourths of all investment is made in a few California locales, Boston, New York City, and greater Washington, D.C.

Venture-Capitalists Are Long-Term Investors

In structuring their investments, venture investors typically provide only enough funding to take the company to its next significant milestone, at which time they can either invest more or cut their losses. The pension-fund managers who invest in the funds are also evaluated monthly, quarterly, and annually, so there is enormous pressure for short-term performance. As a result, investors have shifted from allocating approximately 40 percent of capital to start-up, seed, and early-stage companies in the 1980s to around 20 percent today. The need to realize investment returns by going public or selling the company encourages firms to focus on later-stage opportunities that are closer to exit opportunities, to get strong returns sooner and thereby bolster the reputation of the investment firm.

ANGEL INVESTING

As venture firms have reduced their share of funding seed-stage companies, young companies increasingly turn to the informal risk capital market known as the angel market. The positive connotation of "angel" suggests friendly, supportive investors who care more about the company's future than their own investments. That may be true of some investors, but it is not a valid generalization. Angel investors tend to be wealthy individuals who invest limited funds (typically under $1 million) into a company because it is not yet ready to receive venture-capital funding. While the formal venture-capital industry dates back to the end of World War II, angel-backed ventures can be said to include Queen Isabella and King Ferdinand's sponsorship of Columbus's 1492 voyage, King Louis XVI's $450,000 investment in the

National Bank of Philadelphia, and Boston attorney Gardiner Greene Hubbard and leather-merchant Thomas Sanders's funding of Alexander Graham Bell and the Bell Telephone Company of Boston (after bank officers and the *Boston Post* had ridiculed Bell's idea).[10] Today, angel investors are typically wealthy individuals, such as doctors, lawyers, and successful entrepreneurs.

Because angel investments are harder to track and measure than those from the formal venture-capital market, it is more difficult to estimate the size and impact of angel investing activity. The University of New Hampshire's Center for Venture Research, founded by Jeffrey Sohl, estimates that a total of $25.6 billion of angel investments were made in 2006, almost exactly the level of investments made in the formal venture-capital market. While angel and venture investors invested the same aggregate amounts, angel investments were made in 51,000 companies by 234,000 individuals, in contrast to 3,500 transactions funded by the roughly 2,000 venture firms. That is, the average angel investment per deal was $500,000, versus $7.4 million for venture-capital investment, and the average investment per investor was $100,000, versus $13 million.[11]

Angel investing accounts for a much higher percentage and dollar value of seed and start-up investments—approximately 46 percent, versus 4 percent for the traditional venture-capital industry.[12] That means that the angel market accounts for more than *ten times* the amount of traditional venture-capital invested in seed and start-up companies. One reason angel investors fund earlier-stage companies is their investment horizon. Generally speaking, they are more patient and expect to hold the investment for a minimum of three to five years.[13]

Despite the differences in average deal size and stage of investment, there are many similar characteristics between angel and venture-capital investing. The industries benefiting from angel investments are similar to those receiving traditional venture-capital investments: healthcare, software, biotech, and retail.[14] Convertible preferred stock, which gives more protection to the outside investors relative to the company founders, is the most common form of investment.[15] Angel investors also tend to invest close to home—over 80 percent of angel investments are made within a half-day's travel from the investor's home.[16] One reason angel investors invest close to home is that they prefer to source deals and make decisions face-to-face and to spend time with the company.[17] Another is that they tend to invest with fewer formal terms and conditions. But the biggest reason that angel investing tends to be up close and personal is that it carries relatively greater agency risk—that of conflict of interests between managers and investors—and prospective investments may have significant informational asymmetries between entrepreneurs and potential investors.

The Angel Capital Education Foundation, a nonprofit organization founded in 2005 by the Ewing Marion Kauffman Foundation, lists over two hundred angel groups, capital-source databases, and other angel resources in North America.[18] Many of these groups function as what Sohl calls angel "portals"—that is, "organizations that provide a structure and approach for bringing together entrepreneurs seeking capital and business angels searching for investment opportunities." He describes six different forms of angel portals: matching networks, facilitators, informal angel groups, formal angel alliances, electronic networks, and individual angels.[19]

Matching networks feature matching databases in which the networks screen investor criteria against business-plan submissions. For instance, the New York Angels network meets monthly to listen to vetted business plans. Outside the United States, many of these original networks still operate, such as the Business Angels Party Limited in Australia, Halo in Northern Ireland, and Euroregional Business Angel Network in Germany. But in the United States, most have evolved into the venture forum format with published investment criteria, specific business-plan-submission methods, and formal screening processes that must be passed before an entrepreneur gets the opportunity to make a 30-minute presentation to the investors.

Facilitators tend to provide more educational, less formal opportunities for investors and entrepreneurs to meet in person and share experiences. Facilitators include private-sector organizations as well as public-private-sector hybrids. The hybrids tend to foster economic development in their geographic area (for example, International Angel Investors in Tokyo and Tech-Invest in Wales). In the United States, informal angel networks such as eCoast Angels and Walnut Venture Associates tend to rely on group members to refer deals internally. Formal angel alliances like the Band of Angels can have a variety of structures, some requiring minimum levels of annual investment, regular participation at presentations, formal voting, and pooling funds.

Electronic networks are an intriguing form of angel portal. During the 1995 White House Conference on Small Business, the concept of forming a clearinghouse to improve access to equity capital for young, entrepreneurial companies was conceived. That led to the creation of the Angel Capital Electronic Network (ACE-Net), an internet-based market to match angel investors with new and early-stage companies, by the U.S. Small Business Administration's Office of Advocacy. The target size for the investments was $250,000 to

$2 million, on the assumption that investments of less than $250,000 were likely to be made by friends and family, while those of greater than $2 million were being made by the formal venture-capital market. The Small Business Administration (SBA) also sought to broaden the availability of early-stage financing beyond the concentration of industries and geographies of the formal venture-capital industry. In 2000, the SBA spun off ACE-Net into a university-based operation, and in December 2004, ACE-Net became Active Capital. Overall, electronic networks have as their principal weakness the preference for angel investors to be up close and personal in order to manage the agency risk of their investment.

Ultimately, the opportunity to establish an education industry-specific angel portal appears to be a potentially effective mechanism to promote angel investing in the sector, as well as a good way to create some of the human-capital networks addressed in other chapters in this volume. This concept is explored further as a model later in this chapter.

HOW K–12 DIFFERS FROM HIGHER EDUCATION

The U.S. K–12 and higher education sectors have vastly different public perceptions regarding their overall effectiveness. They also have dramatically different investment characteristics. Despite the higher total spending on K–12 than on postsecondary education, investment dollars have flowed disproportionately to colleges, universities, and the companies that service them. Over one million Americans attend the 2,561 for-profit postsecondary schools. In addition, nine companies running hundreds of schools are publicly traded for-profit colleges (many of which had previously been venture-funded) that now have approximately $25 billion of market capitalization.[20]

In 2005, mergers and acquisitions constituted $300 million in the postsecondary industry and only $64 million in the K–12 sector; 82 percent of all K-16 investment dollars in 2005 flowed to postsecondary education. But the amount of money invested in solutions companies (those that provide services to K–12 institutions and colleges) was approximately the same. So while companies servicing postsecondary institutions and K–12 districts attracted similar levels of investment, few investors seriously consider investing in the delivery of K–12 education.[21] As a result, there is no for-profit operator of a K–12 school system with over a billion dollars of market value. Without industry leaders and scarred by years of failure, investors tend to shy away from K–12 investments.

One notable example was Edison Schools, Inc., which had a market capitalization in excess of $1.5 billion at the time when investors perceived its school management system to be radical, transformative, and welcome. However, it was acquired only a few years later by a private equity investor for approximately 10 percent of its peak stock market value. Another potential example of transformative secondary school delivery is K12, Inc., an online education company (backed by Michael Milken's education industry investment vehicle Knowledge Universe) that serves home-schooled and virtual charter school students. K12, Inc. completed a successful initial public offering in December 2007, but it is a rare exception.

Why do investors focus almost exclusively on postsecondary education? There are four main reasons why they have poured billions of dollars of capital to improve and modernize the delivery of postsecondary education but have virtually ignored K–12 schools:

- The federal government student-loan and grant programs function like a voucher system that encourages competition among all players and generally does not discriminate against for-profit providers.
- For-profit providers have carved out market niches not addressed by traditional nonprofit institutions.
- There is broader public acceptance of for-profit operators in postsecondary education.
- The cost structure of higher education provides greater operating leverage—that is, direct instructional expense is lower as a percentage of revenue so there are greater economies of scale.

The Student-Loan Voucher System

The federal government supports the postsecondary education of its citizens by providing approximately $85 billion of (primarily) subsidized loans and grants each year. Students can use these federally subsidized loans at any accredited institution.[22] Students apply for financial aid, which is disbursed according to a need-based formula.

With the exception of the accrediting hurdle, the government imposes no restrictions on how that tuition money is spent, and there is only slightly greater regulation of for-profit providers. This voucher system has fostered a competitive environment even among the top universities. Harvard and Stanford compete aggressively for the world's top talent, while the University of Phoenix and Strayer Education compete to serve America's working adults.

For-Profits Fill Underserved Niches

When most scholars and policy analysts think about postsecondary education, there is still a dominant notion that universities serve young adults—aged eighteen to twenty-five—who focus a reasonable portion of their time and attention on scholarly pursuits. But the largest and fastest growing segment of America's college population is "non-traditional" students. Sixty-three percent of all students attending for-profit colleges are over twenty-five years old, whereas approximately 40 percent of students in traditional colleges are over twenty-five. The average age of a student at a for-profit college is 27.3 years old; 42 percent of such students are white, and only 39 percent are male.[23]

Traditional schools—even community colleges—have shied away from serving this population. Instead, virtually every nonprofit and state school has focused its attention on gaining ground in the *U.S. News & World Report* rankings by competing to attract top-flight professors and applicants with higher SAT scores. Meanwhile, for-profit colleges have targeted a new type of student: working adults more interested in furthering their careers than in receiving a traditional liberal-arts degree.

For-profit colleges also embraced technology before their nonprofit peers. Today, 10 percent of all postsecondary degrees are granted online and for-profit colleges have a disproportionate market share, estimated at 30 percent. The University of Phoenix alone enrolls approximately 200,000 of the country's 1.2 million online students. Meanwhile, observers estimate that 55 percent of all online learners are aged 26 to 45—the nontraditional niche that for-profits serve.[24]

Acceptance of For-Profit Providers

While for-profit colleges and universities still face significant discrimination, there is a long history of private operators of postsecondary institutions that makes the presence of for-profit operators less controversial. K–12 education is more politically charged due to its role in our nation's history as a leveling force for social equality, its emphasis on local control, the great strength of teachers unions, and the age of its students. It is important to note that for-profit colleges have suffered a large number of scandals over the years and much criticism of the for-profit sector is well-deserved. While criticism has resulted in some increased regulations (for example, the rule that no more than 90 percent of an institution's revenue can come from federal grants and loans or the limits on each institution's loan-default rates), the federal government has continued to fund student attendance at for-profit colleges. At the local level, certain states and municipalities have restricted the operations of for-profit colleges. Although most states have separate rules governing the operation of schools within their borders, these restrictions have not overly constrained the growth of for-profit providers.

Opportunities for Higher Returns on Investment

Running a college or university is fundamentally a more profitable business than running a K–12 school because the cost of instruction is lower. As illustrated in table 3.2, the cost structure of Strayer Education, one of the more successful publicly traded for-profit colleges, compares favorably to those of even the most successful K–12 school operators.

While for-profit colleges must spend about 15 percent of their revenue on marketing, their total education spending as a percent of revenue is significantly lower than that of K–12 operators. Students pay for their own books, go to class day and night (optimizing space usage), and require less day-to-day guidance. But the biggest difference is the percent of revenue spent on instruction, specifically personnel. Because of class size and the amount of time students spend in class, colleges spend a lower percentage of their revenue on personnel. The math is simple:

- Average price paid per student per class: $1,500
- Average number of students per class: 25
- Average revenue per class: $37,500
- Average pay of instructor per class: $5,000

Conversely, a K–12 school will receive about $7,000 per student, be able to put twenty students in a class, but have to support a full-time teacher at $50,000–$60,000 a year. Investors are generally attracted to higher-margin, lower-capital requirement opportunities. With its low margin structure, K–12 providers are generally less attractive than postsecondary providers.

Ecosystem of Capital and Entrepreneurs

As a result of these four key drivers, entrepreneurial efforts have exploded in postsecondary education. The rapid expansion of the for-profit sector, coupled with the efforts of entrepreneurial nonprofit schools, has created an ecosystem of entrepreneurs and capital to solve real-world problems in postsecondary institutions. For example, new generations of student information systems have sprung up alongside enrollment management companies. E-College (recently acquired by Pearson), Embanet (recently acquired by

TABLE 3.2: Cost Structure (as Percent of Revenue) of K–12 Versus Postsecondary

	K–12	*Strayer*
Instruction	65	35
Selling and Promotion	5	15
General and Administrative	25	15
Profit Margin	5	35

Sources: The percentages in the K–12 column are based on the authors' experience. The numbers for Strayer come from Strayer Education, Inc., "Securities and Exchange Commision Form 10-K," December 31, 2005, http://www.sec.gov/Archives/edgar/data/1013934/000095013606001965/file001.htm (accessed January 11, 2008).

Knowledge Universe), and Blackboard compete to bring courses from both traditional and for-profit schools online. At the same time, enrollment management companies like PlattForm have developed to service the growing needs of colleges as they try to attract students in an increasingly competitive market.

America's colleges and universities are generally considered among the world's best, but its K–12 system is not. While a wholesale restructuring of K–12 school finance is unlikely, there are numerous ways that the government and foundations can foster a spirit of entrepreneurship and capital deployment in the K–12 sector. One of the most powerful ideas is the focus on niche areas of education that are less competitive. Currently, private investors are focusing significant resources in certain areas of K–12, such as companies that run programs for children with learning disabilities (an area traditional school systems have tended to avoid) and K12, Inc.'s successful initial public offering of stock in its online education business.

Focusing attention on niche areas will start to develop the ecosystem required for supply-side school reform. When the University of Phoenix started in 1973 in a single classroom in California serving working adults, no one expected it to become the nation's largest private university. By focusing efforts on such incremental changes, governments and philanthropists can make some significant changes to increase the role of market forces in the K–12 system. The following section proposes three mechanisms that could help create the ecosystem required to create supply-side solutions in K–12. These mechanisms are a prize model for success in niches, an angel investment portal for education, and a government-sponsored education industry direct investment firm.

THE PRIZE MODEL: CREATING A PAY-FOR-PERFORMANCE MARKET IN EDUCATION

The X Prize Foundation calls itself "the leading model to leverage the elements of public interest, entrepreneurial spirit and cross-disciplinary innovation to bring about breakthroughs that benefit us all."[25] It points to the success of the $25,000 Orteig Prize offered to the first person to fly nonstop between New York and Paris. Charles Lindbergh won the prize, but the offer stimulated the efforts of nine different teams, which collectively spent $400,000 to win the purse that ended up being sixteen times the proffered amount. In the meantime, these initial efforts and investments catalyzed the development of the $250 billion aviation industry. X Prize's founder, Peter Diamandis, estimates that in the prize model, "ten to forty times the amount of money gets spent" relative to the prize.[26] Other notable prize offerings include the Gates Foundation and others' Advance Market Commitments to stimulate vaccine production and Sir Richard Branson's Virgin Earth Challenge to award $25 million to the inventor of a commercially and environmentally viable method of removing greenhouse gases from the atmosphere. While the definition of a clear and measurable outcome in the social sciences is more challenging, the following example illustrates how the model could be applied to solve an important problem in education.

Advocates of educational entrepreneurship and the creation of market forces in the delivery of K–12 education since 1990 have focused their attention on charter schools and vouchers. Charter school enrollments have grown steadily to about 1.1 million students in the 2006–07 school year, but that level still only represents 2 percent of total K–12 enrollment.[27] The optimistic advocates of system reform might say that in 1970, virtually no foreign automobile manufacturers sold cars in America, but by 2000, 40 percent of all cars sold in the United States were imports.[28] Pessimistic observers might counter that K–12 does not function like a consumer market and student-achievement results for charter schools are uneven.

Instead of focusing on systemic reforms that are highly politicized and open to subjective evaluation, advocates of market forces could attempt to leverage the concept of a prize to promote a simple educational market that works (for instance, one that creates a prize for achieving a social good). It is difficult to imagine putting up a $10 million prize for, say, improving reading scores for third graders in the Philadelphia School District. Who would receive the prize—parents, teachers, the school, or the curriculum provider? Instead, education could focus prizes on organizations that achieve specific, easily measurable outcomes, such as high school graduation rates.

TABLE 3.3: Cost of High School Dropouts

Category	High School Dropout Cost	Notes
Lost Tax Revenue	$139,100	Dropouts earn less and therefore pay fewer taxes than graduates.
Health Care	$40,500	Dropouts are significantly more likely to go on Medicaid and are statistically sicker than graduates.
Criminal Activity	$26,500	Dropouts are about 20 percent more likely to commit violent crimes and end up in prison than graduates.

Source: Henry Levin et al., "The Costs and Benefits of an Excellent Education for All of America's Children," January 2007, http://www.cbcse.org/media/download_gallery/Leeds_Report_Final_Jan2007.pdf.

High school graduation is the Holy Grail for many education policymakers, as it indicates that graduates have basic skills that help them spend more time employed and less time in prison or on welfare. Educating someone to the level of high school graduate has a high return on investment for both an individual and society. However, the U.S. education system does not reward high school graduation. In fact, most school districts have a variety of policies that allow dropouts to slip through the system. This disparity between the economic return of graduation and the reward structure creates one of the most compelling examples of distorted incentive structures between outcome and investment required. High school graduation, therefore, could be a test case for a prize model because there is such a high potential return on the program sponsor's investment. The average income of a high school graduate is $7,000 (or 30 percent) higher than that of a high school dropout, and high school graduation yields a 7.8 percent increase in full-time employment.[29]

As table 3.3 reveals, the social cost of a high school dropout is extraordinarily high. Henry Levin of Columbia University's Teachers College and his colleagues estimate that each high school dropout costs American society an incremental $209,100.[30]

The problem of low high school graduation rates is not trivial; experts agree that approximately 30 percent of Americans do not graduate from high school.[31] The prospects for dropouts are grim. In fact, prison systems are said to project the number of beds they will require by reviewing the number of high school dropouts in their region.

High school graduation would be a strong candidate for a prize-based, pay-for-performance educational market because it is relatively easy to track success at the local level (high school graduation is defined by each state, and, to a certain extent, the federal government through the General Equivalency Diploma, or GED, program) and because thousands of community-based organizations already deliver many of these services on an ad hoc basis. Many of these programs struggle to raise funds to save children from the streets, and with adequate funding opportunities, the most successful of them would grow to fill the demand. This would cause a significant shift in the funding world. Instead of debating the efficacy of each program, the market would sort out the most successful programs and fund the outcome.

Establishing such a program would be relatively straightforward. A government or foundation could first announce that there would be a prize of $10,000 paid to an educational provider for each high school dropout who went through a course it offered and learned the skills necessary to become a high school graduate. The sponsoring organization would certify providers that wished to offer such services in a consistent and transparent way to control quality. Once registered as a provider, any education organization would receive a small payment to cover the costs of offering a single course (such as each three-credit course completed by a high school dropout). The fee, say $200, would be enough to pay the basic costs of operations. Each successful course completion would be tracked online, and the school district would ensure that the student had not received credit for the course previously. Upon completion of high school as defined by existing state standards (for example, passing the state level exam or GED), the provider would receive $10,000.

The impact of such a program would be immediate, with the potential of substantial multiples of the bonus being invested to solve the problem. Organizations like the Boys and Girls Clubs that already offer such programs would register and get an income stream for providing the services they already do, and they would likely invest in improving quality. To gain extra income, entrepreneurial school districts might start their own programs serving students from other districts. For-profits and other competitors would also likely develop. Companies and school districts with the best high school recovery models would attract investors to fund growth. Before long, educational providers would be advertising to attract dropouts back to class. Imagine signs right next to all those ads for the University of Phoenix, geared toward eleventh grade dropouts, urging them back to school.

Running the program would not take disproportionate dollars away from existing programs. A pilot program, even in a district with 65,000 students, would likely cost approximately $10 million and, according to the numbers in table 3.3, save society countless woes, as well as over $160 million in future expenses.[32] The creation of a high school graduation "market" would be significantly more efficient than the hundreds of millions of dollars spent on supplemental educational services under No Child Left Behind. Most policymakers are unsure of the success of these services, partially because there are no clear metrics to judge effective programs. Even if a benchmark test existed, students are enrolled in school, so evaluators would have to parse out the relative success of supplemental educational services versus that of the classroom experience. Dropouts have no alternative source of education, and success is measured by established state norms for high school graduation. Finally, it is important to note that all school districts, even failing ones, could be eligible for the program. Therefore, school districts themselves would have an incentive to start and support these programs to capture additional revenue.

Today, dropouts are virtually forgotten by traditional school systems. Rewarding institutions that enroll dropouts and turn them into graduates would create competition to service eleventh grade dropouts. In the process, American society would reap a massive return on its investment: $209,100 per graduate minus the cost of running the program.

CREATING A PORTAL TO INCREASE THE EFFICIENCY OF THE ANGEL MARKET IN EDUCATION

A second model that could be employed to increase private capital investment in K–12 education is the creation of an angel investment portal. The angel investing market, as described above, is as large as the formal venture-capital market. One way to promote angel investing in K–12 opportunities is to smooth out some of the inefficiency in the market for education-related angel financing (such as the high costs of matching innovators, entrepreneurs, and investors). This section explores how an education-industry angel portal—sponsored by the government, a foundation, or another nonprofit organization—might catalyze seed and early-stage investment in K–12 opportunities.

There is a precedent in the United States for a government department to create a portal to attract private investment in the areas it targets. DeVenCI's goal is "to speed Department of Defense adoption of promising new commercial technologies, and to encourage broader commercial support of the

Department of Defense supply chain."[33] It was founded on an experimental basis after the 9/11 terrorist attacks, and by the end of 2005, its participants had made suggestions that led to the adoption of fifteen technologies for military and intelligence uses. Based on its initial success, in early 2006 the Department of Defense expanded the project, funded an office with four full-time staff members, and signed up eleven venture capitalists from thirty applicants to serve two-year terms. Bob Pohanka, DeVenCI's director, calls it a search engine.[34]

There are many examples of public sector–sponsored portals (some with private cosponsorship) in other countries. Sohl has analyzed the research on many of them, including Canada Opportunities Investment Network (COIN), Local Investment Networking Company (LINC) in the United Kingdom, Chalmers Venture Capital Network (CVCN) in Sweden, Business Introduction Service (BIS) in Denmark, Matching-Palvelu in Finland, and Business Angel Network Deutschland (BAND). He has concluded that the success of these organizations is mixed. Successful portals, he found, are regional and provide face-to-face interaction between the angels and the entrepreneurs. In general, they undertake marketing efforts to increase awareness, conduct screening, and develop criteria to ensure that the opportunities are investor-ready and remain portals by resisting the urge to become investment funds.[35]

A new education industry portal—call it AngelEd—would draw on some of these recommendations. It should focus on the links between the innovator and the entrepreneur, not unlike the Angel Investors of Greater Washington, a portal that focuses on using federal lab and university liaisons to help entrepreneurs commercialize federally funded research and development. Perhaps the portal could be an offshoot of the Institute of Education Sciences, the research arm of the Department of Education. (Of course, increased funding of basic research under its purview is a sound policy prescription for increased commercial development of that research.) If federal policymakers will not take the lead, a sufficiently large state, say California or Texas, or a consortium of several states could undertake the effort.

AngelEd would be well-suited for government or foundation sponsorship because of the investment and cost of marketing and screening that would need to be undertaken (probably in the range of $10 million) and the importance of giving the portal the proper exposure and profile. Given the growing university connections between graduate business schools and education schools—notably at Stanford and Harvard—a potential source of subsidized screening talent might be provided by graduate students. One other potential feature of AngelEd would be to provide matching funding to leverage third-party investment dollars. The lessons of the SBIC policy notwithstanding, there are examples of monetary incentives that have worked, including the Scottish Enterprise Business Growth Fund and the Scottish Co-investment Fund (which accounted for 7 percent of total early-stage company investment and 55 percent of all deals recorded in 2004, a significant increase in average deal size).[36]

AngelEd could also connect entrepreneurs to customers. Through the portal, for example, entrepreneurs might be able to give products for free or at low cost to a network of early-adopter teachers or school systems. These early adopters could serve as a test of the product's efficacy and help investors make better decisions based on the results of field tests.

Ultimately, there is substantial evidence to support the idea that angel investment in the K–12 sector could be increased and made more efficient through the successful creation of AngelEd. The lessons of ACE-Net, DeVenCI, and other international angel investment portals, along with input from knowledgeable organizations like the Ewing Marion Kauffman Foundation, should all be taken into account in its design so as to maximize the success of such a portal.

CREATING A PRINCIPAL FIRM TO COINVEST IN EDUCATION

In the late 1990s, the CIA realized that the nation's intelligence agencies were not accessing the rapidly expanding field of technology companies. Large firms like Boeing received the vast majority of contracts, while small companies had trouble navigating the complex web of government procurement policies that seemed "custom made to discourage innovation."[37] As a result, the CIA did not have access to the latest technologies, and entrepreneurs did not realize the potential value of their products.

The CIA (and later other agencies) decided to create and fund In-Q-Tel, a venture-capital firm designed to invest in businesses that might prove useful to the intelligence services. In-Q-Tel was built to invest alongside other venture-capital firms to prevent the government from picking winners, to invest in as many companies as possible that would improve national security, and to introduce new ideas to government bureaucracies without committing too much capital. Successful investments have been made in companies that would have been successful on their own, but In-Q-Tel's capital and expertise facilitate the growth and development of products for the agencies. In-Q-Tel structures investments in a variety of ways—including debt, equity, and pay-for-development of specific services. To date, In-Q-Tel has invested in over seventy companies. It has a ten-person staff in Silicon Valley and fifty more workers in the Washington, D.C., area.[38]

What makes In-Q-Tel so successful, though, is that it invests more than just dollars. It also works closely with companies to bridge the gap between Silicon Valley (or other dynamic locales) and the CIA's headquarters in Langley, Virginia. In-Q-Tel's staff includes senior-level investment professionals and technologists from the highest ranks of the intelligence community who can bridge the gap between business and government cultures. The board of directors ranges from the president of Arizona State University, to a former secretary of defense, to the former CEO of Lockheed Martin. Staffers and advisors also help to guide the development of technology and interface with the various government agencies that help them buy products. Each year, Congress appropriates funding for In-Q-Tel and recycles some of the profit from its investments in new companies. Based on its success, Congress has funded similar programs run by the Department of Defense and NASA.

The education industry faces a similar problem about how to encourage entrepreneurs to focus on education and then attract capital so that companies in the sector can grow. Access to capital is not necessarily the issue for educational entrepreneurs; a large number of small education companies do receive some capital. Where education companies typically stumble, however, is the growth from a small company to one of size and scale. In education, it is difficult to cross the chasm from a small company to a big one. The long sales cycles—that is, the time from the initial sales meeting to the contract signing—faced by companies trying to sell to government security agencies is not dissimilar to, and quite possibly worse than, those faced by young education companies.

The largest issue growing education companies must deal with is the sales cycle inherent in selling to school districts—namely, an education company must experience the long sales cycle each time it approaches one of the nation's fourteen thousand school districts. Each district has its own procurement bureaucracy, standards for buying products, and curricular program. The average sales cycle for each district is longer than twelve months, an eternity for a start-up. At a minimum, school districts could agree on a common procurement platform similar to the ones created by the Department of Defense.

However, America's educational establishment could go one step further. The Department of Education, or even a consortium of states or school districts, could create an In-Q-Tel in the education industry—call it EduFund.

There are a few key structural differences between the defense technology industry and education. First, there is only a limited ecosystem of venture-capital and private-equity firms focused on education. Second, K–12 education businesses tend to have fewer opportunities for venture-capital-like returns. And third, not even the largest school districts have the scale of the federal government in purchasing. Therefore, the creation of EduFund would require creative thinking. The first step would be to focus on what types of companies EduFund would target and the mechanisms for funding them. Some possible guidelines for the implementation of EduFund include:

- Employ a funding model akin to the World Bank type of an equity investment. In particular, EduFund needs to receive a return on investment, but without the home run equity returns in some parts of its portfolio, it may be difficult to realize the 20-plus percent returns that most private investors target.
- Focus on enabling technologies (curriculum, software, etc.) rather than the creation of schools or delivery of education, or vice versa.
- Create a network of ten to twenty of the largest school districts to fast-track purchase of services from EduFund portfolio companies.
- Focus EduFund activities on high-need areas of school districts (for instance, special education software, remedial education, or longitudinal student data tracking.).
- Only fund companies with a minimum revenue hurdle (say, $1–2 million) that are investor-ready and poised for growth.
- Build a network of venture and private equity firms with which to coinvest, so EduFund always invests alongside an experienced partner.

PROSPECTS FOR ENHANCED CAPITAL INVESTMENT

This chapter has discussed how some structural differences have resulted in substantially greater investment in the postsecondary education industry than in K–12. Yet several models could be employed to increase private investment within the existing constraints of the K–12 industry. This chapter has also addressed three specific ideas: a prize model to generate high levels of investment to solve problems with a specific outcome (like high school graduation); the creation of an angel portal to improve the efficiency of angel investing in K–12 opportunities and promote such investment; and a coinvestment model to increase traditional venture funding of education opportunities and give its sponsors a window on innovations that could have a substantial impact on the K–12 sector. These models, if constructed with careful research on the lessons of analogous examples from other industries, could effectively and efficiently catalyze an increase in the flow of private capital to the K–12 sector.

Every year, huge flows of private capital fund promising companies through the formal venture-capital market and informal angel-investment market, but very few of those dollars flow to the K–12 sector because of its limited potential for radical innovation. The history of policy efforts to promote private capital investment is mixed at best. The biggest boon to increase private capital investing generally was the ERISA reform that allowed pension funds to invest in venture funds. Less important policy tools have included a reduction in capital gains tax rates. The SBIC example highlights the delicate nature of creating such incentives. Therefore, a warning to policymakers seeking to promote private capital investment in K–12 is this: The problem is not necessarily the supply of venture capital. Venture capital will fund companies that have the opportunity to produce strong economic returns, but it will only find the K–12 sector when K–12 is liberated from the structural constraints limiting the potential returns on investment of that capital.

CHAPTER 4

Social Purpose Capital Markets in K–12

Kim Smith and Julie Petersen

We are not thinking our way into a new way of acting. We are acting our way into a new way of thinking.

—*Katherine Fulton, Monitor Group*

On the outside of nearly every personal computer sold today is a sticker that says "Intel Inside," a reminder from semiconductor giant Intel that the integrated circuits its company manufactures are central to that computer's operation. These small silicon chips have tiny electric circuits etched onto their surface, and their existence has in many ways made possible the proliferation of personal computers, which have transformed the way we live and work. But it might not be so if a group of renegade engineers known as the Fairchild Eight had not left their employer in 1957.

Frustrated by the dysfunctional management of the Shockley Semiconductor laboratory, the group met with a young East Coast investment banker by the name of Arthur Rock—who went on to become a successful venture capitalist and help them raise $1.5 million from a local electronics company. Rock's funds, together with five hundred dollars from each of the founders, helped birth Fairchild Semiconductor, which went on to revolutionize the semiconductor industry. Along the way, Fairchild also helped to spawn a thriving Silicon Valley ecosystem, both as a company and as an incubator for talent. Gordon Moore and Robert Noyce, two of the founding eight team members, went on to create Intel, while Eugene Kleiner, another member, started the legendary venture-capital firm Kleiner Perkins Caufield & Byers, which has since provided funding to dozens of successful start-ups (among them Sun Microsystems, Amazon, and Google). Before long, other start-ups in what was fast becoming known as Silicon Valley began raiding the company for well-trained managers and engineers, pointing the way toward the robust entrepreneurial ecosystem that exists there today.

Like the entrepreneurs who created Fairchild, educational entrepreneurs are in an undeveloped industry, where they must raise financial capital to turn their visions into new enterprises. In industries like technology and medicine, the capital markets available to help entrepreneurs start and grow their businesses have come a long way since the founding of Fairchild, as entrepreneurship has become more accepted and the ecosystem of capital providers has become more sophisticated. The conventional market for private capital is regulated by a number of agencies and operates in ways that have become standard, including a significant amount of uniform and transparent information, and a secure and reliable infrastructure that includes mechanisms like public stock exchanges. These structures and practices have encouraged the development of a wide array of independent intermediary organizations that provide expert analysis, and as a result, a significant and diverse number of capital providers have flourished.

However, the availability and structure of investment capital remains an enormous challenge for entrepreneurs addressing complex social issues like public education—one that keeps many of them from realizing their true potential and prevents the field from growing. This is particularly true for social entrepreneurs in education—those motivated foremost by the desire to improve educational access, equity, and outcomes for students not adequately served by the current system. These entrepreneurs strike out on their own, unencumbered by the restrictions of the current system, to create new organizations that can both provide students with better educational options and spark disruptive change within existing institutions.

We bring to this subject many years of experience in helping social entrepreneurs create and grow new organizations, most recently at NewSchools Venture Fund, a nonprofit venture philanthropy firm founded in 1998 by Kim Smith in collaboration with noted venture capitalists John Doerr and Brook Byers (of Kleiner Perkins Caufield & Byers). The firm's mission is to invest in both nonprofit and for-profit entrepreneurial education organizations and connect their work to systematic change in public education. NewSchools does this by aggregating capital from many philanthropic sources, identifying promising entrepreneurial solutions, and providing both significant capital (most investments range from $1 million to $5 million) and hands-on guidance to a portfolio of organizations. This money and support is generally allocated over the course of several years according to various milestones of organizational progress, with senior members of the NewSchools team taking a seat on each investee's board and each bringing to bear many years of experience with entrepreneurial organizations.

Drawing on this experience, as well as our work with and as entrepreneurs in the business world, we will explore what we call the social purpose capital market—the market of individuals and institutions that provide investment capital to these social entrepreneurs in education. These markets are the engines that enable such entrepreneurs to start their new organizations, acquire the necessary equipment, and grow their operations to a scale that begins to address the magnitude of need in public education. We will argue that this social purpose capital market for education entrepreneurs lacks many of the elements that make the conventional capital market work for entrepreneurs in other industries. Indeed, we believe that the social entrepreneurs in education who have succeeded to date have done so in spite of the current capital markets, rather than because of them. If we can agree that these social entrepreneurs are a potentially valuable mechanism for dramatically improving public education, then we must take action to alter the capital markets that are so vital to their success.

ENTREPRENEURS IN SEARCH OF CAPITAL

When a social entrepreneur decides to create a new organization, one of the first questions that he or she faces is whether to adopt a for-profit structure or a nonprofit one. This is one of the most important decisions a social entrepreneur must make because most capital providers invest in only one or the other. As members of one of the few organizations that invest in both for-profit and nonprofit ventures, at NewSchools we have seen this decision-making process play out many times and watched many factors influence it, including the organization's business model, its theory of how it will create change, the political context, the status of the capital markets, and often the founder's personal preferences and beliefs.

For instance, Don Shalvey—who founded nonprofit charter management organization Aspire Public Schools in California—knew he wanted Aspire to be a nonprofit institution because he felt most comfortable leading and recruiting teams in the public-benefit sectors, and he believed that this structure would allow Aspire to consistently prioritize social impact without any possible conflicting financial motivations. Conversely, when Linda Chaput created Agile Mind to provide online access to Advanced Placement courses, she sought to create a for-profit company despite her explicit social mission to serve low-income communities. Like Shalvey, she was motivated by her past experience, but she also knew that early-stage venture-capital funds were available for such businesses and that she would need to offer stock options to recruit software engineers and the other employees necessary to build this Web-based resource.

Even when the entrepreneur is agnostic about corporate structure, the availability of capital, the specific business model, or the political context may make the decision clear. For instance, technology-related ventures like Wireless Generation, a provider of innovative handheld assessment tools, that need to raise significant capital to develop their products and entice employees will often choose to be for-profit so that they can raise money from venture capitalists who understand this need. On the flip side, most for-profit education management organizations have avoided doing business in California because it is nearly impossible to earn a profit on the per-pupil funding the state provides to public schools, except in the rare cases where their work is supplemented by philanthropic funding. And on the political front, organizing by groups such as the Association of Community Organizations for Reform Now has led to broad mistrust of many for-profit providers in education.

Once the organization's corporate structure has been identified, the entrepreneur then turns to that sector's investors for the financial capital and other support needed to start and grow the enterprise.[1] All enterprises need four types of money:

1. *Start-up capital,* which allows the entrepreneur to hire a team, develop products and services, rent an office, buy supplies, and do all the other things that they need to do to get a new organization off the ground;
2. *Operating or working capital,* which begins to flow in once the organization is up and running, and usually comes in the form of revenue;
3. *Capital expenditures,* which are used for purchasing assets that depreciate in value over time, such as real estate or expensive equipment like laboratories; and
4. *Growth capital,* which is used to finance significant expansion of the organization.

The first, third, and fourth types can together be referred to as "investment capital" because they come from outside investors or donors, who provide the capital in exchange for the creation of some sort of return (growth in the business, repayment of a loan, some sort of social impact on society, et cetera). However, this chapter will not deal with revenue because it is provided not by investors but more often by customers or, in the case of a publicly regulated industry like education, third-party payers who provide funds on behalf of customers (such as states' reimbursements to charter schools for the services that they provide to students).

Investment capital can come from investors in the private, nonprofit, or public sector. When people talk about capital markets, they usually mean the conventional, private for-profit capital markets in which investors provide businesses with capital in the form of either equity (in which investors put their money into a public or privately held company, in exchange for an ownership stake) or debt (in which investors loan money to companies and expect to be repaid). This market is overseen by industry regulators like the Securities and Exchange Commission (SEC), as well as specialized industry groups like the Financial Accounting Standards Board. As former Federal Reserve chairman Alan Greenspan noted, "Our market system depends critically on trust—trust in the word of our colleagues and trust in the word of those with whom we do business."[2] Recent accounting scandals aside, this industry has a robust system of mostly trustworthy information sources and service providers that help both investors and entrepreneurial enterprises do business.

It is important to recognize that this market is not merely an organic system that naturally evolved but is rather a publicly regulated market that has been refined over time to increase trustworthiness and efficiency. A full description of the evolution of U.S. capital markets is beyond the scope of this chapter, but there are five elements that make these markets function as well as they do—elements that will be instructive when we consider the challenge of the social purpose capital markets for educational entrepreneurs:

1. General agreement on the *metrics and definitions* of success, including common methods for calculating a business's profits and losses;
2. Transparency, uniformity, and availability of *performance data;*
3. A *robust ecosystem of independent intermediary organizations* that provide expert analysis;
4. A *secure and reliable infrastructure* including mechanisms like public stock exchanges, where any investor can buy and sell securities, as well as legal enforcement tools such as contract and property law, the oversight of the SEC, and the criminal and civil court systems; and
5. A *large and diverse supply of capital providers,* each of whom has a different preferred amount of investment risk, type of financial return sought

on investments, type of investment tools, and stage of companies that they will invest in.

The nonprofit capital market operates much differently. Donors—whether foundations or individuals—are given a public subsidy in the form of a tax deduction to encourage them to provide funds to organizations that produce some sort of public value. The vast majority of investment activity takes place in the form of grants. Internal Revenue Service (IRS) regulations dictate that 5 percent of the endowment assets of a foundation must be distributed each year, whether to grantees or as administrative expenses; the remaining 95 percent of assets are generally invested in the conventional capital markets so as to maximize financial return and keep the foundation going. The philanthropic capital market is loosely regulated and enforced by the IRS and by states' attorneys general, but most regulations were established primarily to prevent fraud and the misuse of these tax-advantaged philanthropic funds for personal benefit or political advocacy. Comparatively few attempts have been made to put in place the kind of practices, transparency of information, or intermediaries that make the for-profit capital markets so efficient.

Finally, although a significant amount of money does flow through the public sector, little of it takes the form of investment capital. When federal, state, or local governments do provide funds to entrepreneurial organizations, it is less often as direct investments, and more often as investment incentives, such as tax credits, designed to motivate investors to take action in an underserved area or industry.

SOCIAL PURPOSE CAPITAL MARKETS AND EDUCATION

Since we have limited our focus here to the capital markets for social entrepreneurs in education, it is worth turning our attention to the narrow slice of the capital markets that serve them. We refer to these as the social purpose capital markets, and they include a variety of individual and institutional investors from across the public, private, and nonprofit sectors.

Many of these investors have different expectations for the kind of value their investments will create. One of the most common and straightforward measures is the return on investment (ROI), in which a financially motivated investor compares the number of dollars spent or contributed with the dollars generated. But many investors who back social entrepreneurs intend to calculate a social return on investment (SROI), which is a far more slippery notion than the counting of dollars and cents that essentially boils down to: "for each dollar invested, what is the resulting benefit to individuals and to

FIGURE 4.1: Social Purpose Capital Markets

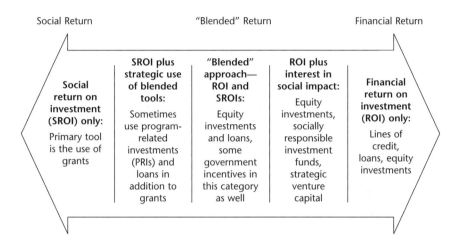

society?"[3] For example, the longitudinal High/Scope Perry Preschool Study—which studies the short- and long-term benefits of a Michigan preschool program—found that the program returns to the public roughly seven dollars for every dollar spent to operate it, given the higher level of schooling completed by the preschool's attendees, their need for fewer social services, their greater job earnings, and the like.[4]

As figure 4.1 indicates, at one end of the spectrum are investors motivated entirely by social impact. These include nearly all conventional endowed foundations that support education, from older ones like the Hewlett Foundation to newer players like the Bill & Melinda Gates Foundation and The Broad Foundation. University of Arkansas professor Jay Greene estimated that, in 2002, private philanthropies gave K–12 schooling only about $1 billion to $1.5 billion, less than .03 percent of the $388 billion spent by taxpayers that year on K–12 education.[5] Of that, it is impossible to calculate just how much went to support educational entrepreneurs—as opposed to school districts or other established entities—but we project that it was a small fraction. The primary nonprofit supporters of social entrepreneurs in education are listed in table 4.1.

As noted, individual donors and foundations have a remarkable degree of flexibility in how to use their funds. This is intended to enable philanthropists to take early-stage risks with important innovations that can later be taken up by the public sector, such as the Carnegie Foundation's work with public libraries back in the late nineteenth century or the Walton Family Foundation's early support of charter schools in the early 1990s. However, this flexibility sometimes results in idiosyncratic and ideological philanthropic funding decisions. Each nonprofit funder has a distinct organizational personality—often informed by the wealthy individual or family whose money endowed the foundation and how they achieved their success—which affects both what they will invest in (such as whether they are for or against school choice) and how they invest (size of grants, level of engagement with grantees, length of grant cycles, anticipated scale of impact).

Generally, most philanthropic funders prefer to invest in specific programs that nonprofits operate, rather than in the general operating expenses that a nonprofit incurs. "Different funders are interested in different things," explained one entrepreneur. "So, you have to pull your organization apart in various puzzle pieces and then sell each one to the funder who cares about that piece. In the end, you put the puzzle together with a whole variety of different funders, all of whom want something a little different and feel they are supporting something different and important."[6] Foundations also tend to give out a large number of small grants that are short-term in scope and, as a result, spend a great deal of time managing the details of selecting and overseeing grants, rather than deeply engaging with grantees in a long-term way.

At the other end of the spectrum are investors whose goal is financial ROI but whose capital is sometimes available to some social entrepreneurs in education. These profit-seekers may be willing to provide funds to for-profit companies or to give out loans or lines of credit for mature charter management organizations. Because of their explicit focus on financial return, these investors consider only an organization's financial viability and potential profitability, rather than its mission or social impact. Traditional lenders like Wells Fargo and Bank of America fall into this category, as do traditional venture-capital firms, such as Arcadia Partners, that seek to make money by investing in start-ups in the education sector.

The size of this financially motivated market pales in comparison to philanthropic support. For example, in 2005, venture-capital investors funneled just $64 million into preK–12 businesses, according to market research firm Eduventures, Inc. That is trivial compared with the $1.5 billion in philanthropic support that flowed into K–12 education that year, not to mention what venture capitalists put into entrepreneurial organizations in healthcare: more than $7.2 billion, according to healthcare market-research firm Irving Levin Associates—more than a hundred times the amount invested in K–12.

Unlike for foundations, the method for selecting for-profit investments is somewhat standardized across venture-capital firms and other private inves-

TABLE 4.1: Nonprofit Providers of Capital in Education

Organization	Background
National Foundations	
Bill & Melinda Gates Foundation www.gates foundation.org	**Founded:** 2000 **Structure:** 501(c)(3) private non-operating foundation **Assets:** $30 billion (2005) **Investment Focus:** First wave invested primarily in "inside" systems change, second wave increasingly combined inside and outside change agents. New leadership in August 2007 may affect focus.
The Broad Foundation www.broad foundation.org	**Founded:** 1999 **Structure:** 501(c)(3) private non-operating foundation (spun out operating organizations include The Broad Center for the Management of School Systems) **Assets:** $836 million (2005) **Investment Focus:** Majority of investments are leadership for "inside" change agents, mostly districts (some data, competition, and CMO grants).
Doris and Donald Fisher Fund *(formerly Pisces Foundation, no website)*	**Founded:** 1998 **Structure:** 501(c)(3) private non-operating foundation **Assets:** unknown **Investment Strategy:** Funds K–12 public education reform efforts with particular emphasis on charter school movement (including schools, human capital and policy/advocacy) and social entrepreneurs, notably the Knowledge Is Power Program (KIPP) and Teach For America (TFA).
The William and Flora Hewlett Foundation www.hewlett.org	**Founded:** 1966 **Structure:** 501(c)(3) private non-operating foundation **Assets:** $7.3 billion (2006) **Investment Focus:** Long-term institutional and field development in education reform, improved instruction, and access to technology (large effort in open-source educational content).
The Walton Family Foundation www.waltonfamily foundation.org	**Founded:** 1988 **Structure:** 501(c)(3) private non-operating foundation **Assets:** $1.3 billion (2005) **Investment Focus:** Strong free-market theory of change, including charter schools and vouchers.
Michael & Susan Dell Foundation www.msdf.org	**Founded:** 1999 **Structure:** 501(c)(3) private non-operating foundation **Assets:** $1.2 billion (2005) **Investment Focus:** Data systems, human resources, leadership development, and charter school organizations.

TABLE 4.1: Nonprofit Providers of Capital in Education *(continued)*

Organization	Background
Tiger Foundation and **Robertson Foundation** www.robertson foundation.org	**Founded:** 1996 **Structure:** 501(c)(3) private non-operating foundation **Assets:** $659 million (2005) **Investment Focus:** Entrepreneurial change from within as well as with charter schools, primary focus on New York City.
Regional Foundations	
Hyde Family Foundations www.hydefamily foundations.org	**Founded:** 1961 **Structure:** 501(c)(3) private non-operating foundation **Assets:** $131 million **Investment Focus:** Revitalization of the city of Memphis, with focus on entrepreneurial human capital and inside change as well as charter schools.
Robin Hood Foundation www.robinhood. org	**Founded:** 1988 **Structure:** 501(c)(3) public charity **Assets:** n/a, $83.5 million in grants (2007) **Investment Focus:** Poverty in New York City through four programs, including two related to education (Early Childhood and Youth, Education). Entrepreneurial education grantees include Achievement First, Building Educated Leaders for Life (BELL), Uncommon Schools, Urban Assembly.
Intermediary Financial Organizations	
NewSchools Venture Fund www.newschools. org	**Founded:** 1998 **Structure:** 501(c)(3) public charity **Assets:** $100 million raised to date; current fund roughly $50 million **Investment Focus:** Highly engaged venture philanthropy; invest only in educational entrepreneurs (both for-profit and nonprofit); large investments in CMOs and entrepreneurs who serve both district and charter systems with human-capital programs and data tools.
New Profit, Inc. www.newprofit. com	**Founded:** 1998 **Structure:** 501(c)(3) public charity **Assets:** $5.9 million (2005) **Investment Focus:** Social entrepreneurs in the nonprofit sector to build scalable organizations that will have a lasting impact.
Chicago Public Education Fund www.cpef.org	**Founded:** 2000 **Structure:** 501(c)(3) public charity, intermediary **Assets:** $8 million (2006) **Investment Focus:** Educational entrepreneurs working in Chicago-area schools, as well as in-district initiatives.

Organization	Background
Venture Philanthropy Partners www.vppartners.org	**Founded:** 2000 **Structure:** 501(c)(3) public charity, intermediary **Assets:** $17.9 million (2006) **Investment Focus:** Washington, D.C. region.
Charter School Growth Fund www.chartergrowth fund.org	**Founded:** 2005 **Structure:** 501(c)(3) public charity, intermediary **Assets:** $35 million (2006) **Investment Focus:** Charter school entrepreneurs growing organizations to large scale.

tors, regardless of industry. They assess the market, the product or service, the financial model, and, most importantly, the team, using a relatively standard model of due diligence that they can apply across a wide variety of companies.[7] The investors who support these start-ups also tend to be professional investors whose job it is to serve on their ventures' boards so as to be engaged in helping the companies develop. They often work together to increase the amount of upfront support that the entrepreneurial organization receives while decreasing the burden on the entrepreneur, by combining their efforts as a syndicate that provides coordinated funding all at once. George Overholser, a founding executive at consumer finance company Capital One who now runs the nonprofit investment firm NFF Capital Partners, explains: "Investing growth capital is a tricky business—it requires a lot of predictions, a lot of judgment and a lot of due diligence. And due diligence is expensive. One of the benefits of writing large checks—and of forming syndicates—is that we can afford to conduct due diligence in an in-depth way."[8]

Because of this high engagement in ventures, venture capitalists tend to invest significant amounts of capital upfront (an average of $3.8 million per early-stage deal compared with an average foundation grant size of $125,000 in 2005).[9] As such, for-profit entrepreneurs are generally able to raise all the initial investment capital they need from just a handful of investors. These investments are allocated toward general operating purposes of the company, and thus the entrepreneur can use them as he or she sees fit to develop the organization. For example, Aaron Lieberman is an entrepreneur who has raised nearly $2 million in early-stage funds for his for-profit preschool management firm Acelero Learning, all of which has come from just three investors. This compares with at least 20 individual and institutional donors from which he had to raise funds to found Jumpstart, a nonprofit focused on the same market, back in 1993. The flipside to these larger amounts of invest-ment capital is that a typical venture-capital investor is often in hot pur-suit of the fastest path to exit—either an initial public offering on the pub-lic stock market, or an acquisition or merger with another company—which often leads them to prioritize rapid growth in revenues rather than long-term, sustainable quality. This can be difficult, or even disastrous, for a social entrepreneur in the public education space, where it takes time and patience to develop a strong company.

Increasingly, the middle of the spectrum is expanding, as more inves-tors choose to include some social preferences in their investment decisions, and some philanthropic organizations are more open to utilizing loans or for-profit tools like equity investments. Some blended-value investors focus on generating economic activity in a specific state or region, such as Pacific Community Ventures, which is a development venture-capital fund located in northern California that seeks financial returns but invests in businesses that employ low-income workers.[10] Other blended-value firms partner with banks to meet federal Community Reinvestment Act requirements that man-date financial institutions to provide a certain level of investment in low- and middle-income communities where they operate businesses.

For example, JPMorgan has spun off the Bay Area Equity Fund, a $75 mil-lion venture-capital fund raised from traditional sources—major banks and insurance companies, foundations, corporations, and private individuals—to invest in "companies that can deliver market-rate venture-capital returns while enabling social and environmental improvement in the San Francisco Bay Area's low and moderate income neighborhoods." Within education, the fund has invested (together with NewSchools) in Revolution Foods, a for-profit company that provides healthy meals to local schools at a reason-able cost. NewSchools is also in this blended middle zone, as a philanthropic investor that clearly prioritizes an organization's social mission but makes strategic use of financial instruments like equity investments and loans where appropriate. Table 4.2 shows the small group of relevant investors who support for-profit entrepreneurs in education.

Finally, despite the public sector's role in holding public schools account-able and providing ongoing operating funds to existing schools, it pro-vides little investment for social entrepreneurs. For example, in 2007, the federal government allocated $214 million to charter school start-up grants and another $36 million to a program that enables charter schools to obtain more affordable facilities loans.[11] This $250 million investment in helping to create new public schools amounts to less than half of a percent of the U.S. Department of Education's $68 billion budget for the year.[12]

Changing this dynamic is essential to the continued growth of entrepreneurial organizations in education. One powerful example of public support for developing supply is the way that the federal government has approached the market for low-income housing, stimulating demand by providing Section 8 vouchers ($15 billion worth in fiscal year 2007) while also offering investment and tax incentives for investors and developers to work together and create an additional supply of low-income housing (approximately $5 billion in annual budget authority for the Low-Income Housing Tax Credit). In fact, the low-income housing market has also been bolstered by public-sector intervention into the housing market as a whole. The private mortgage company Federal National Mortgage Association (FNMA or "Fannie Mae"), for instance, was originally established as a governmentally chartered organization to expand the flow of mortgages to home buyers at low rates, and the establishment of the Government National Mortgage Association (GNMA or "Ginnie Mae") made it possible for the fragmented local lending industry to pool loans into a new class of assets—mortgage backed securities—that could be sold to other investors, thereby helping standardize the mortgage industry nationally (creating a $6 trillion a year industry).

The federal government also invests over $28 billion annually in the National Institutes of Health to support medical research that ultimately helps the biotechnology and pharmaceutical industries with innovation that can later be commercialized—a figure that Larry Berger and David Stevenson note in chapter 5 is a hundred times more than the Institute of Education Sciences's $260 million.[13] Another interesting example of a public policy intervention that affected the capital markets was the revision of the Employee Retirement Income Securities Act in 1979, which dramatically increased the pool of venture-capital funding by allowing public pension funds to invest in venture-capital funds. By 1983, the value of commitments to venture capital had soared from $200 million annually before the regulations were changed to more than $5 billion per year.[14]

The increased involvement of the public sector is particularly important, given how daunting public education is as an investment arena. In the late 1990s, NewSchools saw an increasing number of traditional venture-capital firms willing to take on education investments, only to see them begin to steer clear of the industry after discovering how slow the sales cycle is for companies selling products or services into districts, not to mention the

TABLE 4.2: Providers of For-Profit Capital for Education

Organization	Background
Geographically focused firms that have made at least one investment in education	
Bay Area Equity Fund (JPMorgan) www.bayareafamily offunds.org/funds/ baef.shtml	**Founded:** 2003 **Assets:** $75 million **Mission:** Double–bottom-line investor. Invests primarily in technology, health care, consumer products, clean tech. **Education investments:** Revolution Foods, organic healthy food for Bay Area schools.
Boston Community Capital www.boston communitycapital. org	**Founded:** 1985 **Assets:** $70 million (2006) **Mission:** Social purpose investor; loan fund invests in housing, community facilities, and social services; venture fund invests in product and service companies. **Education investments:** Acelero Learning; management tools for Head Start programs; loan recipients include Jumpstart.
Pennsylvania Early Stage Partners www.paearlystage. com	**Founded:** 1997 **Assets:** $239 million **Mission:** Prioritizes financial returns, focuses on technology and life-sciences companies, some funds required to be invested in Pennsylvania-based companies. **Education investments:** LearnNow, education management organization (sold to Edison Schools).
Financially motivated investors with industry focus on education	
Knowledge Universe www.knowledgeu. com	**Founded:** 1996 **Assets:** unknown **Mission:** Michael Milken founded to invest in cradle-to-grave education ventures (not focused on underserved communities or public education). **Education investments:** LearnNow and Charter Schools USA, primarily weighted toward consumer market products like LeapFrog and higher education and training services.
Knowledge Investment Partners www.kiplp.com	**Founded:** 2002 **Assets:** $200 million **Mission:** Invests in education and knowledge businesses through two hedge funds and a private equity fund. **Education investments:** Eduventures, Schiller International University.
Quad Partners www.quad ventures.com	**Founded:** 2000 **Assets:** $200 million **Mission:** SBIC support for ventures serving mixed- or low-income communities motivates some venture selection. **Education investments:** Teachscape, Platform Learning.

Organization	Background
Socially motivated investors that make for-profit investments	
NewSchools Venture Fund www.newschools.org	**Founded:** 1998 **Assets:** $100 million raised to date **Mission:** Public charity venture philanthropy firm, acts as value-added intermediary between individuals/institutions and K–12 educational entrepreneurs. **Education investments:** For-profit investments include LearnNow (sold to Edison Schools), Teachscape, Carnegie Learning, Revolution Foods.
Raza Development Fund (RDF) www.razafund.org	**Founded:** 1998 **Structure:** 501(c)(3) public charity (community development lending arm of the National Council of La Raza) **Assets:** $50 million School Building Fund developed with Citibank's Community Development Division **Education investments:** Provides loans, financing and lease guarantees for charter schools that serve Latino and other minority students; recipients include Bronx Charter School for the Arts.
Self-Help www.self-help.org	**Founded:** 1980 (venture fund established in 1984) **Structure:** 501(c)(3) public charity **Assets:** Unknown; $85+ million in loans issued to date **Education investments:** Provides loans to charter schools in low-income areas with facility financing needs over $2 million; recipients include KIPP Gaston College Prep.
Other	
Ascend Ventures www.ascendventures.com	**Founded:** 2001 **Assets:** $150 million under management (2007) **Mission:** Venture capital firm that invests in early-stage technology companies that are minority- and women-owned. **Education investments:** LearnNow (education management organization), Platform Learning (supplemental education services), SchoolNet (data tools for districts and states).
Commons Capital www.commonscapital.com	**Founded:** 2000 **Assets:** Unknown **Mission:** Double-bottom-line investor, invests in early-stage companies that promote a sustainable economy and address major social and environmental problems. **Education investments:** Apex Learning.

industry's political volatility and the sheer lack of demand for higher quality products by education consumers.

Meanwhile, for philanthropic funders, the significant funding needed to get entrepreneurial education ventures to scale is daunting in comparison to the smaller grant sizes with which they are comfortable. This dynamic is changing somewhat, thanks to an influx of new education-focused foundations and individual donors willing to think entrepreneurially, but the field of social purpose capital is still small. This sometimes leads entrepreneurs to contort their business models to cater to prospective investors. One entrepreneur went so far as to say, "Some funders think they have hired you to work for them when they fund you." For example, one well-known foundation recently put significant pressure on a nonprofit to dramatically change its growth plans—in terms of both pace and geographic locations—to meet the foundation's own priorities, in exchange for funding. The organization ended up declining the offer, but that discipline is hard to maintain in the face of a multimillion-dollar check and few alternative funders.

MAKING THE SOCIAL PURPOSE CAPITAL MARKETS WORK

Although the conventional capital market in the United States is far from perfect, it is relatively well-developed and efficient and therefore can provide a helpful framework for considering how the social purpose capital markets might be improved in a way that better supports social entrepreneurs in education. As mentioned earlier, this includes all three sectors–public, private, and nonprofit—but because the lion's share of funding for social entrepreneurs still comes from foundations, we will focus the weight of our observations there.

To recap, we identified five main forces that make the conventional capital markets hum: general agreement on the *definitions of success;* transparency and uniformity of *performance data;* a robust ecosystem of *independent, expert intermediary and advisory organizations;* a secure and reliable *infrastructure;* and a *large and diverse supply of capital providers.* Considering the strengths and shortcomings of the social purpose capital markets in this light will help illuminate areas of opportunity for investors and policymakers who wish to better the odds of success for educational entrepreneurs.

DEFINITIONS OF SUCCESS

In traditional capital markets, how to "keep score" is clear because success is defined as maximizing shareholder value, which is calculated in dollars.

This simple metric allows the rest of the system—information, services, and regulations—to function in reasonable alignment. In public education, the definition of success is highly complex and incredibly political, leading to significant problems for the social purpose capital markets, which, after all, place their money with social entrepreneurs with the expectation that some sort of value will be created. There are two primary types of confusion: the first, and most troubling, is the lack of clarity on what we mean by success in education, and the second is how to balance organizational sustainability with social impact.

The question of defining educational success is a complex one. What constitutes a successful student—one who graduates from high school, one who enters college, one who finds a fulfilling career, one who becomes a productive citizen? About which students exactly are we talking? At minimum, the move toward state standards and greater accountability has led to greater attention toward *outcomes* in place of an earlier focus on *inputs and processes,* which has opened the doors for entrepreneurs to innovate with different approaches for accomplishing improved outcomes. This very idea is still under attack by some defenders of the status quo, and there is still plenty of disagreement around priorities (for example, should we focus on adequacy to ensure low-income students do not fall between the cracks, or address our most talented students so we stay economically competitive?) and means (should we provide more funding to back-to-basics curricula, or focus on more progressive pedagogical approaches?). Overall, this market-wide disagreement over what success looks like and what metrics should be used to quantify the value created by a school (or entrepreneurial organization) has created a volatile system in which laws and regulations shift with the political winds, frightening off for-profit investors and doing little to focus philanthropic funding in a coherent direction.

Even when funders generally agree on educational goals, there is still tremendous disagreement over how to balance those with organizational metrics like profits or the ability for the organization to remain a going concern. For instance, when NewSchools first considered a grant to nonprofit principal preparation program New Leaders for New Schools in fall 2000, our investment advisors initially encouraged us to ask founder Jon Schnur to charge districts and schools a fee for each principal they placed. This was common sense to our investment advisors, most of whom have business backgrounds and thus emphasize the ability of an organization to generate enough revenue quickly to become sustainable.

However, both NewSchools's and New Leaders's teams were concerned that its new model—which demanded that partner districts provide their principals with greater autonomy than they would otherwise enjoy—would fail to gain traction with districts if it also charged this fee up front. Ultimately, NewSchools and New Leaders agreed that they should forego the fee in the early years, while its principals proved their merit, and today the non-profit's program has become so sought after that prospective district clients agree to raise half the cost of training the principals. The organization had to wrestle with the fine balance between social impact and financial sustainability, opting to place some of its early emphasis on the former in the hopes that success would manifest as more revenue down the line.

What would improve clarity on metrics for success, and thus help this market better align investment behind social entrepreneurs? Unfortunately, there may always be fundamental inefficiencies in this capital market because the definition of educational success will inevitably involve value judgments that purely financial markets can largely avoid. If industry-wide agreement on the definition of educational success is impossible, it is at least important for investors and entrepreneurs to be as clear as they can about their own goals and how they will measure them. For example, the Bill & Melinda Gates Foundation has developed its own clear idea of success: college readiness. The foundation's grants are measured against that benchmark, which has allowed them to hold their grantees to a tangible standard while also letting them continue refining their specifications of what elements lead to college readiness.[15]

PERFORMANCE DATA

"It is disquieting that philanthropists have access to so little of the kinds of information that private investors rely on," says Paul Brest, president of the Hewlett Foundation. "[Private] investors can make use of a broad array of data, ranging from reports of quarterly earnings statements to the historical and current prices at which stocks are traded—all based on standards that are consistent across many industries, markets, and countries. Based on this information, investors can put together portfolios that are aligned with their investment horizons and tolerance for risks. And at the end of the day, or quarter, they will know their actual returns."[16] Brest is right; it is frustrating for social purpose investors and donors to have so little access to useful, comparable data that they can use to make funding decisions. Three main types of data are lacking: achievement data, organizational data, and financial data.

Insufficient achievement data is a deeply rooted problem in education, where educators themselves are only now beginning to become comfortable with using data to inform their instructional decisionmaking. There have been some encouraging efforts. An increasing number of states are investing in student-level data systems with unique student identifying numbers that will enable them to track over time how an individual student, class, or teacher is doing and adjust interventions accordingly. And efforts like the for-profit Grow Network (now owned by publisher McGraw-Hill) and School-Net offer tools that schools and school systems can use to track and monitor achievement and other data. Online tools like GreatSchools.net and School-Matters.com have both helped make publicly available information about schools and districts easier to access and understand. While these improvements have increased the availability of achievement data within districts and states, it remains difficult to draw comparisons across them or to understand what exactly is behind these differences.

To address this dearth of uniform achievement data, all three sectors must invest in more of the technological tools that make it easy for public school systems to collect, analyze, report, and act on student-level and program data. Such tools would help both entrepreneurs and their investors understand what is happening and what is working and which approaches are leading to more value. Another tactic that might very well enable more comparable data comparisons is the adoption of national standards, which would allow investors (along with other stakeholders) to compare results across states and systems. This is a complicated political challenge, but it is clear that entrepreneurial education organizations of varying sorts have spent an inordinate amount of time, energy, and money to align programs to different state standards of highly varying quality—all of which could have been better used to serve students.

In addition to addressing academic data, investors require better access to organizational data, benchmarks for elements like program design, staffing, and costs. The Center for High Impact Philanthropy at the University of Pennsylvania is one early effort to provide this service for donors. Executive Director Kat Rosqueta explains: "What's really needed is reliable information on the impact and cost-effectiveness of the kinds of activities a philanthropist could fund. Some of this information does exist, but it's locked up in academia, in the gray literature that foundations and policymakers use and generate, and in the heads and experiences of 'experts,' practitioners, and clients. Unfortunately, these are all sources that are inaccessible or unintelligible to the vast majority of philanthropists."[17]

In the nonprofit sector, financial reporting is often presented in an inconsistent way that is less than useful to funders, especially those interested in helping organizations grow to a significant size or achieve a level of sustainability that decreases their dependence on philanthropy. For example, nonprofits do not account for their growth capital separately from their general operating revenue, and thus, according to George Overholser of NFF Capital Partners, "relatively few donors and foundations are willing to provide money for growth because it is difficult to track what their money accomplishes." Overholser notes that if the $18 million his organization helped raise for the youth employment nonprofit Year Up were put toward annual operations, an additional 818 young people could be trained. But if that same $18 million were used to cover operating losses while the organization expands to the point where its revenues cover its expenses, that same money would allow the organization to serve 1,100 more young people each year thereafter.[18] Yet this kind of distinction in types and uses of capital in nonprofits is quite rare. This sort of sophistication will need to become more widespread to persuade more investors to support growth investments.

INDEPENDENT INTERMEDIARY ORGANIZATIONS

In the private-capital markets, a variety of independent intermediary organizations help make the flow of capital and information more effective and efficient. Some of these intermediaries such as bond-rating firms, equity analysts and consulting firms, trade in knowledge and information, while others, such as venture-capital firms and investment banks, specialize in funneling investment funds. Because the private-capital market is so large and diverse, these intermediaries develop valuable expertise in particular types of investments, categories of capital providers, or spheres of information, allowing them to add value to the space between an investor's capital and an entrepreneur's business. Of particular value are independent intermediaries because they provide information and services free of conflicts of interest. For example, a certified financial advisor employed by a bank may try to sell his or her clients money management services, whereas an independent advisor is more likely to provide unbiased guidance.

Because the social purpose capital market in education is young and growing, there are still a limited number of these independent intermediaries and advisors and fewer still who are focused explicitly on education. Thanks to the influx of philanthropic capital into the market over the last five years, several consulting firms have begun to engage with entrepreneurial clients, including the for-profit Parthenon Group and The Bridgespan Group, the nonprofit spin-off of consulting giant Bain & Company. As far as we can tell, there is still just a single organization, Eduventures, Inc., that provides investment analysis of the K–12 and postsecondary education market, allowing investors to track industry trends. Beyond education, a variety of philanthropic advisory firms—including the Center for High Impact Philanthropy mentioned above—provides tools, services, and advice to individual and institutional donors. And groups like the Investor's Circle bring together individual socially motivated investors to help increase each member's awareness of possible investments and give them a peer group of potential coinvestors.

In the private sector, investment intermediaries help add value to the funds they aggregate by specializing in a particular type or stage of investment. Larger investors, such as pension funds or banks, choose to support intermediaries like venture-capital firms because they know that they cannot themselves be experts at everything. For example, the National Venture Capital Association describes venture capitalists as firms that "finance new and rapidly growing companies; assist in the development of new products or services; add value to the company through active participation; take higher risks with the expectation of higher rewards; and have a long-term orientation."[19]

Such specialized investment intermediaries are still relatively rare in the social purpose capital markets. Ten years after our founding, NewSchools is still the only firm that focuses exclusively on social entrepreneurs in education and across both the for-profit and nonprofit sectors. This focus allows us to connect entrepreneurial leaders, track patterns and opportunities over time, and presumably add value to social entrepreneurs' organizations and also to those of our donors. Other investment intermediaries have developed their own specializations: New Profit focuses broadly on social entrepreneurs across many fields and partners with the consulting firm Monitor to provide consulting and coaching to entrepreneurs in their portfolio; Venture Philanthropy Partners in Washington, D.C., focuses on social entrepreneurs within a limited geographic area; and the Charter School Growth Fund focuses exclusively on charter school organizations across the country that are growing to scale. Despite their differences, all of these intermediaries prioritize social impact, aggregate capital from diverse sources to provide larger and longer term grants, and focus on helping social entrepreneurs grow their organizations.

A few new firms have also emerged to help social entrepreneurs in their quest for growth funds, including the NFF Capital Partners, founded by George Overholser within the Nonprofit Finance Fund, and SeaChange Capital Partners, which was created by two former Goldman Sachs partners with a $5 million initial contribution by Goldman Sachs itself. These organizations perform extensive due diligence to choose nonprofits that are poised for growth, present the opportunity to their network of donors, and raise capital from those donors—as NFF describes it, "without major restrictions and with an expectation of return measured by social impact." This approach has helped NFF Capital Partners raise more than $40 million for two education nonprofits, College Summit and Teach For America.

On the for-profit front, there are fewer such intermediaries who focus on social entrepreneurs in education, which means that those social entrepreneurs who choose to create for-profit businesses are hamstrung by a lack of early-stage investment capital and often must seek such funding from individual, or angel, investors. As such, there is a significant need for more investing intermediaries willing to take on early-stage, high-risk, for-profit education investments in the way venture capitalists have embraced healthcare and technology.

In the near term, the political complexity and fragmentation of this industry may continue to scare off for-profit investors, which means that the philanthropic sector and even the public sector may need to step in and create more social purpose investing intermediaries that are able to invest in both for-profit and nonprofit organizations. Such an expansion would allow entrepreneurs more freedom to develop innovative organizations and greater negotiating power by giving them more of a choice of investors. It could also allow different firms to specialize in specific areas of education, such as preschool services, technology tools, or human capital systems. This will require foundations to delegate consciously some investment decisions and organization-building to such intermediaries. Given the sizeable need that social entrepreneurs in education face, it is crucial to figure out how to provide strong, successful, well-run organizations with greater long-term growth capital, allowing them to spend less time fundraising and more time building their team and delivering services.

INFRASTRUCTURE

The most obvious infrastructure supporting the conventional capital markets is institutional or regulatory in nature, such as the public stock markets or specific financial reporting or accounting requirements. As noted earlier, there is little regulation of nonprofit funders other than the prohibition to use these tax-advantaged dollars for personal gain or political advocacy and the requirement to disburse 5 percent of their assets each year. This is designed to allow such donors to innovate and to encourage experimentation. Paul Ylvisaker, former dean of the Harvard Graduate School of Education, has referred to philanthropy as "society's passing gear" for this very reason because these loose regulations allow donors to move society forward by developing new solutions.[20] However, the unintended consequence is that there is little incentive for donors to be disciplined about how they manage or measure their impact, which makes for a seemingly capricious funding world for social entrepreneurs. Public oversight agencies have become increasingly concerned over the past several years about the way foundations spend their money. It seems that the best way for foundations to get out ahead of this scrutiny is to make their grant-making criteria and success metrics more transparent.

Meanwhile, investors who choose to back for-profit social entrepreneurs are a new phenomenon and are generally held to the same regulatory constraints as their peers in the sectors in which they operate. One new development that may help to clarify this field is the work by sporting apparel entrepreneur Jay Coen Gilbert, who is trying to create a new kind of corporate class, called "for-benefit corporations" or "B Corporations," that would make clear that a for-profit company has chosen to balance both financial and social impact.[21] Gilbert's new investment fund B Lab is developing legal frameworks and other infrastructure that would allow this to happen. It has recently unveiled a slate of twenty-one charter B corporations that have, among other things, modified their articles of incorporation to account for nonfinancial impact and agreed to transparent reporting of their performance.[22] There are no current tax incentives to encourage social-purpose investors to try this blended approach to investing; thus, for-profit social entrepreneurs must either raise money from for-profit investors who expect a standard rate of financial return (difficult to accomplish in an early-stage education organization) or try to raise capital from philanthropic donors (few of whom support any for-profit entities). We support the development of B Corporations and other innovative approaches to resolving this challenge.

Further, the development of human and intellectual capital will go a long way toward supporting educational entrepreneurs and will also strengthen their ability to raise capital. In particular, greater attention must be paid to programs and organizations that help prepare leaders with experience from across the public, private, and nonprofit sectors. We call this hybrid leadership and believe that this combination of expertise and capital savvy from across sectors is crucial to the development of the social purpose capital markets. Some programs have begun to address this need for cross-sector leaders, including the dual master's degree in education and business at Stanford University and The Broad Center for the Management of School Systems, which identifies and prepares leaders with varied backgrounds for roles within school districts, not to mention the increasing number of universities with specializations in social entrepreneurship. Because this field is still emerging and is led by relatively young managers and entrepreneurs, more energy and resources will need to be spent on professional development for these leaders and on developing the pipeline of next generation leadership. An increase in industry-specialized strategy consultants, recruiters, and executive coaches would help bolster this aspect of the social entrepreneurship infrastructure.

LARGE AND DIVERSE SUPPLY OF CAPITAL PROVIDERS

In the conventional capital markets, there is a broad and diverse set of capital providers, ranging from small, community-oriented lenders to large-scale investors who manage the billions of dollars in public pension funds or foundation endowments. Most of these large capital providers diversify their investment risk by placing their funds across a broad array of investment tools, stages of development, and industries. Indeed, a quick look at any newspaper's business pages shows the mind-boggling array of stocks, bonds, commodities, and mutual funds available through public exchanges, demonstrating that there seem to be as many investment opportunities available as there are individual and institutional investors. The bottom line is that for conventional for-profit businesses, there is an immense amount of financial capital available in the United States, and it is available in a variety of mechanisms, ranging from start-up equity investments to loans of varying degrees of risk to shares of stock offered to the public on stock exchanges.

Contrast this with the social purpose capital market, which as described above is still relatively limited in terms of the number of players, the coordination of these, and the types of investment vehicles available—all of which significantly hamper the growth of entrepreneurial solutions in education. The responsibility for fixing this is shared among the nonprofit, private, and public sectors. Specifically, the biggest financial challenges facing these entrepreneurs are an almost complete absence of early-stage investment capital available to for-profit social entrepreneurs in education (as Larry Berger and David Stevenson detail in chapter 5); a severe lack of nonprofit capital for organizations that want to grow to scale (at both the early and later stages); and a shortage of supply-side investments or incentives in this important arena by the public sector.

As Joseph Keeney and Daniel Pianko explain in chapter 3, most for-profit investors are intimidated by public education, despite the relatively large and recession-proof nature of the industry. It is not difficult to see why: Each of the fifty states has a unique set of education laws, standards, and mechanisms for assessment; the sales cycle into each of the country's 14,000 districts is long, idiosyncratic, and relationship-based, making it difficult for new entrants to gain traction; and there is general resistance to adopting new tools and technologies. As such, few private investors are willing to take a risk on unproven for-profit enterprises in K–12 public education, making it difficult for social entrepreneurs to create new businesses in some of the areas where for-profit business models appear to make the most sense—such as technology tools to manage achievement and program data.

Meanwhile, social entrepreneurs in the nonprofit sector—particularly those taking on an ambitious project designed to address the vast scale of the problems in public education across the country—find themselves forced to spend at least half of their time cobbling together dozens of early-stage grants from philanthropic donors. According to consulting firm McKinsey & Company, for-profit companies spend between $2 and $4 raising capital for every $100 that they bring in, compared with $10 to $24 spent for every $100 brought in through fundraising among nonprofits.[23] One social entrepreneur who had a track record of success with earlier companies, Randy Best, found that to raise the capital he needed he actually had to change his organization's corporate structure from nonprofit to for-profit. "I would tell a foundation that we needed a three-year grant of $500,000 per year and they would award me a one-year $20,000 grant and tell me to reapply next year," says Best. "I was spending all of the time fundraising and I needed to be focused on building the business. I changed our status and went to friends and investors who had supported my previous business ventures. We raised $40 million, and I had the money we needed to get started."[24] That company became Voyager Learning, a provider of research-based reading curriculum and professional development programs that grew to almost $100 million a year in revenue before it was bought in 2005.

Moreover, established nonprofit organizations trying to raise funds for growth often find themselves stymied as well. As social capital markets investor Tim Freundlich of Good Capital points out, nonprofit donors tend to "nickel-and-dime social change leaders to death" by providing small grants and then cutting off their funding when they begin to demonstrate positive results and reach toward more growth.[25] This is what Bridgespan consultant Jeff Bradach calls the "paradox of success" in the nonprofit sector. "At precisely the moment when large amounts of capital would flow to a proven idea in the for-profit sector, funders in the nonprofit sector frequently back away," he writes. "There are many reasons—donor fatigue, a belief that equity requires spreading money around, hesitance to make 'big bets'—but the consequence is that proven solutions to pressing problems do not spread."[26]

Certainly not all nonprofit investors shy away from providing growth capital to these organizations: both NewSchools and the Charter School Growth Fund aggregate capital from other donors and provide large, long-term grants and loans to charter school management organizations that are trying to grow and serve more students. Some newer foundations established by wealthy entrepreneurs from the business sector—whose founders have an appreciation for what it takes to grow an enterprise to scale—have been willing to offer bigger grants to organizations seeking to provide large-scale change, thus allowing those entrepreneurs to focus more of their energy on running the enterprise. For example, the Doris & Donald Fisher Foundation (benefactor Donald Fisher founded the Gap clothing empire) and the Bill & Melinda Gates Foundation have both given many millions to the nonprofit charter school network Knowledge Is Power Program (KIPP) to sustain that organization's ambitious growth plans, including at least $40 million from the Fisher Foundation and $17 million from the Gates Foundation.

In a bold move, some exceptional foundations, including the Atlantic Philanthropies and the Gates Foundation, have announced that they plan to spend down their endowments. Rather than allocating only the minimum legally required amount of 5 percent of their assets each year, they have set a deadline by which all of their funds will be put to use. This strategy stands in sharp contrast to the vast majority of foundations, whose growing endowments allow them to grant more money to nonprofits but also to support enormous staffs and occupy lush office buildings and operate in perpetuity. These bold decisions by Atlantic and Gates will no doubt increase the amount of philanthropic capital available in this century, but because only a small percent is expected to flow into public education, this will not come close to filling the gap of nonprofit growth capital for social entrepreneurs in this market.

Foundations can take a number of steps to address this shortcoming. The simplest is to recognize the capital needs of social entrepreneurs and provide them with larger, longer-term grants. Further, more foundations could take a page from Atlantic and Gates by either spending down their endowments, or at least increasing the percent of their assets that are used toward creating social impact through a variety of program-related investments (PRIs). One of the easiest ways to do this is to provide recyclable grants for expanded operating capital. These interest-free, long-term loans can be allocated toward nonprofits that generate public fees for their services (such as charter school management organizations) and which can therefore repay those loans over time, allowing the same grant capital to be recycled and provided to other organizations.

Another approach is to create an equity equivalent that would allow foundations to provide nonprofits with growth funds without saddling them with debt liability that reduces their access to private-sector debt. Although such a tool might look much like a recyclable grant or loan, it could be structured so that it would be accounted for and function more like equity (only to be repaid if certain financial accomplishments were met). Another way to use PRIs is to invest in independent intermediary organizations that could then specialize in selecting and supporting higher risk early-stage organizations—whether for-profit or nonprofit–within areas that complement the work of foundations themselves. These firms could then leverage the funds with later-stage funds from the private sector or from foundations.

Similarly, the public sector could and should do a great deal more to mobilize private capital into entrepreneurial education organizations by creating new tax credits to reward investment in specific areas of need, such as more sophisticated assessment tools that measure the higher-order skills we hope to see in students. Another change might be to revise the New Markets Tax Credits—originally created to mobilize private-sector investments into low-income communities—to make them more amenable to education investments by eliminating the requirement to hold investments for 10 years. The public sector could also stimulate the supply of entrepreneurial solutions in education by establishing a pool of funds that would be available through a competitive request for proposal process to investment intermediaries to use in supporting organizations that address key areas of need (such as assessment tools or teacher and principal preparation programs) and could even require that these funds be matched by private-sector commitments. Finally, the public sector should attend to the needs of one of education's largest entrepreneurial movements—charter schools—by increasing funding to these schools in a way that enables more of them to get off the ground (expanding federal charter school start-up grants significantly), helping more of them to obtain and pay for facilities (by expanding the federal Credit Enhancement for Charter School Facilities program), and encouraging more established operators to develop new schools in the communities that need them (through a new competitive grant program designed to support quality scale organizations).

CALL TO ACTION

No matter how fertile the seeds of entrepreneurship, they wither without the proper economic soil.
—*Dwight R. Lee, University of Georgia*

This volume assumes that educational entrepreneurs are important change agents, are here to stay, and require additional support from their surrounding ecosystem to have the strongest positive impact on the public education system. This chapter goes one step further, arguing that social entrepreneurs—who seek to improve outcomes for those underserved communities and transform the system so it better meets those needs on an ongoing basis—occupy an especially valuable niche within the broader entrepreneurial space. We further argue that it is important to consider this field—both entrepreneurs and sources of capital—across the traditional boundary of the economic sector. That is, given the import of this work and the scale of the problems we seek to fix, it will take leaders and resources from all of the nonprofit, private, and public sectors. And last, we point out that social entrepreneurs' ability to create significant change has been hampered by the limited size and relative immaturity of the social purpose capital markets intended to serve them.

It is worth remembering that the conventional capital markets have only come into their present structure through the intentional actions of a variety of means—namely, government regulations to establish and refine the ground rules and help guide the flow of capital, and business and nongovernmental organizations to create a range of institutions, practices, and investment tools within those constraints. It will be no different in the social purpose capital markets for educational entrepreneurs. Specifically, for this movement to continue to develop and increase its impact, our most important recommendations include:

More Growth Funding

The field needs much more funding, both at the early and latter stages of an entrepreneurial organization's development, and it should be committed in larger amounts via multiyear investments and grants with fewer strings.

More Patient Capital

Building quality in public education takes time, and investors need to recognize that the best way to build financial or social value is by providing consistent quality over time.

A Strong Ecosystem

Any mature industry needs substantial specialized human and intellectual capital, so investments in entrepreneurial ventures need to be accompanied by greater support of entrepreneurial team capacity, as well as a more robust ecosystem of financial, intellectual, and human capital intermediaries.

Move Past Old Ideologies

Just as we expect entrepreneurs to think creatively—beyond the bounds of the status quo—so too must their capital providers. Foundations need to expand program-related investments and support a stronger for-profit field through the creation of nonprofit investment intermediaries. For-profit investors need to work toward supporting blended-value or double-bottom-line investments. Finally, public-sector leaders—who bear ultimate responsibility and accountability for ensuring that the needs of public school students are met—must expand supply-side support for these entrepreneurial organizations by devising approaches that bring together resources from across the public, private, and nonprofit sectors.

CHAPTER 5

Barriers to Entry

Tales from a Tool Builder

Larry Berger and David Stevenson

From 32,000 feet on a recent flight, we declared the tangle of lights out the left window to be a "37." An hour later, the dense cluster by the river was a "54." When we landed, Google Earth revealed that we have gotten disturbingly good at this game: Little Rock (40 elementary schools) and Wichita (51 elementary schools).

We play this game because, as educational entrepreneurs, we are desperate for scale. We operate in a $500 billion market, but the dollars are scattered among 14,000 school districts, few of which are large enough to see from midair. We also play this game to distract ourselves from the thought that, while we are flying over these districts, the vast sales forces of the big publishers are already on the ground in them, meeting the deputy superintendent at the Rotary Club, luring away the last few discretionary dollars she has.

* * * * *

Our company, Wireless Generation, was founded in 2001. Our goal was to build mobile software that would give teachers new diagnostic insight and new capacity to adapt their teaching to precise student needs. In our most popular product, elementary teachers use our software to record, on a handheld computer, their students' reading and math progress. These observational assessments are preferred for children who are not old enough to take standard tests, and they provide a more nuanced picture of student learning than multiple-choice tests. The data on the handheld computers are then synced to our website, where we offer reports that help teachers understand

and address their students' needs, letters that give parents customized learning activities for the home, and analysis that helps districts provide instructional leadership.

We have grown to 300 people, serving more than 2.5 million K–6 students, including most of the K–3 classrooms in New York, Chicago, Miami, Houston, Washington, D.C., and more than a thousand smaller districts. We are considered a preliminary entrepreneurial success story, but we will just barely make a profit for the first time this year, and we remain vulnerable to political funding shifts, to the various ways that the culture of education is slow to change, and to competition from "Big Edu" (the three dominant educational publishing companies).

Our perch above "start-up" and below "established player" might be a useful one from which to explore the barriers to entry that entrepreneurs face as they try to succeed in the educational marketplace, as well as to consider the barriers to exit that keep most educational ventures from reaching initial public offering or other impressive liquidity events. Without such exits, investors and entrepreneurs will be reluctant to invest in K–12, and entrepreneurship will continue to be an underfunded force for improving the education sector.

In this chapter, we will discuss several of the barriers to entry that our company and our colleagues in other education start-ups have encountered, will touch on the barriers to exit that peer companies have faced (we are not interested in exiting anytime soon), and then will make a few suggestions about how schools and policymakers could begin to dismantle these barriers.

A NOTE ON TOOL BUILDERS VERSUS SCHOOL BUILDERS

We should note that our perspective on educational entrepreneurship is that of a builder of tools, systems, and services for schools. It will therefore differ in important ways from that of the entrepreneurs who start and run schools. School builders would not be interested in our airplane game, since most of them work in limited geographic areas and hope to be left alone by the school district, whereas we tool builders tend to work nationally and need to work *with* the school districts. School builders can be considered successful when they have built one successful school; tool builders generally need to demonstrate success in thousands of schools. School builders thrive in environments of decentralized local choice; tool builders thrive in environments of centralized leadership that can purchase our products at scale.

One irony of the current fashion in K–12 philanthropy is that the same entrepreneurs who made fortunes in other industries through highly centralized systems that crushed local variation—for instance, Wal-Mart, Microsoft, Gap, and Netflix—have tended to focus on educational entrepreneurship in the form of local, decentralized, often boutique entities and are surprised to learn that their philanthropy can be counterproductive for our type of educational entrepreneur.

That is, Wal-Mart and Microsoft dominate because they have the scale to make huge investments in innovation and improvement and can standardize tools and practices across vast organizations, thereby achieving economies of scale unavailable to smaller competitors. But when they turn to education, they are drawn to the decentralized niche players and choice. For example, the NewSchools Venture Fund set out to build one fund to invest in school builders and another to invest in tool builders. The school builder fund has attracted more than $100 million in philanthropic dollars; the tool-builder fund has not quite gotten off the ground.

In fairness to these philanthropists, this state of affairs may simply be a matter of where they are in a longer-term strategy, since there is a growing focus among these philanthropists, and among the school builders, on scaling these start-up schools into larger networks of schools. The largest of these networks will soon achieve the scale of a small urban school district and will thereby become a viable customer for tool builders. The meeting of these two forms of entrepreneurship strikes us as a thrilling opportunity (as Kim Smith and the NewSchools Venture Fund saw from the outset). We will discuss this further in our concluding section about overcoming barriers to entry.

ELEVEN BARRIERS TO ENTRY

There are many more than eleven, but our goal is to speak about barriers that we have actually encountered as practicing entrepreneurs.

Barrier 1: Lack of Investment in Innovation

The macroeconomic barriers constraining entrepreneurship in the education sector can be distilled down to three numbers:

1/100. Chris Whittle has noted that the annual federal investment in healthcare R&D outstrips that of education by a ratio of 100 to 1: The National Institutes of Health's annual budget is $27 billion versus an unpacked Institute of Education Sciences R&D budget of $260 million.[1] While Big Pharma and the medical device makers like to present themselves as engines of innovation and discovery, it turns out that the health sciences R&D climate in the United States—and most of the breakthroughs—depend largely on government funding of innovation through the NIH and at universities.[2] The public willingness to invest, at large scale, in educational innovation has not yet generated anything comparable.

3.5. Keeping the lights on and a teacher in every classroom consumes most of the annual money spent on education; little is left over to generate or try new tools, techniques, or approaches. Of every dollar spent on education in 2005, only 3.5 cents went to materials, tools, and services.[3] Subtract the big mandatory purchases of textbooks and annual testing, and one is left with almost no free funds to deploy creatively. With class-size reduction and teacher incentive pay ramping up around the country, the pressure on these budget lines continues to increase, reducing the dollars available for investment in breakthrough tools and services.

1.8. The public school system spends roughly 1.8 percent of its annual operating budget on information technology (IT).[4] IT here refers to hardware, software, and related services, along with a generous 50 percent of the total spent on assessment (because some assessment is automated). In healthcare, the comparable investment is 4.1 percent of revenue. The construction sector spends 5.5 percent.[5] It is clear that education is not making a competitive effort to harness IT, a key engine for innovation and a key door through which entrepreneurs enter a sector. At the heart of the matter is that K–12 education, for the most part, does not invest in IT—it spends on IT, because parents and politicians want to see computers in classrooms. But IT for the sake of appearances rarely delivers any important educational benefits to schools, which, in turn, limits future willingness to invest, which, in turn, shrinks the supply side of initiatives worth investing in.

Barriers 2 and 3: Oligopoly plus Decentralization

These next two barriers need to be understood in concert: The existence of a Big Edu that dominates the national distribution channel in education combines with extreme decentralization (the large number of small districts and the small number of large districts) to create converging barriers. Only Big Edu has the resources to thrive on the vast national scale, while the local field is crowded with "lifestyle" businesses (retired teachers and principals hanging out shingles).

In 2007, there was a consolidation within the oligopoly: Reed Elsevier decided to exit the K–12 education market. It sold Harcourt Assessment to Pearson, and the rest of Harcourt—including core and supplemental publishing—to Houghton Mifflin/Riverdeep. That leaves three major publishers controlling almost 85 percent of the K–12 textbook market.[6] It is telling that each of these three members of Big Edu has congealed around a core publishing business that is at least 125 years old.

As illustrated in figure 5.1, the K–12 publishing industry can be visualized as a modified Pareto distribution with an unusually big head and an unusually long tail, but a slender midsection. That is, there is an abundance of small companies off to the right, and there is Big Edu controlling most of the revenue in an unusually big spike to the left, but there is not much of a middle. The big three—Pearson, McGraw-Hill, and Riverdeep/Houghton-Mifflin—command annual revenues in the billions.[7] Scholastic's education division and two others are next, with annual revenues in the high hundreds of millions. But then there are fewer than a dozen companies in the $100–200 million range, among them Renaissance Learning, Cambium, and Voyager. Follow the curve out to the right and you find fewer than you would expect in the $25–100 million range (Wireless Generation is in this group), then there are many companies between $5 million and $25 million in revenue, and many hundreds at $5 million and below, most of which are still founder-run and serving specific regional and subject-area niches.[8]

This distribution may or may not be transparent to customers in schools, as the biggest players are aggregations of smaller players, often with retained brands (for example, "Saxon, a Harcourt Achieve Imprint" and "SRA/McGraw-Hill"). Sales forces, distribution, shipping, offshore call centers, and other functions are consolidated to support expansion and discover efficiencies, to develop up-sell and cross-sell opportunities, and to provide more level earnings across buying cycles and even pedagogical fashions.

One of the reasons for the continuing consolidation is that the market is expanding from core, or basal, textbook purchases toward supplemental or intervention materials. The basal programs were developed to be a complete curriculum for a year or sequence of years and are purchased via an arcane, political adoption process in about half of the states, including Florida, Texas, and California.[9] But as assessment instrumentation has gotten better and easier to use and adequate yearly progress pressure has increased focus on students at all achievement levels, many schools and districts have turned to more specialized, focused materials designed to be used with small

FIGURE 5.1: Pareto Distribution of K–12 Education Companies by Revenue

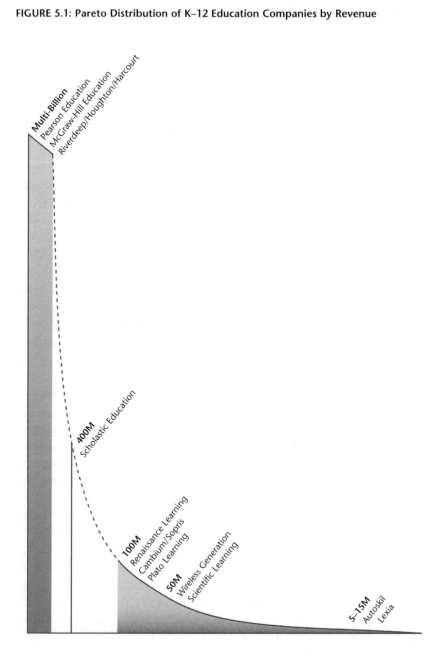

groups of children with specific needs. While this does represent an opportunity for innovation in curriculum design, Big Edu has spotted the trend and has acquired a string of supplemental and intervention companies. They are able to drop these programs into their existing sales channels. Different states are headed in different directions on this. In Florida's reading and language arts adoption this year, there was a separate process for supplemental programs. In the 2008 California adoption, the specifications expect an integrated intervention program as part of the core program (thereby making it hard for the smaller intervention-only providers to participate).

Another reason for the consolidation is the decentralized demand in the sector. With 50 state education agencies, 14,000 districts, intermediate units in most states, and 65,000 schools, there are a lot of decisionmakers. Big Edu solves this problem of radical decentralization by building enormous sales forces of more than a thousand representatives each. Arming these forces with a broad and deep stack of products, they can leverage personal relationships with enough of the local decisionmakers to be successful. Whether a district's focus next year is reading or math, high school or preK, phonics or whole language, the local Big Edu representative has a solution waiting. Indeed, she probably helped the district write the grant proposal that attracted the funding, and her colleagues on the government relations team probably lobbied for the legislation that created that grant program in the first place. Entrepreneurs generally cannot afford to play this game. In our case, we confess that we did not at first understand that there was such a game.

The smaller companies are forced to make difficult choices to secure a distribution channel that can find its way around the oligopoly. Ramping up a sales force around a single product or small mix of them is risky and difficult to accomplish (salespeople in the industry understand this dynamic better than anyone and will often require significant cash guarantees in order to work with a small company). There are two alternatives: regional selling by company founders or sales via independent resellers. Founder selling is often well-received by the schools (especially if the founder is a local small business), but it is difficult to scale and tends to hit a wall at around $5 million in revenue. Independent resellers (who carry the products of several small publishers) can help a company get to $20 million in revenue but usually not beyond it, and the eventual transition to internal sales representatives is often wrenching (the independent reps keep the customer relationships, so when a given company drops them, the independent reps can swiftly tilt their relationships toward other companies they represent).

The large number of small businesses, and the success of the founder sales model in getting these off the ground, indicates that the market has plenty of room for new entrants. There are a few hundred players between $1.5 million and $15 million in revenue. So in what sense is the oligopoly really a barrier?

The problem is not in the first moves but in the middle game. The small business owners in education are not necessarily entrepreneurs. Many of them are building lifestyle businesses to keep themselves engaged after they retire from a school district. They are not attracting investment capital to drive accelerated growth and in many cases do not want to grow beyond a certain size. They get to know the landscape of their local communities, just like the local Big Edu sales rep, and they learn to thrive in that small pond. They are not entrepreneurs who want to innovate across the sector, create value by redeploying resources, and take high levels of risk for high levels of reward—potentially high enough levels to justify gambling years of low salary, high stress, and uncertainty. The would-be entrepreneur scans the educational landscape, sees the crowded field of small companies, notices that few are crossing the chasm to become big, and starts looking at other sectors.

A primary reason Wireless Generation has grown to its current size is that we had a rare opportunity to sidestep some of these distribution barriers. The Reading First component of No Child Left Behind created an unusual amount of liquidity centralized at the state level (about $200 million per year) that did not already have a bureaucracy designed to spend it and that was distinct from another $800 million per year for the districts. So we were able to visit state capitals and win more than a dozen state Reading First assessment contracts, rather than having to visit the thousands of districts those contracts comprised. The founding executive team was able to do much of this selling, so for the company's first five years we were able to keep the sales force under five people.

As we opened up opportunities in new states, we hired regional representation to expand our presence beyond Reading First (we have 10 representatives today), but we did this expansion once we already had momentum and thus never had to make the big up-front investment in a standing army. Such legislation is almost unprecedented and certainly has not repeated itself for any of our other products. The hope that we might repeat this phenomenon (the Math Also First Act?) has prompted us to try to figure out the game of big-league lobbying and government relations—but we are still very much in the minor leagues, and such investments are a drain of resources away from the core educational innovation on which we prefer to focus.

Barrier 4: Vicious Sales Cycles

At a recent presentation we made to Stanford Business School students interested in education, a student provided what was almost the right diagnosis of the industry: "From the complexity of the district decisionmaking process you just described, it seems that in education, no one is in charge."

Our wistful reply: "If only that were the problem. But the situation is much worse: In education, *everyone* is in charge."

Our sales process often involves winning the support of state policy people who oversee the relevant funding streams, academic consultants who advise the districts, key school board members, the district curriculum leadership, the special education department, the office of research and assessment, the chief information officer, the director of IT, the principals, the reading coaches in the individual schools, the district lawyers (we store personally identifiable student data)—and then finding the person in procurement who can figure out how the district will pay for it all. It should be noted that of this long list of people who are "in charge," most of them are only authorized to say "no." Only a few people have the budgetary or instructional authority to say "yes."

This mob of stakeholders means a long sales process that often surfaces political tensions that further complicate matters; several of our sales processes are four years in the making. Our average sales cycle is about eight months to get some of the schools in the district as customers and about 18 months to expand to the whole district. Fellow education entrepreneurs tell us that this is comparatively fast. Slow sales cycles make things hard for entrepreneurs who need capital to keep operating and need to prove to investors that they have created something worth supporting. The typical investor does not understand that in education a product could be "hot" and yet take two years to sell.

There is one precious, if disturbing, exception: In the final days of the fiscal year, schools sometimes find themselves with money that they must use or lose. At this time, the long, involved process goes out the window, and we get a breathless call: "How much of your product can I buy for $61,000?" One of the most useful things we have learned from our veteran salespeople is always to leave a price proposal behind when we present our product, even if the district does not seem ready for one. If your proposal is in the desk drawer when use-it-or-lose-it time rolls around, you might just get the lucky call. We have sometimes gotten this call two years after a sales lead had apparently gone cold. But these last-minute calls, while delightful, represent less than 1 percent of our sales.

The longer and more political the sales cycle, the less attractive a market will be for an entrepreneur hoping to inspire rapid change. Still, it would be possible to overstate the importance of the length of the sales cycle. A long cycle with rigorous, adventurous procurement at the other end would still attract entrepreneurs, but if it's only a pilot waiting at the other end, the attraction fades.

Barrier 5: Pilot Error

Even when a district does decide to buy a product, the first instinct of many school administrators will be to pilot in a small number of schools or classrooms. This approach may seem prudent, but it has unintended consequences. Many promising start-up companies have been killed by early interest in their product from people not quite ready to purchase it at an economically viable scale. So the start-up company agrees to do a pilot program at a low price to get in the door but ends up servicing the customer with a lot of expensive onsite handholding because the stakes for success are high. Or worse, the pilot is not successful because the company cannot afford to do this handholding and because the teachers take a "this too shall pass" posture toward "just another pilot."

Even when the pilot is successful, the same decisionmaker who could not pull the trigger at the outset often rewards the successful pilot with an expansion from 10 classrooms to 15 or with nothing but a congratulations, since she never really had much budget authority in the first place. One noble resistor of this dynamic is the Grow Network, a start-up that delivers useful reports interpreting high-stakes test data for parents, teachers, and principals (it is now a division of McGraw-Hill Education). Grow insisted on citywide or statewide contracts and would not entertain requests for pilots. Grow founder David Coleman believes that this policy cost them some customers, but it meant the contracts they did win were economically viable and enabled them to focus on making the product and service successful at scale. As Coleman puts it, "Building for scale transformed our product development and professional development from the beginning. We knew that since we were working with four thousand teachers, we couldn't make a thick, difficult product that required in-depth, one-on-one training. This approach is very different from the notion of building something that will work in one school and hoping it will go to scale. The pilot notion (as well as the charter approach) raises the danger that we will develop micro solutions that only work at the school level and very few truly scalable approaches."

Barrier 6: No Return

A few years ago, in a mid-sized suburban district, we had prepared a comprehensive proposal to provide early literacy screening, diagnosis, and progress monitoring, plus training for all teachers and principals in how to use this literacy data. The new director of reading objected that our $160,000 proposal was too expensive. We asked if the problem was a budget limitation, but she assured us that the district had adequate funding. We asked if the product was insufficiently valuable to justify the price, but she assured us that she thought the product was great. "I guess the real problem I'm having," she gradually admitted to herself and to us, "is that $160,000 is more than I spent on my *whole house.*"

Few school administrators have a formal training in business decision-making or in calculating return on investment. They are often promoted from the classroom, and we find that they are often more comfortable with teaching and learning than with procurement and negotiating private-public partnerships. The problem for education ventures is that such administrators will tend to make decisions within their comfort zone; they will usually choose to solve a problem with additional district people and processes rather than with tools, systems, or outsourced resources—without regard to whether the additional district people might be the more expensive or less effective option. The return-on-investment mindset that drives other sectors to replace expensive labor with technology, and that sees the logic of scaling such efficiencies rapidly, does not come naturally to K–12.

When people ask us about our competitive landscape, we always say that our biggest competitor is the district's decision to create a solution in-house, especially because the district often concludes that using five in-house people and buying expensive servers and databases and people to maintain them and answer support calls costs nothing because the people are "already" paid for and the servers can be purchased using the IT budget. This is not just a middle-management limitation. We had an enlightening correspondence in summer 2007 with an education scholar who has also been a leader in federal education policy. This expert lamented that the educational data and knowledge management system (for which we are a subcontractor) being developed by New York at a cost of up to $80 million over five years could instead pay for building "two new state-of-the-art elementary schools."

We pointed out that, in the corporate world, an organization with a $17 billion annual budget that spent only $18 million per year on its enterprise decision–support system would be considered irresponsible. We also mentioned that two new elementary schools would represent only a 0.4 percent increase in the number of elementary schools in New York and that these schools would not be state-of-the-art if the teachers in them lacked the very things this system is designed to provide—access to attendance data, formative assessment data, and basic electronic communication and research tools that are now taken for granted in other professions and in other school districts. We also made a purely quantitative return-on-investment argument: Given the following ways this system will save many more than 20 hours per year per teacher, it pays for itself. These arguments did not carry the day, perhaps because the expert's issue was not a matter of return on investment but rather a notion that $80 million over five years is an unseemly amount for educators to spend on something other than facilities, people, or traditional instructional materials.

Barrier 7: Viewing Teacher Time as a Sunk Cost

Implicit in the return-on-investment discussion above, but worth singling out, is the problem that teacher time is perceived as a sunk cost (one that has already been incurred and cannot be recovered). The argument goes: We have already paid our teachers, and we were not planning to downsize next year, so there is not any economic benefit to saving teacher time.

Wireless Generation's main reading assessment product streamlines a previously time-consuming paperwork process, which has been demonstrated in several independent studies to save at least 25 teacher hours per year on required tasks. It is telling that our marketing materials almost never use what would seem to be a compelling argument: that 25 teacher hours are worth approximately a thousand dollars, which is more than the cost of our product. We tried using this argument at first, but no one in education seemed impressed by it. Teacher time is viewed as a sunk cost, and therefore saving it does not "count" in economic terms. Sometimes districts must reduce their headcount, but never, in our experience, because of an assumption about increased productivity.

In other fields, many of the compelling applications of technology have to do with making labor more efficient, thereby enabling a reduction in people or an increase in output. Such productivity tools are generally good entry points for the entrepreneur because they have straightforward value propositions and measurable return on investment, such that a new company does not need preexisting relationships or expensive marketing to make its case. Most district programs and initiatives begin by adding adults to schools—

mentors, coaches, achievement facilitators, aides, or just more teachers per child. But even if the education sector is not interested in reducing head-count, it would still be good for the teaching profession, and for the ability of entrepreneurs to articulate their value propositions, if the education system started to quantify the value of a saved teacher hour in terms of its increased instructional output, including the impact on retaining good teachers.

One of the main excuses school people will give for not adopting new tools is that they cannot free up the teacher time for adequate training. This is a genuine obstacle in some cases, often accentuated by union rules, but it is certainly ironic when the tool they would be learning would lead to a net savings in time. Our sense is that the unions want to see time-saving, professionalizing tools for teachers and would adapt their rules accordingly if asked, but we know of no union contract where a district has traded the introduction of time-saving tools for a productive use of saved hours. It would be hard to think of another industry in which 85 percent of the budget is going toward something for which there is so little investment in systems that could make it more time efficient or productive.

Barrier 8: The Brief Tenure of Superintendents

The tenure of superintendents in large districts, while not as brief as has been popularly reported, averages fewer than five years. Substantial innovations in tools and systems tend to take a year or two to create and perhaps three or four years to refine. So if a superintendent does not start such projects in the first year—and these infrastructure projects are rarely considered a first-year priority—then they would launch just as the average superintendent's term ends or under a successor with no commitment to the effort. As a result, many urban superintendents who believe that better instruction and assessment tools, data management systems, and communication systems are essential still have little incentive to invest in them if their position is politically uncertain, if they are under the gun to deliver immediate changes in test scores, or if they are seeking to push every available dollar into salaries or teacher training.

Barrier 9: The Vendor Wall

When Margaret Honey, a respected education researcher who had run a division of the nonprofit Educational Development Corporation, decided to join Wireless Generation this spring, she reached out to many of the people in her network. She was surprised by a new barrier in her path:

From: ——@——.gov
Date: Sat, 14 Apr 2007 10:26:51 -0400
To: "Honey, Margaret" <mhoney@edc.org>
Subject: RE: Early Childhood Assessments

Hello Margaret,

I wish you the very best in your new venture. It sounds very exciting and certainly a key area of expansion at the present time. At the state department, we have a policy that recommends that we not meet with vendors. This protects us but also protects you. If we were to issue an RFP and you had met with us prior to the issuance, it might be construed by others as your having unfair advantage in the RFP process.

Please watch our website for RFP releases and best of luck in your new work.

Margaret was taken aback by this message and cut straight to the problem: "If this is the policy, how do they ever become informed about anything?" Every sales process has obstacles between the seller and buyer, and in cases where public procurement is involved, some formal obstacles may be necessary to ensure the integrity of purchasing with public funds. But in education, the obstacles are unusually dense and only occasionally attributable to actual procurement policy (though it is often used as an excuse for not taking meetings).

The vendor wall should not be blamed entirely on educators. Vendors, especially those bearing technology, have sold some dreadful things to schools over the years. The gap between what was promised and what was delivered has been vast enough to inspire lasting mistrust. And there are many education salespeople who have not made an effort to understand the actual challenges educators face.

Whether learned or innate, the culture of education is, as discussed above, often quite insular and is not inclined to be interested in what an innovator from the outside might offer. There is no one that we know of, in any district, whose primary role is to be on top of the latest innovations or to be an expert at managing relationships with outside providers.

Educational decisionmakers are particularly inclined to see newer ventures as risky (and they are right in a self-fulfilling way, because many ventures fail, or never achieve excellence, in part due to the expenses and difficulties they encounter trying to overcome this very barrier). Inexperience, project delays, and failure are often tolerated within district organizations but are deemed conspicuous and embarrassing when they come from an outside partner. As Charley Oswald, perhaps the twentieth century's most successful educational entrepreneur (he led the National Computer Systems for 30 years, until its $2.4 billion acquisition by Pearson), said to us on the day he agreed to provide a start-up investment in Wireless Generation, "There is one basic principle of success in education: The School Man doesn't want to be embarrassed."

Innovation, however, involves taking risks. Innovative organizations develop cultures in which they are expected to take these risks—and as a result they develop expertise in mitigating these risks—often through establishing deep partnerships with collaborators. One thinks of the relationship between the engineers at Toshiba, who were trying to develop tiny hard drives, and those at Apple, who were trying to design a new digital music player. They had to be curious about, and responsive to, one another's goals, business models, supply chains, design processes, and timelines. And there were professionals at both companies whose job it was to make such relationships sing. There are no "business-development" people in education, and this sort of close partnership is rare indeed. Only twice in more than a thousand district sales have we been asked what type of relationship, or what size of contract, would help our company succeed.

Barrier 10: Start-Up Capital

Taking an innovation quickly to market requires capital. In most sectors, professional venture capitalists provide it in the form of early-stage investments, followed by later rounds of investment if the innovation looks promising. Venture capital funds range in size from a few million dollars to a few billion, but all of them are looking for the same thing: opportunities for ten times or a hundred times returns on their money. They expect to have a few hits and a bunch of misses, with the returns from the hits more than compensating for the misses.

Venture capital is K–12 education phobic. There are a few firms that focus on education, like Quad Partners, Ascend Venture Group, NewSchools Venture Fund (a nonprofit), and a few others that have made an education investment or two and then lost interest. The barriers to entry described in this chapter constrain the size of a potential return in the sector, and education companies require too long—five years, at least—to garner a meaningful return. (Because venture-capital funds are measured by their internal rate of return, the timing of the return matters a lot).

In our case, we failed to convince professional venture capital firms to fund us—even the smaller mission-driven and nonprofit ones. We turned instead to angel investors, individuals with sufficient personal wealth to make independent investments in small, early-stage companies. If an investor does not think in detail about all of the barriers above, sticks to the big numbers (a $500 billion market), and has a personal interest in making a difference in education, then an education business seems like an interesting risk to take, especially for someone wealthy enough to have made the same size philanthropic gift to an education cause.

All of Wireless Generation's investment to date is from such angels. The advantage of angel investors is that they tend to be more patient than venture firms that often have five or seven year clocks. As one of our investors told us, "If you sold Wireless Generation today at a good price, I would just have to go find a less interesting company to put all the money I made into." So we are not under pressure to meet an external deadline for value optimization and exit. That is good for us—it has given us time to find ourselves and establish some genuine value in our products and relationships—but it might prove bad for the sector overall. Wireless Generation, even if it succeeds over 15 years, may be yet another proof point that education takes too long for institutional investors to take seriously.

Another subtle disadvantage of angel investment can be in attracting veteran executives experienced in helping companies transition from medium to big or from early success to successful exit. A key part of the compensation package that would enable a cash-poor company to recruit such an executive is stock options that give the individual a stake in the ultimate value of the company. It is a form of profit-sharing that recognizes that growth companies do not often generate profits at first and reinvest what profits they do generate rather than distribute them. But for stock options to have value, there has to be a liquidity event on the horizon—a sale or an initial public offering that converts shares to dollars. Those experienced executives know that angel investors often signal a company that will take its time getting to a liquidity event, so they prefer venture-capital-funded companies, of which there are few in education.

Barrier 11: Free Things

The dual status of education as both a public good and a private industry leads to uncertainty about what aspects of education should be addressed by market forces and what should be addressed by government or philanthropic funding. A resulting barrier is the proclivity of public and private funders to give away for free the very things that entrepreneurs are trying to turn into businesses. When the funders come up with something they believe is innovative, they rarely ask whether there are existing organizations that might already be working on this idea or might like some help creating a market for it. Instead, with the best of intentions, they pay for someone (usually at a university, but sometimes at the foundation itself) to do the whole thing—research, development, distribution, even marketing. And then they give the product away, or even pay people to use it. And they never even notice the small company that they are quietly putting out of business in the process. And then they lament the sustainability problem they have created for themselves—as soon as the funding is gone, the project goes away, because only the funder was committed to paying for it.

At Wireless Generation, we live in fear of all of the foundations that have decided that educational data management and formative assessment are priorities. They are right that the current state of the market suggests a need for their help, but we also know that some of them are incurious and dismissive about what is already out there or is in development. They have not yet invested enough time or money to give away what we do, but we never know what might happen (we recently failed to recruit a great candidate because he was offered a dramatically higher salary at a foundation funded initiative in formative assessment). While we look forward to competition from organizations that have to play by the same rules we do, it is difficult to win against a competitor who can spend more than we can building the product and intends to give it away for free.

To clarify, it is not "freeness" itself that has a chilling effect on entrepreneurship. As we will discuss next, many of the most exciting new business models revolve around free things that create new markets (for example, free internet search funded by paid advertising or free Linux software funded by fee-based service and support). It is things that are artificially free (no business model, no loss-leader strategy) that make an unfair fight.

REMOVING THE BARRIERS

While it was cathartic to get all of these barriers off our chests, we should confess that we love the field we work in and look forward not only to having a positive impact on education and succeeding as a business but also to dismantling some of these barriers and thereby transforming the sector. We believe there are some relatively simple steps that districts, policymakers, foundations, and entrepreneurs can take to work around the barriers or remove them entirely.

1. Achieve Scale through Consortia

A simple path around the barriers of lack of R&D funding and the decentralization of command would be for districts and states to form consortia in which they pool their resources and their expertise to help bring a new product or service to market.

The New England Compact brought Maine, Rhode Island, New Hampshire, and Vermont together to develop new state tests in ways that these states could not have afforded on their own. The top assessment companies might not have pulled out all of the stops to win a contract with just Rhode Island, but together these states were big enough to command more attention. The compact was an opportunity for the states, researchers from the Education Development Center, and the assessment companies to work together on an agreed-upon set of grade-level expectations that would drive the assessment. Nine states and for-profit and nonprofit organizations similarly collaborated this year to create an algebra II assessment that would provide a foundation for middle and high school math reform.

When Wireless Generation wanted to extend its work in early reading to the less-well-funded world of early math, we formed a consortium of districts and universities to help us understand the different ways districts and researchers are approaching math assessment, instruction and professional development, and issues of local standards alignment. This allowed us to test whether there was enough agreement about what needed to be created, rather than give each district a custom solution that would be more expensive and harder to maintain and improve over time. The consortium was invaluable to the creation of our math product, and the districts who participated have received a substantial discount for their participation, as well as a product that responds to their particular concerns.

Such consortia are a simple way to consolidate demand, save money, and avoid reinventing wheels on the supply side. There is usually much commonality in what neighboring states and districts are trying to achieve, but it is rare that they work together. Their procurement processes are different, they imagine that their state standards are unique, and they sometimes want to outperform their neighbors rather than collaborate with them. But state and district leaders can overcome most of this after a few minutes in a room together. When these leaders need to assert that this sort of collaboration is a priority, the process usually happens naturally. Foundations could review their one-off investments in individual districts and then invite other districts and other foundations to form a larger team to achieve the same goal.

The consortium model not only pools resources, but it signals to the entrepreneur that this is a problem for which many customers beyond the consortium may be seeking a solution, and it suggests to future customers that this is a solution that has already been vetted by several school systems. In this global era, it would be exciting if some of these consortia were global—perhaps triggered by pooled funding between departments of education in different countries, thereby providing an opening for more international trade in education products and services.

2. Commission R&D—Not Finished Products

Most of the big-ticket items in education are purchased in competitive bidding processes. In most of these cases, the product to be bid needs to be largely finished before the contract is even awarded. For example, for a textbook to be adopted, it has to be written in advance. As a consequence, the big publishers invest a large amount of money upfront in the hope of designing the right product. Smaller players generally cannot afford to take this risk, and the big publishers admit that they could invest even more if they were not hedging their bets against the chance that they might not get adopted.

Compare this to how procurement works in more R&D-friendly sectors. When NASA wants a new spacecraft, it does not expect Boeing to build one at its own expense and Lockheed to build a different one, also at its own expense, and then fly around a bit to decide who gets the contract. Instead, it invites the industry to submit proposals and sometimes even funds the early development of competing designs—and then it picks a team with which it will work closely to bring a new product into existence.

There are some bids that work this way in education (in assessment more than in instruction), but not many. If textbook adoption rules were to change so states could simultaneously adopt finished products and provide R&D commissions for compelling proposals to work toward the next adoption, there would likely be a line at the door for entrepreneurs, as well as a chance for dramatic improvement in what gets submitted in the next adoption.

3. Create a Welcoming Climate for Promising Disruptions

Entrepreneurship is often driven by the discovery of disruptive technologies and business models. It is not easy to put out a welcome mat for disruptions and innovations that do not yet exist, but a simple first step would be to ask for them—to articulate the demands that would inspire entrepreneurs to try to create a supply. The work Tom Vander Ark is doing to launch an education

X-Prize is a good example of putting the desire for certain innovations into the public eye with incentives to whet the entrepreneurial appetite.

Another promising example of an emergent disruption is the work on open source curriculum promoted by the Hewlett Foundation, Curriki, CK12. org, and Wireless Generation's own open-source reading intervention. Open-source business models have transformed software, news, and reference industries, among others. By making an expensive part of the value chain (for example, a textbook or a university course) free, these projects promise to create new points of entry for entrepreneurs by directing new resources to the work of professional development, data, and personalized instruction. As happened with open-source software, it is likely that when the expensive commoditized product becomes free and open, the services that surround the product and support its high-quality implementation become all the more valuable.

4. Products Plus Services

The education procurement process is designed to buy products, such as books, computers, tests, and training workshops. It is not as good at buying services. Indeed, in many cases, the services are expected to be "free with order"—the textbook comes with a consultant and a handful of training sessions, or the test comes with perfunctory data analysis.

However, the more innovative solutions being designed for schools are complex combinations of products and services. A key ingredient to overcoming several of the barriers—especially barrier 9, the vendor wall—is to make it easier for schools to buy these product-service bundles. Entrepreneurs are much more drawn to markets that are receptive to product-service combinations because they do not yet have finished products, so they need to work closely with initial customers in a service capacity to figure out the final form that the product should take.

It is possible to buy our assessment system as a product: a one-year subscription plus a standard training on how to use it. But the impact of our system is dramatically improved by various services that surround the product, which we often design collaboratively with our customers. For example, we are working with the state of Oklahoma to find in our data the top reading teachers and top schools in terms of promoting reading growth. We are accompanying state literacy leadership on visits to these schools to understand what is happening in them that is not happening elsewhere. Then we are working on innovative ways of sharing what we learn and supporting the necessary changes to see these practices travel. Finally, we are using our data to evaluate whether this whole process is working. These are complex, highly collaborative service offerings, not shrink-wrapped products. This is possible in Oklahoma because of an unusually engaged state superintendent, who has demanded a more ambitious approach from her team and ours, and a particularly entrepreneurial Reading First director, but such collaborations are rare.

There is one simple change and one complex change necessary to make this kind of procurement more widespread. The simple change is to revise procurement documents and define the initiatives that these procurements support in such a way as to invite rich product and service combinations of the sort the entrepreneurs will be eager to provide. The change that will be harder to effect is for districts to look objectively at what their core competencies are and to make it part of their standard practices to invite service partnerships with outside providers for things that are not core competencies. The reforms occurring in New York City are a great example of a district doing exactly this.

The newer foundations that are active in education (for example, the Gates Foundation and The Broad Foundation) are particularly fond of involving management consulting firms in their funded reform efforts. While this has been a target of some criticism, it has helped to establish the precedent of outside providers offering services in support of the core activities of education leadership. It remains to be seen whether this precedent transfers from established, elite management consulting firms to start-up service providers.

5. Tool Building for School Building

Tool builders have taken a bit of a backseat to school builders in recent efforts to support educational entrepreneurship. The reformers and funders saw the importance of creating an alternative system that would have many benefits, one of which might be creating a market for tools large enough to define a new demand side with fewer barriers.

We are now reaching the moment when the school builders like KIPP, Aspire, Achievement First, and YesPrep are trying to scale rapidly from a handful of campuses to dozens or even a hundred of them. As they push toward scale, they have become more interested in tools. Many of these school models have been able to depend on superhuman efforts by unusually dedicated teachers, but now they need to maintain quality without being able to handpick talent quite as carefully or expect quite as much entrepreneurial zeal from their employees. They also have important practices and cultural norms to define and instantiate more explicitly than when new employees could simply absorb them from the founders, and they need to figure out how to support schools in remote cities.

We are in a few conversations with different school builders about products and services they need. The conversations are inventive, refreshing, and, indeed, more entrepreneurial. For example, with KIPP we are talking about what "sharing" means to them, how their people learn from each other, and how to embody certain qualitative elements of KIPP-ness in a software system. It is too soon to say whether these will lead to substantial tool-building collaborations. At least one of the school builders has made the decision that school districts often make (to build its own tools in-house). And we have not yet tested whether the influential funders see the power of these "school builder plus tool builder" collaborations and the importance of seizing this moment when the two primary paths of educational entrepreneurship are finally crossing.

CHAPTER 6

Supply-Side Reform
on the Ground

Matt Candler

I am about to enter my tenth year as a school starter, and I hope to share here some of the lessons I have learned about life on the supply side of school reform—from my time at the Knowledge Is Power Program (KIPP), where I led the new school development team, and in New York and New Orleans, where I have helped build two new organizations dedicated to improving the quality of charter schooling citywide. All of these are about a commitment to quality—in existing schools and in those still in the pipeline. I will try to draw lessons that might inform new supply-side reform efforts elsewhere.

LESSONS FROM KIPP

Soon after his new foundation director, Scott Hamilton, explained the potential he saw in KIPP, Don Fisher, the founder of Gap, invested $15 million to take KIPP to scale—from two schools in Houston and New York to as many as it could without sacrificing quality. The earliest versions of the business plan had KIPP's national footprint at well over a hundred schools within less than five years. In fact, the growth came more slowly. The first year, Dave Levin and Mike Feinberg, cofounders of KIPP, identified three educators who displayed leadership potential and alignment with five pillars that expressed what their schools held in common: high expectations, choice and commitment, more time, power to lead, and a focus on results.

These teachers, the first three Fisher Fellows, would each become a leader of a new KIPP school a year later, and they went straight to work learning leadership basics from Nancy Euske at the University of California–Berkeley's business school and from Mike Feinberg and Dave Levin's schools in Houston and the South Bronx neighborhood of New York City, where they shadowed the two founders and watched KIPP in action. Someone had to write the charters, build the boards, talk to the superintendents, and drive around looking for buildings, and nobody thought that was a good use of time for future school leaders. Their priority was learning the model and getting "KIPPnotized." Mike was running his own school in Texas, setting up the new foundation team based in San Francisco and meeting with the people who were calling in orders for more KIPP schools. Before those first three school leaders even opened their doors, it became clear that Mike would need some help. He asked Jill Joplin, a Teach For America alum based in Atlanta, to help him with the start-up effort, and they proceeded to submit applications and prepare for the three new schools.

Meanwhile, a couple of my friends in the charter world had heard of the new KIPP expansion. One sent me a copy of the business plan. Another told me I should get in touch with Mike. When I first sat down with him at a Holiday Inn in Raleigh, North Carolina, I walked him through what I had been doing for three years with individual mom 'n' pop schools in North Carolina. Each fall, I would reach out to founding teams that I thought had potential and offer to coach them through the charter application process. If they made it through the application successfully, I would work with them as a consultant to help them build the board, hire a principal, find a building, and get through the first few months of school. Once the dust settled, usually in November, I could start again with the next round of applicants. Considering the state's distaste for for-profit management companies, business was good. I had worked with about ten schools so far but questioned the impact I was having on kids since leaving the classroom a few years earlier. I picked clients as wisely as I could, but some were more interested in trying out a neat idea than building schools like KIPP, which I had seen earlier that year in New York.

Trailblazers—Clearing a Path for School Leaders

Mike hired me a few weeks later as the vice president of school development in charge of three functions—facilities, recruiting new principals, and trailblazing. Mike used the term "trailblazer" to describe what he and Jill were doing for the three new recruits. They would blaze a trail through the brush of a school start-up so fellows could stay focused on learning the KIPP model. To begin constructing schools at a quicker rate than three per year, we built a team of trailblazers based in San Francisco, Chicago, Washington, D.C., Atlanta, and New York City. Blazers picked the cities in which schools would open, garnered political support, evaluated and engaged critics, built boards of directors, looked for buildings, and told the story of KIPP while school leaders were busy learning how to run schools.

In interviews, we would drill trailblazer candidates for at least three traits. They needed, first, to display enough tenacity to get multiple school deals going in different states; second, to have the humility to do whatever it took to set each future school leader up for success; and third, and most important, to have capacity to read people and communities. We had calls coming in from across the country, both from folks who wanted to become KIPP principals and from community members asking us to start schools in their town. Training for the team centered on picking apart requests from different cities to determine which deals were best and which might collapse at the last minute.

Funding, facilities, and freedom—the three Fs—were the deliverables required of every trailblazer in any new school deal. It was easy to train blazers on how to diagnose the fiscal and facilities landscape in a city, but teaching folks to have a good read on the freedom we needed was harder. We were looking for congruence, especially between those folks who wanted us in town and those who were going to be our bosses—the state and district staffers or board members who authorized and oversaw charter schools. Our first all-blazer road trip illustrates how important diagnosing freedom was to KIPP.

In late 2001, the blazers all flew to Atlanta, and we headed south out of town in my SUV, rigged with the CB radio and multiple cell phones that made my road-warrior consulting gig in North Carolina bearable. Our destination was Thomasville, Georgia, a small city I knew better as an early-morning coffee-and-biscuit stop on the way to dove hunts with my dad and brother than as a bastion of school reform. But other folks, including Governor Roy Barnes, had made a compelling case to the superintendent, and we were an item on the Thomasville School Board agenda that afternoon.

In Georgia, the local board had to approve any new school for it to receive full funding, and we wanted a unanimous affirmation of KIPP from the board. We walked the superintendent through our presentation, and he explained that we might meet some resistance from the school board. It was the first public presentation for Marni Mohr, the newest member of our team, and we wanted her to be prepared. We took off for lunch and, to get her psyched up, we found the best barbeque joint in Thomasville and splurged. It was day one, and I was as concerned with expressing my well-developed barbeque palate as I was in showing strong support to our newest teammate. We learned at lunch that we had until almost 5:00 p.m. to wait for the board, and instead of giving some speech about leadership, I figured we should blow off some steam. We bought five tickets to *Legally Blonde* and loaded up on Twizzlers and Gummy Bears.

Later, coming off our sugar highs but empowered by Reese Witherspoon's graduation speech at the end of the movie, we filed into the board room behind Marni. She delivered a flawless explanation of KIPP and explained what the foundation would do to support a new KIPP school in Thomasville. She finished up and asked for questions. She got nothing. Not a question. Not a single comment. No "thank you," no "no thank you." Marni would summarize the situation later: "Crickets. I could hear crickets chirping outside."

We did not open a school in Thomasville, but we learned our first great lesson in alignment. The authorizer—in this case the district itself—had little interest in KIPP, much less in new schools as a vehicle for change in its system. Even though others really wanted it there, their passionate calls were not enough. If leaders in a city really wanted KIPP to be a part of their reform agenda, they had to make sure the people who would actually approve schools—the authorizers and those who run the system day-to-day—were on the same page and valued new high-quality school creation. That was not the case in Thomasville.

After the Green Light

In the ten cities from which we did get a green light that year, the three F's were in place, and we had solid school leaders under "fellowship." We kept an eye on start-up progress using Gantt charts that tracked progress on each deal; I had learned how to build them when I worked on the Atlanta Committee for the Olympic Games. For each venue we managed, we listed the tasks that had to be completed and by when. We then built a giant map of miniature timelines—one for each task—that provided an easy way to see the whole project and discuss dependencies between tasks. There were 406 items on our 2002 Gantt charter template. Early on, we handed each founder a four-foot-long Gantt chart rolled up in scroll fashion with a bow tied around it. This was partly to scare them about how hard starting a school was and partly to assure them that we had a handle on what it took. Too often, charter-centric reformers focus on getting deals done and then wait until later in the process to find the school leader. For us the Gantt roadmap did not happen without the school leader already in place. Starting a good school takes a

year of planning—and that is after the principal has been hired. Any successful significant supply-side strategy must prioritize getting the school leader
on the ground at least a year ahead of time.

Having the three F's in place is critical to any great supply-side effort. The
most critical F is freedom. Supply-side reformers must prove to the best operators (whether they are KIPP or individual educators) that their future bosses—the people who authorize schools—have a good sense of what strong
schools look like and will not only let them open but keep weaker schools
from muddying the reform effort. They should assure school founders that
they will not face death by a thousand paper cuts at the hands of bureaucrats
who do not really feel responsible for setting them up for success.

NEW YORK: THE THREE F'S SECURELY IN PLACE

On March 27, 2004, in his second year as Mayor Michael Bloomberg's new
chancellor of schools, at the State Charter Association Conference, Joel Klein
declared his profound support for charter schools: "I am an unalloyed supporter of charter schools. From the day I arrived as chancellor, I made clear
that charters are a critical leveraging force in public school reform." Few large-
city superintendents had made such commitments, but it made sense that
he would support charters. The guy who busted Microsoft for stifling competition in software was bound to be a champion of accountable schools
that had to prove their worth in a more competitive market. He understood
that for supply-side charter reform to work in New York, the best operators
would need to be convinced that the right environmental conditions were
in place.

Joel was not the first person to champion charters in the city, and it would
be important for him to align his effort with others in the charter game. In
fact, after five years of investing in charter schools, New York's most active
charter supporters were showing signs of fatigue. With dozens of school openings now under way, donors were starting to lose a sense of which schools
were the strongest targets for further investment.

The Robin Hood Foundation had been building a brilliant philanthropic
brand, attracting powerful fund managers and celebrities to join its effort to
eradicate poverty in the city. Charter schools like KIPP in the South Bronx
made sense, since they were helping kids get to college and break the cycle of
poverty. Julian Robertson, founder of the Tiger Fund and one of the most successful hedge fund managers in history, had hired a smart new director who
was convinced that charter schools held great promise for their new philan-

thropy. Joe Reich, an extremely successful entrepreneur and banker, and his wife, Carol, a developmental psychologist, had been working since 1989 to start a new public school in Brooklyn's District 14 and eventually succeeded after years of skirmishes. They wanted to see more charters in the city but did not think it should be as hard as had been for them in the 1990s.

Joel did more than any authorizer in the country to ensure that the three F's were in place. He promised existing facilities at a dollar a year, carved out $250 million of the capital budget for new charter buildings, allocated funding from his own budget to offset start-up and special education costs incurred by charters, and promised freedom from red tape by authorizing schools directly out of the brand-new Office of New Schools, which reported straight to him. Joel thought there was more to do. He saw the need for an independent entity to advocate from outside the system. His Office of New Schools was intentionally thinly staffed, and he wanted a strong presence outside his administration to keep pressure on the bureaucracy he was trying to dismantle. This was a key feature of the New York supply-side strategy: tight alignment with the current Klein administration to get things going quickly but also independence that mitigated the risk of future administrators that might be less committed than Joel.

The funders loved the idea and got together with Joel to start the New York City Center for Charter School Excellence. Tiger and Robertson committed $15 million each, and Joe and Carol Reich committed $10 million. Another $1 million from the Clark Foundation brought the total to $41 million. Joel and the CEO of New Schools, Kristen Kane, each had a seat on the board, as did each of the three lead investors and a few other respected leaders in the city, including Geoff Canada, founder of Harlem Children's Zone, who was starting a network of charter schools. The size of the financial commitment was certainly important, but the alignment between Joel as authorizer and external advocates with financial and political resources was far more significant. The partnership unclogged the supply pipeline in New York. After our first year of operation, we had more than ninety groups expressing interest in new schools.

The first time I heard about the center was when Phoebe Boyer, director of Robertson's Tiger Foundation, pitched the concept at a national conference a couple of months after Joel spoke to the charters. I was intrigued. As we built KIPP schools across the nation, we struggled with the impact we were making in each city. Should we hunker down in one town or keep going to new cities when we sniffed out good conditions? New York presented a real chance to show quality at scale in many great schools, and since KIPP was there already, I felt at home. Before KIPP, I had actually worked for New York State as an independent reviewer of new applications. The State University of New York's Charter Schools Institute (CSI), established as an independent entity by the charter law in 1998, was dedicated to charter school authorizing and oversight. Its director, James Merriman, was committed to keeping the bar high for new CSI schools. In 2004, 11 of 16 charters serving fourth graders outperformed their district averages, as well as five of six serving eighth graders. Most of these schools were authorized by CSI.

Launching the Center

I joined the center as chief operating officer in October 2004, less than a month after Paula Gavin signed on as CEO. Paula was a New York native and former CEO of the YMCA. She had the street credentials with CEOs and political power brokers in the city, allowing her to spread the message of the new charter effort. At the current pace, we would be hitting the statewide cap of a hundred charter schools in less than two years, and Paula's network would be instrumental in building support for a change in the charter law to lift the cap. I would build a team of educators committed to supporting charter schools in the city, especially those in the pipeline. Paula knew the political landscape, and I knew what good schools looked like. We agreed it would be critical to get out to the schools as soon as possible. Since the money had been raised months earlier, schools were starting to get suspicious about where it was going.

Paula and I used those visits to get to know one another, to get a lay of the land, and to explain to schools what we were going to do with the money. We heard more than once this question: "Why don't you just split the $40 million up between the schools that are running now and be done with it?" We broke the bad news to them directly. Most of our money—at least 50 percent—would be spent on schools that did not even exist yet. We would spend another 10 to 20 percent on advocacy and informing elected officials and influential leaders about charter schools. Only about a third of our money would be spent on existing schools, and much of it would be in the form of advice and coaching, not cash. The investors refused to subsidize operations in schools and wanted us to focus on quality. Those early visits were critical for the center, as we established up front that we were about quality in charters, not about charters alone. We would not protect weak schools. In fact, we pleaded for school leaders to self-police and put pressure on one another. This proactive stance was a departure from most traditional charter support efforts, and one that we worked hard to communicate.

In fact, many folks thought the Center for Charter School Excellence was an old-style charter school resource center on steroids. Charter resource centers were typically led by policy folks involved in the early stages of passing charter laws. Their primary goal was to get schools approved, helping applicants navigate the charter approval process. If they did anything for schools beyond this, it was typically called technical assistance and centered on interpreting charter law and state policy.

I admit that I was obsessed with destroying the perception of being a resource center. I had good friends running resource centers, but I was not a good policy wonk. I was a school starter. I wanted to build a team of seasoned and accomplished educators—folks who would have credibility with our client base in both existing and pipeline schools. Our first goal was to get control of the pipeline and put KIPP-like practices in place, in terms of both picking quality operators and getting them ready for opening day. Then we would move on to the existing school portfolio.

Managing the Quality of the Pipeline

We had two goals in our pipeline work: be attractive enough to all applicants to have them want to work with us, and steer only the very best of that group to the authorizer. Twice annually, we hosted free sessions for the public in which we explained the basics of charter schools, taking up most of the time explaining how hard we thought starting a school really was. Leading this effort was Jessica Nauiokas. Jessica had recently completed New Leaders for New Schools's residency-based principal training and had earlier learned the workings of the New York system as a corps member in Teach For America. She had a tremendous eye for school leadership capacity. She was able to gracefully steer passionate school founders toward either submitting applications, if she thought they had potential, or delaying, if they were not ready.

After the free sessions, Jessica would get to work with those still interested in pursuing the new school idea. She would ask them to fill out a simple technical assistance application, our first screening device. If approved, they would be eligible for $10,000 worth of free start-up advice. This was not a grant, but it was free help provided by hired consultants working on loan to us. We checked in monthly with our team of consultants and asked them to steer the most promising toward applying to the authorizer for a school and for a larger, more intensive $35,000 planning grant. We asked each consultant to mine less promising groups for individual talent that might be ready someday, looking for good jobs in existing schools where they might be exposed to strong leaders. We also studied the non-educators who were most influential in each founding group and looked for other roles for them, either as volunteers or as board members at other schools.

We were willing to lose the planning-grant investment in a school if during that grant period we learned a school was not up to the challenge. This was a simple cost-benefit calculation for us—the funds were a small price to pay to keep a bad school off the street. We did not do it often, but it only took one or two examples to send the message to applicants that we were critical investors. For example, in 2005, a handful of groups were working with Imagine Schools, a management company considering expansion in New York City. Weeks before their applications to operate a new charter school were due, they got nervous about the lack of control that they had under the state law and pulled out of the city, leaving multiple applicants in the lurch. We met with each group and advised delay. One group refused and moved forward with an application, claiming enough political juice to get the deal done regardless. We agreed to disagree, but let the group know that we would share our perspective with authorizers if they asked.

Against our advice, the school was approved, and its leaders did not spend much time with us after the school opened. Their school is doing okay, but it is not a standout. There was real tension between Joel's desire to open lots of schools and our push for quality. This tension continues to define the supply-side work in New York, and I think it is healthy. Today, Joel's team stays in close touch with the center regarding the pipeline each year and coordinates closely on applicant readiness. The independence we have keeps their authorizing more honest and rigorous. Their demand for new schools keeps us focused on developing capacity where we see potential in the pipeline.

Critical Friends for Schools

Once schools made it past the formal application process, they applied for $50,000 Post-Approval Start-Up Grants and got to know the rest of our team. Jessica introduced each group to two operational and two instructional teammates and got to work on the next pipeline cycle. The director of school operational excellence (we still hate that title) was Laura Smith, a fellow alum from business school who was fresh out of a Broad Fellowship stint with innovative superintendent Alan Bersin, with whom she helped 15 small San Diego high schools open in one year. Florence Adu, another Teach For America alum, had worked for the New York City Economic Development Corporation and had a strong base in facilities development in the city. She, like Laura, was able to engage schools quickly, given the universal need to find affordable buildings, whether in Joel's school buildings or elsewhere.

On the instructional side, I looked for educators who had been at the center of strong charter schools. If we were to build any real trust with schools, this part of the team had to earn the right to talk straight with school leaders. Heather Caudill, a founding teacher at the KIPP West Atlanta Young Scholars Academy in Atlanta, had moved to New York to teach and knew what a start-up looked like. Glenn Liebeck was second in charge at what I thought was Boston's best high school, Media and Technology Charter High. He was splitting his time between teaching science and serving as dean while Charlie Sposato, the school's principal, observed instruction. Glenn had a relentless need to call fellow school leaders out for setting low expectations for their kids. He best embodied what I was looking for in a critical friend for schools. He would spend some time watching instruction with school leaders and go right at them with crisp details from the classroom where teachers had let kids off the hook and missed chances to deepen student understanding of a topic. This kind of dialogue disarmed school leaders and proved we could talk shop.

The postapproval grants were designed to deliver the same kind of support to schools that blazers had provided at KIPP. We asked each school to use part of its start-up grant to hire operations directors early in the year. This paid off, as our grant recipients entered the school year with strong financial and operational controls. These schools were able to avoid the most common threats to charter school failure—poor internal controls—and focus from day one on school culture and instruction.

Extremely Critical Friendship

Once we had the start-up process relatively organized, we started to discuss how to engage existing schools. The most important factor in choosing schools was buy-in. After one of those early visits with Paula to the ReadNet Charter School in the South Bronx, the school's founder walked us out the door, down the street, down the steps to the subway, through the turnstiles, and onto the number six train, begging us for advice all the way to the southern tip of Manhattan. The visit revealed a school struggling financially, resulting from under-enrollment and a bad facilities deal. Instruction was poorly aligned because of a weakly developed reading curriculum. The school was approaching its five-year renewal mark, and we were deeply concerned that it might not pass the test. I started meeting frequently with the board and urged them to voluntarily withdraw their charter renewal petition. Deciding on their own to pull the application and take responsibility for closing the school instead of waiting for the state to decide at the end of the year would be gutsy, but it would be in the best interest of kids and families. In a high-profile closure a few years prior, the school had done little to help families relocate because it was fighting the closure case. We needed to prove that weak schools could be held accountable without causing such pain for families and kids.

Instead of waiting for the state to decide the school's fate, the board voted unanimously in November to voluntarily pull its renewal application. We provided pro bono counsel for dissolution and other legal efforts and hosted, less than 24 hours after the board decision, the first of many parent information sessions designed to support each family in its search for a new school. We met with all teachers to finalize their certification papers and help them find jobs. We reached out to charter schools nearby and to regional placement officers—encouraged by Joel to work with us—to provide families with waivers that most were unaware they could apply for and notices of new openings in other schools. The board members showed great leadership, admitting that, while they may have been able to fight for the school's life, it did not have to be that way. They had neither closed the achievement gap for their kids nor established a sound footing for the future, and they were willing to own that failure.

This board's self-policing was a huge win for the movement in New York. It gave the first proof-point to authorizers, the press, and the public that charter schools could self-police quality and that the accountability of schools need not translate into chaos for families or teachers in schools that need to close. It also sent a strong message to other schools that we were serious about ensuring quality in the portfolio.

Replicate and Share Practices from the Best Schools

The other end of the quality spectrum was easier to diagnose. Some of the highest performers in the city, led by KIPP, were already working on replicating. We did what we could to support those efforts, subsidizing the recruitment of new principals through a creative deal with New Leaders for New Schools that allowed trainees and charter schools to get to know one another and arrange residencies in schools that they would later replicate. We bundled planning and start-up grants and got them to replicate schools early. For charter groups like Achievement First, we provided air cover with state bureaucrats who worried that such groups were carpetbaggers who did not understand New York.

For existing high-performers, we focused on building trust and asking for help in leveraging their best practices to benefit other schools. For example, we worked with the Uncommon Schools network and KIPP to pilot rigorous interim assessment practices that we could someday share with others. We tapped leading teachers in each school and taught them how to align curriculum with state tests. They, in turn, taught other teachers to build custom interim assessments to help predict year-end performance early enough to do something about it in the classroom. This was a higher-order instructional strategy that less stable schools would not be able to execute well but which the stronger schools saw as valuable to them and could be more efficiently done in a group of trusted peer schools.

Managing the Rest of the Portfolio

Our strategies for the extreme ends of the quality spectrum made sense— close the worst and replicate the best. We had no idea what to do with the rest of the schools. We studied 990 returns and school budgets provided to us by schools. We created a weighted, running average of academic achievement and compared it to the district and city averages over the last two years of operation. We then plotted schools from best to worst along each axis. Deeper analysis on some schools helped us refine the y-axis based on multi-day school reviews, in-person interviews, and day-to-day interactions with school leaders.

Figure 6.1 shows our first complete picture of the portfolio. The scatter plot of schools spread loosely from the lower left to the upper right, with a few noticeable outliers. We did not have scores for every school but guessed for those that had not posted yet (those are depicted in short lists in each sector of the map without a corresponding dot). We defined our work with schools based on where they fell on the map. For the schools on the far left, we considered whether closure was possible. For others on the left, we focused on diagnosis and then advocated for boards to replace weak leaders. For those on the right, we looked for replication candidates and best practices that we could capture and share with others. We were not sure about the middle and threw a variety of strategies at these schools.

Diagnosing Failing Schools

We were direct and hard-hitting in our dialogue with the weakest schools, at least for those that wanted our advice. For example, Geoff Canada's first school, Promise Academy, posted weak scores in year one (represented by

FIGURE 6.1: A Map of the New York City Charter School Portfolio

Existing Schools

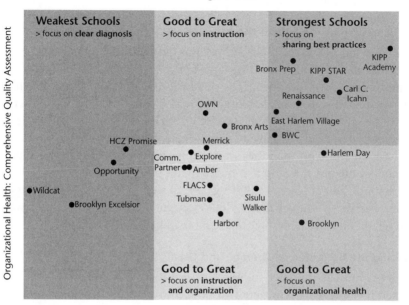

Academic Achievement: Comprehensive Average: ELA & MATH (combined)

the HCZ Promise dot in the left third of the scatter plot). Geoff asked for help, and we assembled a team of center staff and outsiders to do a multi-day review of the school. Soon, Glenn was spending every Wednesday morning there, coaching the middle school director on culture. Halfway through the year, he was convinced she could not turn it around and advised Geoff to look for a new division director. We helped connect him with a successful New Jersey principal and helped Geoff recruit him to take over the middle division, where scores were weakest. The school's dot has since moved to the right; in 2007, Promise sixth graders scored three points above the district average in English language arts and ten points higher in math.

Formal school reviews raised the level of urgency for school boards and principals, but even with the professionals we hired, we had to coach them on making their school reviews more actionable and critical. The growing demand for school reviewers makes those who review schools for a living a little less willing to upset current clients and risk losing future business.

That is unfortunate, and supply-side reformers who want to use external review mechanisms should demand detailed and timely advice that forces a response from school leaders.

Dealing with the Middle of the Pack

What we did not do well in New York was deal with the schools in the middle. I think everybody managing large portfolios of schools, including KIPP, struggles with this—we spent way too much time giving feedback to schools that had not bought into our role as a critical friend. Maybe we spent less time with the schools in the middle precisely because their performance was just mediocre. They did not have to worry about closure since there were other schools far worse off than they were. Some also felt the high-profile support of the foundations behind and buzz around schools like Achievement First were simply out of reach. I still struggle with what to do in these schools and think passive incentives that lay out clear guidelines for monetary rewards for school improvement might have more impact than coaching.

Raising the Bar between Average and Great

Another mistake we made in New York was defining excellent performance at too low a level. There were two perspectives within the team for where to set this bar. One camp advocated for setting it much higher than 10 percent above the district trend, closer to the suburban school district average, to reflect where schools needed to be to close the socio-economic achievement gap. We settled in the other camp, placing the upper bound at 10 percent above the city/district average, mirroring the lower bound for moderate schools at 10 percent below the city/district average.

I think this was a mistake. We did not describe to anyone what we thought excellent schools really looked like or which traits they had in common. In fact, the schools on the far right of the map share some distinct features that, when articulated, can paint a pretty clear picture of what achievement gap–closing schools might look like. Supply-side proponents must clarify what excellence entails by demanding basic structural components like longer school days and longer school years; year-long, residency-based training for leaders; wise use of interim data to modify instruction; and slow growth that allows improved cultures to develop. They also must restrict financial rewards and other incentives like the capacity to grow through replication to schools that demonstrate the highest levels of academic achievement, on par with suburban school performance. Table 6.1 shows what I think, based on lessons learned in New York, a proactive supply-side portfolio strategy should look like.

TABLE 6.1: A Proactive Supply-Side Portfolio Strategy

	Lowest Performers	Moderate Performers	High Performers
Definition	Consistently 10 or more points lower than district/city	Less than high-performing suburban districts	As strong as suburban districts where achievement gap does not really exist
12 month strategy	Focus on clear diagnosis; Support leadership change	Offer incentives for rapid academic improvements (without cheating or teaching to the test)	Help build bench strength; Replicate as soon as possible; Capture best practices
Long-term strategy	Work with authorizer to speed closure	Invest in leadership change	Replicate

Getting lots of charters opened is far less important than making sure the first waves of schools in a supply-side reform effort are of the highest quality. Slow growth will not guarantee broad support, but it holds more promise than a mad rush to mediocrity. In fact, with the cap now lifted, the center is back at it with both Joel's office and others. The tension to rush many schools into existence is at odds with a relentless commitment to excellence. Figuring out the right number of new schools to open always presents a challenge, and the center's independent voice for quality is more relevant now than ever.

TAKING NEW YORK TO NEW ORLEANS

After more than two years of work in New York, it seemed like we were helping improve the quality of charter schools in the city. Charters continued to outperform traditional public schools, and some of the practices we had fine-tuned in school reviews and interim assessments were starting to inform city-wide efforts.

A few days after the levees broke in New Orleans, the Louisiana state school board effort to improve schools there—under way since 2003—took a more aggressive turn. Amid rumors that the local board was contemplating postponing the entire 2005 school year, the state took over every New Orleans school that was below the state average (107 of 125 schools). Suddenly a state bureaucracy designed to oversee local districts was in charge of actually running 80 percent of a 60,000-student system. When the state considered charter schooling as the primary mechanism for getting this done, the once-in-a-lifetime chance to prove supply-side reform as viable was compelling. So was the potential to drag down the rest of the charter movement under conditions that even the strongest advocate for change would not want replicated elsewhere. "Wow, what an opportunity." "Oh man, if they screw this up, we are all toast." This was the nature of conversations charter folks were having after hearing about the state takeover.

I felt the call to New Orleans when Sarah Usdin, the former New Orleans executive director of both Teach For America and The New Teacher Project, came to visit the Center and see what Louisiana could learn from our work. She seemed to understand the complexity of rebuilding the city while focusing relentlessly on quality. State board members and staff in charge of the takeover were asking for help and seemed capable of the same alignment that Joel demonstrated in New York. It would take work, but there was potential. I felt that my skill set as a school starter was something that could be put to use in New Orleans, and after sharing everything we had done at the Center, including some of the mistakes and lessons learned, I found myself convinced that I needed to be there. I joined Sarah as the CEO of New Schools for New Orleans in October 2006, a few months after she filed for incorporation.

Our mission at New Schools for New Orleans is threefold: attracting and preparing talent to teach and lead, launching and supporting open-enrollment public charter schools, and advocating for accountable and sustainable high-quality public schools. Everything I have covered about launching and supporting schools in New York is being applied in New Orleans, so I will not repeat any of that. The most important distinction between the Big Apple and the Big Easy is human capital. It is much easier in the Big Apple. And if this volume is to inform future supply-side efforts, this is a critical topic to cover. When it comes to human capital, most cities have more in common with New Orleans than New York.

Building a Talent Pool in New Orleans

It was much easier to get people to move to, or stay in, New York than it is post-Katrina New Orleans. Even with the recent positioning of post-storm New Orleans as the place for passionate do-gooders, the extremely low expectations placed on educators for decades is profound. Sarah has built a decade of experience in the human capital business in New Orleans and was right to make this our primary area of investment. It will make or break us.

To build capacity in the teacher and principal pipeline, we have solicited the support of many partners, such as The New Teacher Project and New Leaders for New Schools. Both are used to working with large school districts as clients where the relationship is more turnkey. As a nontraditional partner, we do two things that make their models work in New Orleans. We provide a one-stop shop for their engagement with charter schools. First, in New Orleans, where charters are half the market, that lack of access is a deal-breaker. Being willing to strike a deal with charters also incentivizes the district—in this case the state-sponsored Recovery School District—to get on board. Second, we lower fixed costs for each provider, giving free office space and subsidizing a portion of staff costs to make it hard for the district to say "no." This makes the pool of new human capital larger and increases competition for talent, injecting oxygen into a very stagnant labor market.

As we move into the next round of negotiating with each partner, we will propose incentives to motivate placement in the strongest schools, aligning their effort with our school quality investments. Along with Teach For America, which is expanding its effort into the city, these providers will attract and train almost half of all the teachers and principals in the city over the next three years. This injection of new talent into the market is not sustainable forever, so we are studying the potential of starting a new local-teacher development organization, either in partnership with existing degree-granting institutions or as an entirely new institution similar to Teacher You, a partnership among KIPP, Achievement First, and Uncommon Schools in New York.

The Need for Strong Leaders

Charter school leadership is not just about school principals. With half of the schools in the city operating as charters, the sudden need for strong board members is acute. Boards, not school leaders, have legal accountability for school performance. In addition to training existing boards and those still in the start-up process, we actively recruit charter school board members from the New Orleans community. We host "speed-dating" sessions and citywide orientations designed to match potential board members with schools. Having a steady and capable pipeline of potential board members at our disposal provides tremendous leverage in our existing school improvement work. Too often, we have avoided the brutal facts that many charter board members do not take seriously their commitment to deliver high achievement to the citizens who are funding their school.

As Joel did in New York, we are courting great operators to come to town. I do not think we will get much traction with most large operators, since their growth is best done near their home base, but we do think that there are other ways to attract great school founders. Taking another page from New York, we are partnering with Building Excellent Schools to start new schools. This Boston-based nonprofit manages a residency-based training program that exposes promising school leaders to highly effective schools in the Northeast. We front the costs of the program; help recruit board members, business managers, and teachers for their schools; provide office and meeting space for each founder; and share training components with our own School Incubation Program.

Our School Incubation Program, a 12- to 14-month residency-based training program that prepares promising educators to open their own charter schools, is designed to recruit talent from the rest of the country and to train bench players in the strongest local schools to speed replication efforts. Glenn is now running a similar program in New York to build program strength, but ours is, for now, positioned to train more new founders than successors in existing schools. Growing local school leaders is a riskier strategy, which may not be required in New York, but it is likely to be necessary in any new supply-side reform effort located elsewhere.

FIGHT TO FIGHT THE FIGHT

I hope that some of the lessons we have learned at KIPP and in New York can help inform new supply-side reform efforts elsewhere. We are doing our best to leverage those lessons in New Orleans. Supply-side reform architects in other cities must understand what quality operators are looking for in the landscape. At KIPP, we made sure that the three Fs—facilities, funding, and freedom—were in place. Starting truly excellent schools is difficult work, and the most talented operators, whether they are KIPPsters or starting their own schools, need to know that they will not have to, in Dave Levin's words, "fight to fight the fight." A commitment to new schools in a city must be shared by political and business leaders, philanthropists, and, most critically, authorizers.

Supply-side reform architects should be clear about what they mean by excellence. I think it means closing the achievement gap. Any effort that aims lower is likely to die a slow death of regression to slightly above the mean. Reformers cannot be satisfied with solutions that are slightly better than the miserable status quo. We need to aim higher. Radically improving the quality of schools in the pipeline by proactively maximizing the impact of gap-closing schools and finding elegant exits for less capable founders is critical work, best done in tandem between authorizers and independent organizations. Replicating the best and closing the worst schools, also best done via collaboration between authorizers and independent groups, can have a profound effect on supply-side reform.

Entrepreneurs need to attract and then develop the raw materials for great schools—talented educators, board members, and operational leaders. A combination of national and local tactics can yield results here, but the effort must highlight needs in truly excellent gap-closing schools that will attract the best educators. Supply-side reform holds great promise for children stuck in our weakest public school systems. If done by a well-coordinated group of leaders committed to closing the gap in new schools, it can not only change the lives of the children in those schools but also catalyze reform in the larger system for every child in that city.

CHAPTER 7

Quality Control in a Dynamic Sector

Chester E. Finn Jr.

The old, bureaucratic model of public schooling came with its own versions of quality control, mostly of the old, bureaucratic sort. If those had been effective, we would have less angst today over the performance of American K–12 education and would not be trying so many different schemes to reform, renew, and reinvent it. Traditional approaches to quality control, however, have not been effective in assuring high-quality performance from traditional education providers.

The old quality-control model was built for an education system that lacked good data on student performance and academic outcomes, one that presupposed educators were state (or district) employees governed by an oligopoly with plenty of regulations, and one in which the monitoring of inputs was assumed to be both efficient and equitable. In other words, traditional quality-control arrangements were—and largely remain—part of the "one best system" that characterized U.S. public education during most of the twentieth century. Today, however, given new tools, a flood of outcomes data, clearer understanding of the shaky relationship between school inputs and academic results, and widespread discontent with the latter, we are able—indeed, we are obliged—to rethink quality control for American primary and secondary education.

Because U.S. education is not delivering the results we demand from it, since at least 1983 we have been attempting to revitalize it. These attempts take too many forms to catalog here. But prominent among them, and getting more so, is entrepreneurship: the entry of new participants, providers, and models into K–12 education. In addition to having cookie-cutter schools operated in bureaucratic fashion by a state near-monopoly that is regulated, standardized, and homogenized in a hundred different ways, America is more open than ever to alternative sources of schooling, school designs, curricula, instructional materials, technology, governance arrangements, financing, and even personnel. Some of these entrepreneurial entrants are profit-seekers, some are nonprofit but private, and some are governmental. But they are proliferating, experimenting, competing, often boasting, and certainly absorbing vast sums of money—though never as much as they would like.

For three compelling reasons, however, we are not prepared simply to turn them loose in the marketplace to forage for themselves. First, children are involved, and society is obligated to safeguard their welfare. Second, for the most part, public dollars are involved, and sound fiscal practice calls for steps to ensure that these are not wasted, much less stolen. Third, because the backdrop to all this activity is discontent with the performance of old-style public education, new models are of value—and the hassles, tussles, and risks associated with putting them into place are worth enduring—primarily to the extent that they yield better performance, which needs to be determined by suitable metrics and comparisons.

Yes, you could say that those same three conditions also apply to traditional public education in today's context and thus explain why schools are enmeshed in so dense a quality-control web of precautionary, regulatory, bureaucratic, and accountability schemes and are thereby deterred from innovating on their own. And you would be at least partly correct.[1] Indeed, if we trap the new entrepreneurs in that same web, we can be pretty sure that they will not be able to do much differently or better. If, on the other hand, we have no quality control, then these anxieties will be inflamed.

So the question arises: Can we think differently about quality control with respect to K–12 education's entrepreneurial sectors and new entrants, attending to the welfare of children and the taxpayer's dollars, as well as academic performance (and other important school outcomes), without stifling innovation and scaring off innovators? Or will this goose be strangled before we can determine whether any of its eggs contain gold?

Plenty of would-be stranglers lurk by the roadside—both those that want to kill off entrepreneurial competition to traditional providers of K–12 education and those that simply cannot imagine fresh approaches to quality control. Yet if we truly make it easier for unfamiliar people and organizations to flow into this enterprise, to start new ventures and change familiar practices, it would be absurd to be dynamic on one side of the equation and bureaucratic and inflexible on the other. Still, we do not want entrepreneurs rifling public funds to pay for goods and services and models that do not work (even if they pad the entrepreneur's bankroll or burnish its reputation).

Unfettered markets also carry costs and risks (for example, harm to innocent youngsters) that society will refuse to pay. Nor is casting off the fetters and letting it all rip a good long-term environment for nurturing entrepreneurialism in education. Since eagle-eyed, politically powerful, and media-savvy defenders of the present system will noisily publicize every single cost, failure, even hiccup in the entrepreneurial sector, those who believe that sector has something to offer American education need to be smart—and proactive—on the quality-control front.

QUALITY CONTROL: OLD AND NEW

Historically, private schools and their operators had their quality controlled almost entirely by the marketplace—and all of the usual dynamics still prevail there for good and ill: word of mouth, reputation, hearsay, advertising, family custom, price, status, ability to raise money (philanthropy or, in the case of profit-seeking private schools, investors), geographic convenience, et cetera. Nearly every state insists on a license before one can operate a private school, and in a few places those requirements are fairly stringent. In most states, however, they are easily met. On the other hand, many private schools feel it is important (if only for marketing purposes) to be accredited, which means that they are also subject to the more persnickety (and conformity-inducing) quality ideas of private accrediting organizations.

By contrast, traditional public schools historically had what passed for quality control carried out via a thicket of state regulations and licensure requirements for schools, teachers and other staff. (Many also take part in state or private accreditation.) At the district level, the central office bureaucracy controls many school decisions (for example, budget and personnel assignments) and monitors their compliance, later to be double-checked by auditors. In many jurisdictions, textbooks and other classroom items are subject to separate state approval processes. And, of course, in public and private schools alike, certain generic control mechanisms operate (for example, fire and safety norms for buildings, licensure for bus drivers and school nurses), and specific goods—such as cafeteria food—are subject to their own regulatory processes.

Oversimplifying, we might label yesterday's quality-control model "Regulating Inputs and Process," or RIP, and we might term the one we need today "Producing Academic Results Efficiently and Safely," or PARES. Both are concerned with the welfare of children and the integrity of public resources, but RIP paid scant attention to effectiveness denominated in terms of academic achievement. This is partly because there were few sure ways to monitor results, partly because policing processes and resources is how any bureaucratic near-monopoly instinctively approaches quality control, and partly because RIP dates to the pre–Coleman-Report era when educators sublimely assumed that proper management of sufficient inputs would yield acceptable outcomes.

PARES, by contrast, needs to address today's demand for stronger academic performance (and the narrowing of gaps), the entry of multiple providers, and our keen awareness that the path from intentions and resources to results is twisty indeed. PARES also has to be more versatile because its users have varying quality-control needs and make different demands. For example, a district considering whether to outsource its personnel operation to The New Teacher Project will be interested in very different performance metrics than parents comparing schools for their children or monitoring the quality of teachers within a school. RIP really had just one client and could rely on one approach. But PARES may turn out to require multiple quality-control mechanisms for different purposes and users. It probably also calls for different data. We do well to bear in mind that conventional discussions of education data assume the current delivery system; reconceiving quality control so that it is better suited to the needs and idiosyncrasies of a more diversified and entrepreneurial system means that we must uncouple ourselves from habits of mind that have become reflexive in the mostly-monolithic, top-down systems of the No Child Left Behind (NCLB) era.

The Charter School Lesson

Until the last fifteen years or so, quality control throughout public education focused almost entirely on RIP-style inputs and was hardly affected by market forces or school results. But the near-simultaneous arrival of market-driven public schools (for example, charters and magnets) and standards-testing-accountability regimens has forced our sense of the quality of public schooling to be influenced by parents' choices and students' test scores—that is, to deviate from (or at least augment) the old RIP model.

NCLB has made that vivid for district-operated schools—both the test-score part and, to a lesser extent, the choice part. But the charter school example is even more instructive because these new schools are subject to both sets of forces, as well as compliance with sundry RIP-style laws and regulations that bear on them along with district-run schools. Though nobody would contend that today's charter universe exemplifies effective educational quality control in action, one could fairly say that charter schools, at least in theory, are subject to more quality-control forces than either traditional district schools or private schools. This is particularly relevant because charters are also one of the most dynamic sectors in K–12 education, and are the main doorway through which new school operators have been able to gain entry.

The spread of market-based education reform has not, however, done a good job of integrating Adam Smith's market mechanisms with illuminating and well-tailored school performance indicators or academic-quality gauges. It has, for example, relied on assessments keyed to fixed state standards, the results of which may be useful for public accountability purposes but tell consumers little about whether a given school is effective with its pupils. Over-reliance on K–8 math and reading assessments to measure performance also means that families have scant information to inform their choices among schools and must therefore rely largely on inputs (for example, pupil-teacher ratios) and school-generated razzle-dazzle. (If, by contrast, one is shopping for a new car, one can turn to multiple sources for trustworthy, comparative information on various models' price, mileage, safety, trunk capacity, handling, reliability, resale value, and much more.)

Organizations that promote school choice have invested in giving parents pamphlets and making them aware of their choices but have not matched this investment with an aggressive effort to build good quality-control metrics or cultivate better information sources. And the schools have not put much value in transparency. Much as private schools shun external exams that might yield comparable data on their educational performance, charter operators are far more apt to market their schools on the basis of educational philosophy and parent-friendly extras than as effective engines of teaching and learning.

Charters thus illustrate the frailties of today's quality-control arrangements in K–12 education. The market works imperfectly, but so does the top-down, results-based, standards-driven accountability system to which charters (primarily via their authorizers) are subject. On the one hand, many parents—perhaps because they are ill-informed or easily satisfied—continue sending their daughters and sons to mediocre charter schools rather than trading up to those with stronger academic records. On the other hand, NCLB and state testing systems yield plenty of proof that some charters are delivering abysmal results, yet nothing much is done by public authorities to change (much less close) them. One can lay a good share of this blame at the door of charter authorizers, who are more apt to police their schools' RIP-style compliance than their academic effectiveness and who are reluctant (and perhaps incompetent) when it comes to putting low-performing schools on probation or shutting them down. (Fiscal mismanagement is more apt to trigger such draconian steps.)

What leads charter authorizers to provide weak-kneed quality control? Are there programmatic or structural alterations that would render them more effective? Consider the extent to which authorizers feel pressure—political, economic, civic, even racial—to open more schools and how little incentive they have to police entry in a rigorous fashion. To be sure, a few authorizers have done a fine job of this, often because they had relatively few charters to give out and were thus forced to select carefully among would-be school operators. But especially in the early days of the charter movement, getting schools open seemed more important to most authorizers than ensuring their future quality—and many of those same authorizers had little expertise by which to make informed judgments in the first place.

One ought not be surprised that such expertise is scarce, given the inherent difficulty of determining in advance what will be a good school and doing so based largely on information contained in a paper proposal. That is not too different from staring into pigeon entrails to foresee one's own future. Indeed, we may even need to question whether initial authorization of a school can provide rigorous and reliable quality control. Perhaps the renewal of a school's charter rather than its initial granting is the true quality-control checkpoint. But that is not easy either, due to political pressures that inevitably bear upon sponsors weighing non-renewal of a popular but low-performing school.

I am aware that charter school doctrine puts enormous stock in the wisdom, perspicacity, and courage of high-quality authorizers, and in its work in Ohio, my own foundation strives to behave that way. But our on-the-ground experience in the Buckeye State also underscores both the difficulty and the rarity of such sponsorship practice, as does much evidence from the business world on the difficulty of predicting in advance which start-ups will succeed. (Business has less trouble than education and other public-sector fields in bidding adieu to the failures.)

THE BUZZING WORLD OF EDUCATIONAL ENTREPRENEURSHIP

Charter schools are by no means the full story of entrepreneurialism in American education circa 2008. Innovation and enterprise come in many forms, but five categories embrace most of them:

- *Providers of specific goods and services.* These include a host of non-instructional items such as pupil transportation, technology, data management, food services, laundry, and building maintenance. Increasingly, they also include professional services such as counseling, school psychology, school health care, library items (and operations), social work, pupil personnel services, school security, and professional development for school staff.
- *Providers of new instructional materials, pedagogies, assessments, and such.* These include publishers, media firms, testing companies, curriculum vendors, virtual schools, and homeschoolers (for example, SchoolNet, K12, Inc., Connections Academy). Some specialize in school report cards for educators, policymakers, and parents (for example, GreatSchools.net, Just For the Kids). Other recent arrivals tutor kids (countless Supplemental Educational Services providers) and deliver outsourced subjects (for example, online APEX courses).
- *Providers of new people in teaching and school-leader roles.* These include as Teach For America, New Leaders for New Schools, The New Teacher Project; and their regional, state, and local counterparts.
- *Firms and organizations that serve as expert advisors, turnaround specialists, management consultants, and the like.* These range from classic all-purpose consulting firms (for example, McKinsey & Company) to nonprofit specialists (for example, The Bridgespan Group) to a host of even more specialized "school doctors" like the Center for Performance Assessment, Virginia's School Turnaround Specialist program, and the American Institutes for Research's School District Consulting Practice.
- And, of course, *entities that run whole schools.* These range from one-off, mom-and-pop charter operators to state and national organizations like Green Dot, National Heritage Academies, Aspire Schools, Edison Schools, Modern Red Schoolhouse, and KIPP.

Some organizations have varied product lines. Edison Schools' website, for example, lists five main services that span at least three of the categories above. The Success for All Foundation also cuts across multiple categories, as do Catapult Learning, Kaplan, Inc., and a host of other diversified for-profit and nonprofit organizations. (Some also go beyond K–12 education to include preschool- and college-related programs and services.)

That is a lot of actors in many roles in numerous education dramas. How does anyone know which of them are any good? Effective? Safe for kids? Offering value for money? Which to choose for one's state, one's school, one's child, one's new curriculum? They are all at least somewhat self-interested, eager to grow, to polish their reputations, to make money, to educate more kids, and to propagate their ideas. All will naturally put their best sides forward, making claims intended to persuade others to participate or purchase or permit. All will understate their shortcomings, inadequacies, and unevennesses. That is true in every field and must be expected in this one. (It is also true of conventional public school systems. Thus came John Cannell's "Lake Wobegon" report of two decades back and today's tendency for states to fiddle with their standards, tests, and accountability regimens to make more kids appear "proficient.")

What sort of new-style quality-control system could education use that would foster entrepreneurship and innovation while protecting the public's several interests here? The answer surely begins with realization that not everything can fruitfully be shoved under the same quality-assurance regime or judged in exactly the same way. Quality control does not necessarily lead to simple "yes-no" decisions; often it serves first to ensure a floor under product quality, then to provide consumers with guidance to help them determine how the prices of various options (above that floor) match their marginal utility for that particular product or service.

For example, *Consumer Reports* often suggests best buys in several price ranges; whether you think the $4,000 or the $1,500 flat-screen TV is a best buy for you will depend on your budget, how fussy you are, and how important the extra features are to you. There is a parallel here for, say, a superintendent trying to choose between rival custodial services, alternative math curricula, or Title I tutoring firms. It is different, though, in the case of parents selecting among district and charter school options; their out-of-pocket costs will be identical—zero—and their decisions about "best in category" will instead rest on such factors as school reputation, convenience, size, course and extra-curricular offerings, and maybe even academic performance.

Some quality-control strategies work better for some goods and services, in some contexts, and for some users, than for others. Apples-and-oranges problems are common in a field as multifaceted as K–12 education. The criteria one might use in appraising providers of in-service training for primary teachers, for example, are likely to differ from those one would use in

TABLE 7.1: Education Quality-Control Metrics

	Basis for Informed Private Choices (retail)	Basis for Government Decisions (wholesale, mainly)
Relatively Easy to Quantify	• Is this school accredited? • Which states have regulatory and fiscal environments in which my EMO can thrive? • Which of these schools made "adequate yearly progress" last year?	• How does this school's performance rate vis-à-vis state academic standards? • What is the financial stability of this SES provider? • How does the CMO perform in other states? • Did this reading program pass muster with the What Works Clearinghouse?
Difficult to Measure Objectively	• Which teachers in this school are most effective? • How suitable is a given school for one's child?	• What is the prowess of the new, would-be charter operator? • How effective is this vendor of professional development to middle-school math teachers?

determining which online calculus course to bring into one's high school or which charter school to send one's children to. A diversified firm that offers, say, both SES math-tutoring services for sixth graders and data management systems for superintendents' offices deserves to have its product lines examined in different ways. This is illustrated in Table 7.1, which distinguishes two kinds of demand for quality-control information—consumer-style and government-style—and two levels of ease in obtaining reliable data on which to base decisions.

DOMINANT APPROACHES TO QUALITY CONTROL

How is quality control tackled in dynamic sectors outside (as well as within) education? Four models predominate, each with distinctive strengths and weaknesses.

A. The Invisible Hand

The first model is the invisible hand of the marketplace, though this need not be purely a popularity contest or price competition. It may also include much specificity from would-be purchasers as to what a product or service must do and how it must work, as in the Request for Proposal (RFP) process. Of course, that process can also lead to over-prescriptiveness and market-stifling by customers so fussy that few suppliers can meet their requirements, and market entry by newcomers is thus deterred. (Think of the Air Force purchasing fighter planes or the transit system procuring new subway cars.) Indeed, the risk of market concentration and dominance is so acute that the United States has developed an entire antitrust system to mitigate it. Government can also facilitate vibrant markets in other ways, such as the federal Health and Human Services department's provision of comparative data on hospitals' quality of care for heart-attack patients. Indeed, as we will see below, governments can even help to create markets where none previously existed.

Concentration is not the only risk associated with markets, especially in education. Some entrepreneurs (for example, profit-maximizing Education Management Organizations) are so enchanted with marketing and market share that they do not pay much attention to product quality or academic performance, only to whether customers will buy what they offer. Others engage in misleading advertising or offer ancillary services (for example, afterschool programs) that they know will be popular among parents without paying due attention to the effectiveness of the core school program itself. And parents, it must be said, are often undemanding consumers, willing to settle for such features as safety, convenience, intimacy, and a welcoming atmosphere without much regard for curricula and instruction. (That is not to deprecate sometimes-desperate parents' most urgent needs, only to note that once those needs are met, the parents do not necessarily go on to demand evidence of academic quality.)

Families are not the only shoppers in today's education marketplace. School districts are customers, too, for technology, services, and so forth. And, like parents, districts have frequently shown themselves to lack the expertise or incentive to scrutinize the quality of goods or services they purchase. (Recall the Los Angeles school system adopting a reading program a few years back without—apparently—even glancing at relevant research and evaluations.) Too many procurements simply follow the patterns of previous years, go to the lowest bidder, or hinge on the right salesman having treated the right assistant superintendent to a particularly gratifying game of golf.

In industry, firms such as J. D. Powers and Morningstar play the useful role of selling quality-control-type analyses to would-be purchasers and investors. Something like this is probably appropriate to assist districts or Charter Management Organizations (CMOs) to monitor the quality of the goods, services, and technology that they procure. Indeed, new entrants have greater need for such guidance than traditional districts because the former will inevitably be held to a higher standard of probity and performance. To the extent that CMOs, say, begin to displace districts, they will be expected to do a bang-up job of policing the products they purchase for their schools. Nobody expects individual shoppers at Wal-Mart to worry about the inventory software the company uses, but we do expect Wal-Mart and its competitors to be persnickety consumers of inventory software, thereby imposing quality control on the providers of such software.

B. RIP-style Government Regulation

The second model is RIP-style government regulation of various kinds, whether it is the Agriculture Department inspecting meat packers, the FDA requiring evidence of safety and efficacy for new drugs and medical devices, the state licensing beauticians and nursing homes, the SEC insisting on disclosure of information by publicly traded companies, or a town demanding that building plans be vetted before a permit is issued and, later, that the edifice be inspected before it can be occupied. All of this, too, may serve to reward large operators (with, for example, sufficient capital to underwrite field trials of new products) and stifle new entrants. It may or may not regulate key elements (for example, the building may be safe, but is it environmentally and aesthetically friendly?). And it can be vulnerable to bureaucratic miasma, political manipulation, and corruption.

As we have already seen, education is full of such regulation and some of it (for example, fiscal audits, building safety inspections, etc.) is not going to go away, even for new entrepreneurs. Neither are state academic standards, tests, and accountability mechanisms (and their federal counterparts). But these, too, have plenty of shortcomings: weak standards, bad (or misaligned) tests, botched scoring, erratic and uneven accountability systems (for example, the kind that crack down on kids and schools but not teachers or principals), late data, inflated scores, and such.

A particular problem in education is that failings of the standards-and-testing system create more troubles in the marketplace by denying parents (and other purchasers) the clear, comparative data that might help them be more sophisticated retail consumers. Looking ahead, one must ask whether government entities could play more helpful roles in encouraging better and more complete school data or encouraging—and assisting—independent quality-control monitors of schools as well as vendors of education services.

C. Self-Policing

The third model is self-policing. Consider the movie rating system (PG, R, X, etc.), school and college accrediting bodies, or the ways a bar association designs and oversees qualifying exams for legal practice in a state. Peer review in its many manifestations can also be seen as a form of self-policing, often by experts in a particular field or specialty. With all forms of self-policing, however, comes a risk of "restraint of trade" and discouragement of innovation. (One recalls the oft-told tale that crabs waiting to be steamed will drag back down into the bucket any of their mates that gets a claw over the edge and tries to escape.) But there is also the stimulus and quality encouragement afforded when, say, a school joins the Core Knowledge network or the Coalition of Essential Schools.

Can we imagine incentives that would encourage such education networks to provide greater quality control—and make them more effective in doing so? Off the record, people affiliated with them admit that their police powers are weak and that they have a stronger incentive to add members than to bar those that do not faithfully adhere to the model. One assumes that private funders of such networks could use their dollars to encourage greater fidelity; perhaps government policy could do likewise via, say, deregulation of certified network members.

We know that McDonald's or Quizno's would move swiftly to intervene if franchisees used the wrong-sized bun or altered the standard operational model—unless, of course, it were one of those nouveau franchisers that, within clear bounds, welcomes site-specific or regional variation. (A burger chain is more apt to add tacos to its menu in San Antonio than in Buffalo.) Indeed, corporate America, despite many mistakes, does a fair amount of internal quality control. Wal-Mart, Burger King, and Gap inspect their own stores, monitor their own products, and ferret out problems because they must worry about the consequences of failing to do so. Hotel chains send anonymous inspectors to check on cleanliness and service.

Today's education market includes some proprietary monitoring, especially by CMOs and EMOs that operate multiple schools in various places. The KIPP organization is famous for enforcing its own performance standards among schools that want to fly the KIPP flag—and withdrawing its imprimatur when warranted. Other firms, however, use such monitoring more for internal management purposes than assuring uniform quality for consumers. Edison is but one of many such enterprises in which it is widely known that some schools are far better than others. Nor is it clear that other vendors of education goods and services feel much incentive toward self-scrutiny. Consider textbook publishers, for example, and the wretched quality of so many of their wares. Is this because there are no consumption consequences? Is it because it is costly and arduous for districts to switch to new texts, and thus the customer is a captive of the vendor?

D. Independent Reviews

The fourth model is independent reviews akin to Frank Bruni's restaurant ratings, the AAA and Mobil star system for hotels, Fiske's college guides, the *New Yorker's* film and theater reviews, Walter Mossberg's appraisals of the latest technology, *Consumer Reports*'s comparisons of toasters, or *Car & Driver's* evaluations of new autos. Some of these qualify as expert reviews, others simply as user opinions. Some rely on data, lab tests, and formal comparisons, others purely on taste and preference. Many are idiosyncratic (what if the restaurant reviewer dislikes shellfish or the music reviewer cannot abide hip-hop?); they can also be formulaic (for example, using rigid checklists that may not do justice to innovation); and they depend for their integrity on the incorruptibility of the organization, publication, or individual (is *Wine Spectator* influenced by wineries that buy advertising inches?). Still, we rely on them for many decisions, sometimes where objective data are lacking—there is almost no such thing to be had when it comes to movies, plays, books, and concerts, for example—and sometimes because we want to be guided by another person or organization whose judgment we have come to trust.

AND YET MORE

Those four models are dominant, but they do not exhaust the list of quality-control mechanisms already in use in education and other domains. Here are six more variants that do not fit neatly under those headings, though I have noted in parentheses the categories that they most closely resemble:

1. Expert Judgment

When the What Works Clearinghouse reviews reading or math programs, it is looking—like the FDA—for hard evidence of effectiveness. Yet it is not a regulatory agency, and its approval is not mandatory before a reading program can be deployed and purchased. Arguably, it is closer to the *Consumer Reports* model. "Expert judgment" can take other forms, too. Consider, for example, the influential report of the National Reading Panel (as well as sundry other commissions), which established criteria by which specific reading programs and providers can be appraised. The panel did not itself evaluate individual offerings but made it possible for others (such as those running the beleaguered federal Reading First program) to do so. (A, C, D)

2. Audits and Evaluations

Audits and evaluations are typically after-the-fact or mid-course reviews, yet they may determine a provider or program's future prospects. Audits are often strictly financial, while evaluations are more apt to look at performance. Still, from federal agencies such as the Government Accountability Office to state auditors to innumerable private firms (for example, Mathematica or RAND) that perform program evaluations, there is no shortage of entities whose business is to engage in such reviews, the results of which can powerfully influence markets, government funding decisions, and the like. (B)

3. Inspections

Inspectors play a somewhat similar role, checking to see whether a provider is following the rules and doing what it promised. This can lead to constructive feedback (as in the British system of school inspections) or immediate police-type action, as when the health inspector spots signs of vermin in a restaurant and padlocks its door. It is far from foolproof, though. The corrupt building inspector is no urban legend. Neither, I fear, is the school inspector who dings a school just because he does not agree with its pedagogy. (D)

4. Voting

Everyone is familiar with the formal election ballot, of course, and indeed it serves as a form of populist quality control. Everyone is also familiar with opinion polls. Starting in 2007, Mayor Michael Bloomberg has New Yorkers grading Gotham schools via almost two million learning-environment-survey forms distributed to parents, students, and teachers.[2] Even newer—and dependent on modern technology—is "voting" via "wiki" methods, YouTube showings, instant web-based surveys, Zagat-style restaurant reviews, and TripAdvisor.com evaluations of hotels and such. Here, inexpert consumers provide feedback on the quality of their experience with restaurants, hotels, airlines, and everything else. As with Amazon or eBay, one cannot claim that such ratings are scientific—hence, they would, for instance, be vulnerable to courtroom challenge if used for awarding government contracts—but for individual consumers, they can be extremely helpful, aggregating and synthesizing a slew of isolated data points that cannot otherwise be accessed or understood. In K–12 education, GreatSchools.net is beginning to amass such information from parents, and in preK education, one can find a version of it at "The Savvy Source for Parents." (A)

5. Artificial intelligence

The Google system, for example, has its own proprietary criteria and decision algorithms for determining which among millions of websites are best suited to certain needs, purposes, or questions. Of course, it, too, can be manipulated, and an entire cottage industry has arisen of consultants and firms that help organizations adopt terminology and links and other tricks believed to boost their search-engine rankings. (A)

6. Data Aggregations

These are often based on expert judgments about what data matter, followed by gathering those selected facts. Examples include the *U.S. News & World Report* college rankings and *Newsweek's* listings of the "best" high schools. Typically, professionals within the field suggest criteria and categories, then journalists struggle to gather the information, aided by public sources of data and by many institutions' hunger to boost their own status in the academic pecking order by appearing on such lists. (Others shun such "popularity contests.") (A, C)

CRITERIA

Given so many different quality-control options and methods, how can one make prudent decisions about which to deploy in which circumstances? We might begin by suggesting generic criteria that could legitimately be applied to many parts of the education field—and, for that matter, to many other fields. Five are pretty obvious:

- Does it (the provider, intervention, specialized program, et cetera.) do what it claims? That is, does it actually provide the service it promises for the price that it states?
- Is there evidence of cost effectiveness? Is it worth the money? This may matter less for parent consumers of public education (who are spending taxpayers' funds), but it is certainly a question for districts or schools that must stay within budget when procuring goods and services.
- Is there reliable evidence (preferably from trustworthy third parties) that it accomplishes what it claims? In many instances, this would include evidence of enhanced student learning, but different evidence may be bet-

ter suited to other kinds of providers (for example, food services and data management).

- How reliable and consistent (and replicable) is it from one place to another, and how much does its performance depend on specific and thus variable implementation?
- What are its strengths and weaknesses compared to other providers of similar services?

If we knew those things about every educational entrepreneur, service, program, or intervention, we would know a lot more than we do today, and our quality-assurance efforts would take a long step forward. Our schools would likely be more effective, too. Are there other quality-control methods and variants waiting to be devised? Surely there are. The most obvious involve unconventional ways of structuring markets. For example, we have had too narrow a view of the charter school marketplace, viewing it as entirely parent-driven, whereas it should also be seen as authorizer-driven. Picture, say, an authorizer staging an RFP-style process in which it invites would-be school operators to compete for a limited number of charter slots.

Another example comes from New York City, where Chancellor Joel Klein's team has sought to devise market mechanisms and install them within that sprawling public education system. The city has devolved certain funds and decision-making authority to its "empowerment schools," in such areas as teacher professional development. In turn, it has created inside-the-system "learning support organizations" from which principals may purchase such services on a competitive basis and has also authorized a number of external (private) "partnership support organizations" (PSOs) that schools may opt to work with instead. A fifty-seven-page principals' guide published in April 2007 explains how schools can determine which of these to work with and the mechanisms (some of them complicated) that they must use when contracting with those organizations. A small "market-maker" office within the city education department facilitates these arrangements while also providing quality control via a competitive process in which would-be providers of such services have to present evidence of their past performance. The education department guide says that these PSOs "are led by nonprofit groups that have strong records of supporting schools and communities. The DOE selected these groups through a rigorous competitive process."

The New York example is interesting because it signals that three things are happening at once. First, the system is trying—albeit so far in limited ways—to give more choices to schools as to what packages of services they can select and where they can obtain these. In other words, it is allowing markets to develop where none previously existed. Second, the system is trying not only to invite new providers to compete with one another in delivering such services but also to transform some of its traditional internal providers from monopolists into competitors for schools' business. Third, the system is trying to develop quality-control mechanisms that are attentive to both provider performance and the conscientious stewardship of public dollars.

All this is far too new for any definitive judgments as to what is and is not working. But it signals an imaginative attempt by the traditional system itself to beckon entrepreneurs to enter in a structured way that captures at least some of the benefits of the marketplace without trusting the law of the jungle to assure quality.

TRIAL AND ERROR

American education would benefit from hundreds more such experiments, both for institutional purchasers like schools and districts and for families trying to make good decisions for their own children. We do not yet know exactly how best to do this, which is to say, there is at least as much need for innovation and experimentation on the quality-control and rules-of-the-entrepreneurial-road fronts as among educational entrepreneurs themselves. This will, however, likely prove even more challenging. After all, entrepreneurs have their own motives—some nobler than others—for entering the education space and doing their best to innovate, distinguish themselves, and succeed in that territory. This is the great virtue of the private sector. By contrast, the rule-makers, quality-control enforcers, and data-gatherers tend to be creatures of government, with all of the ponderousness, caution, and politics associated therewith. The entrepreneurs will almost certainly run faster. But it would surely be good for American education if the quality-control systems could be made to keep pace with rather than left to retard—or ignore—the entrepreneurs.

Public policy works best with tidy distinctions between what is and is not acceptable, between black and white, yes and no, permissible and forbidden. Yet education quality control is full of grays, maybes, and subtle balancing acts. Mom-and-pop entrepreneurs will arise in any deregulated space, including education. Some are excellent—the local dry cleaner or chef-operated restaurant—but some are awful. (Consider the cleaner that mangles clothes or the greasy spoon that induces heartburn.) It is not always easy to determine early on which is which, and consumers may have trouble collecting reliable information.

That uncertainty often propels them toward big brands (for example, Car-Max, Olive Garden, Holiday Inn, etc.) that typically offer a degree of consistency and predictability and that, because of their size and reputation, can monitor their own operations and be readily monitored by third parties. Yet these big chains are often risk-averse and bureaucratic, even oligopolistic, and cater to established markets with established habits rather than innovating. Hence, good quality control and monitoring are important to keep consumers from being frightened away from start-ups and small-timers, to keep the market open to unknown brands—and yet to ensure that people do not make bad mistakes (for example, feeding their kids tainted food, sending them to dreadful schools, etc.) as a result of having insufficient information.

Too much exit and entry in a market is hard on consumers, yet too little breeds homogeneity and complacency. It is at least possible that better quality-control information would entice new entrants where they are needed—where there is no acceptable dry cleaner, restaurant, or school within miles, say—and perhaps bring a measure of stability to locales or niches where small-scale providers are doing a decent job.

But quality control in education, as in most fields, will not come from the entrepreneurs themselves, or necessarily from boosters of entrepreneurialism. This is clearer than I like to admit in the school choice domain, where advocates have been swifter to emphasize deregulation and parental freedom than school effectiveness and where school operators are more apt to wow parents with nifty technologies, snazzy buildings, and smiling teachers than by carefully displaying their value-added test score results alongside those of other schools. I sense that this is slowly changing in the charter school space—after years of being hammered by adverse studies, mediocre results, and political opposition, and because NCLB and other results-based accountability regimens are slowly but surely requiring evidence of school effectiveness. Unfortunately, with that sort of top-down quality control comes deadening sameness and inattentiveness to crucial consumer differences and provider distinctiveness.

Our prospects for developing varied and flexible quality-assurance systems and applying them where appropriate would be strengthened if all could access the same reliable—and comparable—data on school performance, budgets, and staffing. This brings us back to the need for rethinking our education statistics and also to America's long-running debate about the pros and cons of developing a single set of education standards and achievement measures. I am confident that diverse analyses and tailored applications of information would prove far more credible—and, hence, far more likely to be deployed—if all could draw on the same core data and comparable test results, set alongside shared and mutually understood standards for educational performance, at least with regard to student learning. Where we cannot agree on the numbers—or the goals and metrics—is where we are most apt to be rigid and formulaic with regard to inputs and processes. That is as true of entrepreneurial quality control as of teacher certification or lesson planning.

To be sure, public policy does best with simple distinctions (for example, does your school make adequate yearly progress or not?). But that is only a fraction of the quality-control information that customers need and entrepreneurs deserve. Disappointing as it is to conclude this discussion with a plea for greater experimentalism, I see no honest alternative at this time but to try a number of different approaches and see which ones—perhaps in combination—do more good than harm. Agreement on definitions and measures of success would simply make it easier to experiment in the domains where innovation is most needed.

CHAPTER 8

Reinventing a Research and Development Capacity

Anthony S. Bryk and Louis M. Gomez

School improvement efforts have typically focused attention on particular instructional practices and school activities. There have been efforts, for example, to develop more rigorous math and science curricula, better mechanisms for integrating students from different ethnic and cultural backgrounds, enhanced strategies for meeting the educational needs of English language learners, more challenging academic courses for high school students, and so on. But throughout all of this, the basic institutional structure of schooling was never questioned as it is today. Now, everything is up for grabs—from the design of new curriculum; to who teaches; to how individual educators are prepared, enter the field of teaching, and are rewarded for their work; to even who actually gets to run schools.[1]

At base here, a combination of economic, social, and technological changes now challenge the historic foundation of the "One Best System" of public education.[2] Educators are under tremendous pressure to help all students achieve at high levels. What historically we have asked for only a modest portion of students has now become a universal goal. This goal is especially ambitious given increasing numbers of immigrants, including many students with limited English proficiency. The changing demography of many school systems, especially in urban areas, poses enormous challenges for the existing teaching force. And then there is the whale of technology, which has changed virtually every workplace except schools.

In other sectors of society, leaders confronting such challenges would turn to their research and development (R&D) communities for guidance.

Put succinctly, it is inconceivable to respond effectively to the demands for better schools without also seriously transforming the ways we develop and support school professionals; the tools, materials, ideas, and evidence with which they work; and the instructional opportunities we afford students for learning. Unfortunately, the current R&D infrastructure for school improvement is weak and fragmented. The core institutional arrangements of public education, the work of universities, and the commercial sector combine to form a market failure for educational innovation. All of this exists within a political environment that presses for quick fixes at improving schools rather than investing in the long-term work, including the necessary R&D capacity, to advance instructional productivity at scale.

A CAPSULE ANALYSIS OF THE STATUS QUO

First and most obviously, education research is poorly funded. In fields such as medicine and engineering, spending for research amounts to about 5 to 15 percent of total expenditures, with about 20 percent of R&D expenditures going toward basic research and about 80 percent toward design and systematic development.[3] In contrast, even though education is a $500 billion a year enterprise, we spend well less than a billion dollars a year on educational R&D, or less than a quarter of 1 percent of the overall education budget.[4]

Second, most education research is conducted in university settings, where new theory development is more valued than practical solutions to real problems. Faculty members are rewarded for their individual scholarly contributions, with the singly authored paper in a refereed journal considered the prize accomplishment. Not withstanding a renewed rhetoric in research universities around multi-disciplinary studies, their institutional culture and incentive structure is not conducive to the long-term collaborative work required to produce practical educational innovations.[5] Ironically, across the social sciences, important new knowledge is being generated that has salience and could have significant effects on improving schooling, were this practical task viewed as central to the work of universities. To the point, we have more useable knowledge than ever, but little capacity to exploit it systematically.

Third, while considerable wisdom of practice is surely developed by educational practitioners through their daily work, there are no extant mechanisms to test, refine, and transform this practitioner knowledge into a professional knowledge base.[6] Moreover, the preservice preparation and socialization of teachers into the profession is typically devoid of significant exposure to educational statistics, research design, and measurement topics. The teacher-education programs and applied research activities within schools of education are often entirely separate enterprises. Not surprisingly then, the research developed in the academy tends to be viewed by practitioners as primarily for other researchers. Under these circumstances, even when relevant research exists, educators and policymakers are just as likely to rely on ideological preferences, customary practice, or conventional wisdom to guide their decisions.[7]

Fourth, most school districts operate in a short-term reactive environment vis-à-vis innovation. Absent in most districts is any strategic vision of the core problems of practice that merit their sustained attention. Moreover, districts are not proactive in developing and refining new instructional materials, practices, and organizational arrangements based on careful design. Instead, in attempting to respond to new policy demands, they look to buy tools and quickly implement new services. In the process, however, districts often subvert the more ambitious intents of the new policy.[8] Ironically, while school systems rarely have the time and resources to do it right the first time, they always seem to have the time and money to go back and do it again and again. Chicago's end of social promotion initiative provides a good example of this. The policy was immediately applied districtwide, even though extensive prior research in other cities had found that simply retaining students in grade often failed to advance their achievement. Subsequent studies by the Consortium on Chicago School Research found that the same proved true in Chicago, even as multiple waves of students were subject to a costly, ineffective intervention that sounded good.[9]

To be sure, there are notable exceptions, such as the literacy initiatives in District 2 in New York and the technology-supported curriculum efforts in Bellevue, Washington. In the New York case, a full literacy instructional system was developed over a decade.[10] Anchored in the practices of comprehensive literacy, the initiative included substantial budget reallocations to fund intensive staff development of teachers and principals. For instance, a new organizational role of school-based staff developers and new practices to advance teacher learning such as the professional development lab were instituted. In addition, from the classroom to the central office, a new system of professional accountability was introduced, which included school walkthrough processes and regular use of evidence to inform new protocol.

In the Bellevue case, an integrated program of curricular development and lesson planning was developed and refined over time so that even relatively novice teachers might be able to advance high academic attainment for all students. A vibrant technological infrastructure was also put in place to support the enactment of the curriculum and to enable teachers' use of new materials. Both of these intensive efforts at school improvement were marked by extraordinary, sustained local leadership coupled with keen professional resources operating in unusually stable political environments. That such successful, sustained design and development efforts remain few in number speaks in volume to the overall R&D infrastructure problem that we now confront.

Fifth, the commercial sector, which plays a powerful role in education practice (through the development of textbooks, curriculum materials, and teacher professional development programs), is also not a major R&D player. Commercial firms have to sell goods and services to districts and states, and they understand the factors that shape these purchasing decisions. Not surprisingly, their efforts are primarily influenced by political realities of coping with state and district approval mechanisms.[11] While the press for evidence-based practices is encouraging more formal evaluations of commercial products and services, this research continues primarily as an extension of the marketing objectives of the firm. It has not, to date at least, signaled a new commitment to sustained design and engineering of educational innovation.

Sixth, the nature of federal and state funding for school improvement creates distortion effects and adds uncertainty to the overall marketplace. Because virtually no local general fund revenues are used to purchase innovations or support their development, externally provided resources from federal and state sources, as well as private philanthropy, exert extraordinary leverage here. For example, we witnessed in the 1990s the growth of efforts such as Success for All (SFA) and Reading Recovery (RR) because program costs could be paid with available discretionary funds. Interestingly, both SFA and RR have strong applied research underpinnings, and both support ongoing R&D efforts on their programs. SFA, for example, is involved in a major randomized field trial, and in 2008 the research on RR was reviewed and found effective by the federal What Works Clearinghouse. Although these two entities represent good models of evidence-based practice, neither has fared well as federal support and guidance under Reading First have shifted attention in other directions. In the process, both organizations have been substantially weakened.

The overall effect of policy has been to create an unpredictable marketplace for innovation. From the perspective of a social entrepreneur, even if one builds good products, districts may not purchase them, for reasons unrelated to product quality or even the improvement problem that these new tools and services address. As Joseph Keeney and Daniel Pianko point out in chapter 8, this difficulty of selling products and services to districts is well understood by venture capitalists, which quite reasonably depresses their willingness to invest in such undertakings.[12]

In sum, a complex set of institutional dynamics combines to form an unproductive environment for R&D. Absent substantial and reliable external funding, the risks and market uncertainty for commercial firms are high. School practitioners and school districts that ought to be active players and send appropriate market signals to developers have little incentive to do so. Finally, the expertise and institutional resources of the academy tend to be misaligned with the needs of sustained improvement.

PROBLEM-CENTERED DESIGN, ENGINEERING, AND DEVELOPMENT

Observations such as these have led to a growing recognition that a new R&D infrastructure is needed to support school improvement in the United States. Although the analyses of the problems differ somewhat and proposals vary, there is broad agreement that such an infrastructure should focus on pressing problems of practice in school settings, aim to find solutions for these problems, contribute to a gradually expanding knowledge base about improving schooling, and ultimately hold its own work accountable against evidence on enhancing productivity.

A leading statement in this regard was a 1999 report by the National Academy of Education that called for programs of use-inspired research to address broad-based problems critical for educational improvement, where researchers and practitioners work together to frame the problem and its solution, where there is long-term engagement in the refinement of these innovations, and where this is complemented with a commitment to general knowledge development about how and why things work (or do not).

This report in turn inspired a 2003 National Academy of Sciences study calling for a new genre of problem-centered R&D. As its authors noted:

> There is currently no institution in which education practitioners and researchers from a variety of disciplines are provided with support to interact, collaborate, and learn from each other. Thus, researchers often fail to bring important understandings to the stage of usability, and practitioners have no way either to analyze and systematize their own wisdom of practice or to influence the directions and shape of the research agenda.[13]

This proposal for a Strategic Educational Research Program (SERP) has given rise to an initial round of efforts in Boston, San Francisco, and other locations to bridge the academic research-practitioner gap, with new forms of collaborative district-based R&D. In its original vision, SERP sought to create a new independent institution, supported by private philanthropy and a federation of states, to carry out and direct an ambitious R&D agenda.

More recently, Chris Whittle, founder of Edison Schools, has proposed a major new federal investment in R&D.[14] Whittle envisions the commercial sector as taking a lead role in seeking, nurturing, and inspiring educational breakthroughs. He argues for substantially expanded funding for new school designs, better strategies for developing teachers and principals, and targeted efforts around critical instructional components such as new science programs. Whittle envisions that much of this R&D would occur through federal contracting with private firms and argues that federal funding should rise to $4 billion a year to vitalize all of this.

Along a similar line, but taking a different tack, has been a response by the Learning Federation (a group composed primarily of learning scientists) working in partnership with the Federation of American Scientists (FAS).[15] This group has argued for a major new federal R&D investment effort to support the development of information technology that might transform education both in the home and the workplace. FAS's emphasis is on long-term initiatives that might fundamentally reshape learning and schooling. It looks to build productive partnerships among scientists and industry as the key mechanism to advance these goals. Of note, both Whittle and FAS argue for a new institutional platform, akin to either the Defense Advanced Research Projects Agency or the National Institutes of Health, to operate and oversee such activity.

Although each report brings a somewhat different perspective, there is a growing consensus that a major new investment in R&D is needed to support school improvement in the United States. Also of note, no one appears to argue that simply putting more money into existing institutions is likely to solve the problem. Rather, a new infrastructure is required, its agenda built around the core problems of practice improvement rather than isolated academic theories or currently popular, but ungrounded, policy ideas. Productive innovations need to be codeveloped by researchers and practitioners, tried out in schools, refined, and retried. Such work entails an engineering orientation where the varied demands and details of local contexts are a direct object of study and design, rather than being decried as a failure to implement properly. Finally, in various ways, most proposals also envision

FIGURE 8.1: A New Domain of Work: Design, Engineering, and Development to Advance School Improvement

new mechanisms to draw in the commercial sector as a partner during the actual R&D phase, not just at the end of the chain. During early stages of R&D, these firms can bring to the table significant technical resources and practical perspectives. They, in turn, can learn valuable lessons through partnering in this work and build along the way their own capabilities to support more productive school use of R&D.

In sum, we need to catalyze and nurture a new design-engineering-development (DED) enterprise around schooling.[16] While significant individual capabilities exist that can be drawn on, no extant institution can amass and mobilize the needed talent and develop the necessary know-how to make this all come together. The academy and expert practitioners are very good at identifying problems of practice and documenting how they look in the context of day-to-day work. Commercial actors, on the other hand, have very good mechanisms for creating technical applications that are robust and useable. Past failures to blend these diverse forms of expertise have produced research insights that fail to yield effective products. Future DED must engage in more direct partnerships among schools, the academy, and commercial firms to advance a better educational R&D enterprise. Figure 8.1 captures the spirit of these new collaborative forms.[17]

DEVELOPING A ROBUST DED INSTITUTIONAL INFRASTRUCTURE

While sweeping proposals of the sort outlined above are the meat and potatoes of special panels and committees, the successful launch of such an effort will depend on both visionary leadership and thoughtful institutional design. The remainder of this chapter focuses on some key considerations in this regard and outlines some plausible courses of action. These observations draw heavily on our experiences since 2001 as collaborators in the Information Infrastructure System (IIS). The IIS has drawn together diverse academic colleagues with strong educational practitioners and select social entrepreneurs who seek to bring the resources of their commercial ventures to bear on improving schooling in disadvantaged urban communities. Specifically, we ask: How might a combination of technology and new social practices guide classrooms and schools toward more ambitious instruction for every student?[18] This question has led us to develop a formative assessment and data visualization system for primary literacy; work on a web-based multimedia environment to support professional learning in comprehensive literacy (including now a multisite trial of its effectiveness); create a clinical case-management system to support operations of the diverse academic, social, psychological, health, and mental programs typically extant in disadvantaged urban schools; and generate an increasing array of technology-based tools that both students and teachers use in their day-to-day activities. The comments offered below draw heavily on the lessons learned in conducting this work, as well as more general observations taken from efforts over the last half-century at seeking to bring applied research to bear on school improvement.

The Varied Nature of Educational Innovations

First, we need to unpack our operating assumptions about the nature of educational innovations. Some innovations are relatively simple and, as a result, can easily be implemented and taken to scale very quickly. An example is the recent introduction of ten-week benchmark assessment systems in many school districts across the country. These tests are designed to track closely with the end-of-year state accountability exams. Administered periodically throughout the academic year, test results are fed back quickly to schools and are typically used both to modify instruction (for example, reteaching lessons of which children failed to achieve mastery) and manage an accountability triage (for example, identifying the subset of students near the accountability targets who can be moved past the target with some short-term intervention). We have witnessed an expansion of these activities from almost zero five years ago to widespread use.

Certain features of these innovations have made this rapid expansion possible. First, the innovations themselves require only modest changes in schools' existing practices and make only small demands on new teacher learning.[19] They are relatively easy to absorb within existing school operations (the time and resource demands are modest), and they do not represent a fundamental challenge to prevailing school norms. Second, the DED activity for such interventions tends to follow a relatively straightforward process (referred to as a "research→practice" model): 1) develop the tool → ; 2) evaluate efficacy (ideally through a randomized trial design) → ; and 3) implement (or make findings available to practitioners). If one places ample discretionary resources and policy incentives behind such activity—voila—a rapid change in practice occurs. This is the typical working model assumed by most innovators and in many policy discussions today.[20]

Unfortunately, many educational innovations, especially those aimed at grander outcomes, do not share these characteristics. In general, as reforms become more ambitious—in the sense that they aim at more complex intellectual work for students, require more teacher learning, or demand more expert management systems—many more design problems arise, demanding greater and more diverse expertise.

Framing the Reform Goals for DED

Embedded in any list of problems of practice that might be the focus of DED are basic assumptions about what schools should seek to accomplish. Thus, a new DED infrastructure needs some clarity about the educational goals we aim to advance. For some, this means higher standardized test scores, lower dropout rates, and increased numbers of students in college. Others argue that while all of this is important, it is just not enough. In a global economy where increasing numbers of students around the world are now achieving basic academic skills, the United States must do more if it is to maintain preeminence as a first-world economy and sustain a national belief in opportunity for all. Success in a "knowledge economy" within a "conceptual age" poses new demands on students to be able to apply basic skills and conceptual knowledge in the analysis of complex problems.[21] It demands more sophisticated social communication skills and the ability to use these effectively in working with others. It also entails efficacy in supporting new technologies and deploying multimedia tools to enhance communication and learning.

In truth, no one knows exactly what all of this really means for the future of schooling in America. However, from the point of view of building a vital infrastructure to support educational improvement, it seems prudent that we aim high in our R&D efforts as the long-term costs of underestimating the target are unacceptable. Quite simply, we cannot afford to fail. Thus, in the following pages, we accept as a working hypothesis the implications of a "world is flat" analysis for dramatic changes required in U.S. public education. We will attempt to flesh out some of the implications of this perspective for future educational R&D.

A Primer on Organizing Schools for Improvement

It is widely argued that instructional reform on a broad scale requires challenging basic routines and organizational norms deeply entrenched in schools. Most reform proponents embrace an imposing set of new expectations for school practice and the organization of schooling that include:

- A reflective teaching practice where day-to-day decisionmaking is based on regular observations about students' work in the classroom, clear understanding of the appropriate aims for instruction, and deep content knowledge about specific grade-level topics;
- A teaching practice open to examination by colleagues, organized around a common system for both describing the development of students as learners and the pedagogical options available to teachers in advancing such learning;
- A norm among teachers that the critique of one another's practice is essential to improvement and that such commentary does not mean that one is "criticizing the people";
- An ethic that ongoing adult learning to improve practice is a core professional responsibility; and
- An internal school accountability process aimed at continuously improving student learning.

Central to school transformation are a tightening of the connections between teaching practice, evidence about student learning, the communication and use of evidence, and structured opportunities to learn from all of this. Such a dynamic must occur in multiple contexts:

- In the work of individual teachers, where instructional decisionmaking is firmly rooted in the day-to-day evidence about student learning;
- In the social learning of a community of school professionals, as teachers plan, engage, and learn together about efforts to improve their instruction; and
- In the internal management of an instructional program, where principals, staff developers, and other school- and district-based instructional leaders make critical resource allocation decisions.

In short, moving toward an evidence-based culture requires replacing the traditional loose coupling characteristic of schools (where teachers work independently behind closed doors, where much of the system-level activity bears little relationship to teaching and learning, and where adult political considerations regularly trump concerns for students' educational needs) with more coherent, strategic, and coordinated action. The backbone for all of this is a shared language for teaching, learning, and schooling that is made visible within new systems of tools and protocol designed to support practice transformation.

The efforts that emerged in literacy instruction within New York's District 2 during the 1990s represent a working example of this at scale.[22] These reform efforts viewed teaching as a complex task that makes substantial demands on teacher cognition, both in the planning of lessons and when instruction is carried out. This reflective practice was supported by teachers working with common instructional materials, tools, classroom practices (including routines to organize and manage instruction), a shared framework for detailing instructional objectives, and common evidence about student learning. This instructional system provided both supports for the development of new teachers entering a school (it did not assume that each new teacher must develop her craft from scratch), while creating ample ground for more expert teachers to engage in professional activities that advance the collective work of the community. We note that this conception of teaching practice—working within a professional community anchored in a common instructional system—is an attractive middle ground in the classic polarity between scripting instruction (where the objective is to standardize teaching around a common script) and the organizing belief that every instructional situation and child is unique and therefore every individual classroom must be a unique masterpiece.

An Intrinsic Dilemma

Educational innovation is not just a technical act of tool design; it is also intrinsically a social and political activity. Effective DED entails a deep understanding of the institutional arrangements of schooling that can strongly influence the introduction and adoption of any innovation. While DED may seek to change the way teachers and students work in classrooms, ambitious instructional reforms (like District 2) typically require concomitant changes in the overall organization of schools and the district and state policy frameworks within which they operate. This makes the conduct of DED both ambitious and challenging in terms of the breadth of expertise needed. Moreover, it also means that DED will likely be embedded in the same political dilemmas that confront school reform itself. The more ambitious the goals we set for reform, the more likely it is that many practitioners will encounter failure at least initially. How to anticipate and analyze such failures and then manage their consequences may well be key to keeping the reforms (and the new tools and practices designed to advance them) on course. [23]

Historically, these problems have lingered in the chasms that exist among research, practice, and the commercial sector. Academic researchers build innovations and then decry the failure of commercial firms and districts to support and implement them properly. The latter, in turn, complain about the lack of attention in the academy to real-world conditions. Observations such as these undergird the conclusions that a more effective DED in education will entail inventing a new infrastructure to advance this work. The organizational and political dimensions of reform must have a place at the design table along with the practical expertise of principals and teachers, the technical expertise of commercial designers and engineers, and the social-cognitive perspective of learning scientists. Currently, there are few places where such expertise regularly intersects.

Assembling a Diverse Colleagueship of Expertise

Ambitious educational innovations require individuals with diverse expertise (academic, clinical, and commercial) working collaboratively for sustained periods of time. In our IIS initiative, for example, we formed an academic group consisting of subject-matter experts, learning scientists, technology designers, and organizational scientists. This academic expertise has blended with clinical expertise in principals, staff developers, teachers, and other professionals who we sought to assist. We also joined with commercial firms, Teachscape and Wireless Generation, whose technical resources were central to our R&D efforts and whose field capacity would be essential for subsequent growth of this DED work.

Much of the initial design work of rapid prototyping, field trial, and redesign (we call this the alpha phase) has been carried out in North Kenwood Oakland professional development charter school (NKO), established and operated by the Center for Urban School Improvement within the University of Chicago. From its very beginning, NKO was organized to support ongoing R&D to improve practice. Likewise, we built on a decade-long partnership with the Literacy Collaborative and the national network of schools with which they work. Their expertise and large number of affiliated school sites have been essential as IIS has moved into large-scale beta-phase field trials, in which issues of tool design and building capacity for working at scale have become a central focus.

This type of collaboration in education is difficult to create and sustain because no existing institution provides an especially hospitable home for such boundary-spanning activities. Universities are not particularly well-structured for assembling in-house the expertise necessary for such complex problem-solving because the diverse academic appointments needed must typically be approved by multiple, independent departments or faculty groups. Similarly, absent an established practice of clinical professors and well-defined cooperative agreements with school sites for R&D, building and maintaining productive clinical collaborations can be highly problematic. Then there is the cultural divide between the academy and the commercial sector and the residual distrust that needs to be deconstructed. Without a stronger base of institutional ties, an enormous overhead in time is imposed to secure the people and to continue to nurture the basic work relationships necessary to execute this activity.

In short, a more vital DED infrastructure requires a more hospitable institutional design. The current forms of partnership are far too brittle of a base on which to build the vision described above. While IIS achieved some success in this regard and others have as well, this work remains fragile.[24] Far too much time and leadership energy is spent on holding the enterprise together (and thereby diverting attention away from the actual work of innovation development to support school improvement).

Securing a More Sustained, Stable Funding Environment

A serious DED infrastructure will entail a substantial commitment of new financial resources over sustained periods of time. DED needs regular access to clinical expertise and field sites for prototyping and developing its innovations. Funding must not only provide sustained support for designers, developers, and researchers but also address the demands placed on schools and practitioners who collaborate with them. In particular, as one moves into more complex innovations that make more extensive demands on individual practitioners and schools, a reasonable mechanism to support and remunerate these efforts needs to be developed.

Currently, most educational R&D is carried out as an add-on activity alongside regular school work. It depends heavily on the voluntary commitments of teachers and other educational professionals who take on these tasks in addition to their day jobs. The role of developing professionals and the tools, materials, and ideas with which they work imposes additional costs and demands on these organizations. In general, few schools are organized and financed to undertake R&D as a regular function. The institutional analogy would be to the teaching hospital, which by design is a more expensive operation than a typical community hospital, we need similar organizational innovations in education.[25]

Establishing Authority to Conduct R&D

The distribution of power between R&D centers and public school systems creates serious challenges for innovation. Carrying out reforms in schools requires that a modicum of authority be vested in R&D teams. Moreover, these needs amplify as the innovations become more expansive in scope (whole school transformation, school-community partnerships, et cetera) and where the initial development phase may span multiple years. Normally, a shared understanding is needed among clinical participants that R&D is a regular part of the job. Currently, R&D efforts must compete for staff time, attention, and commitment against many other initiatives from the district, state, or teachers' organizations.

Since districts generally do not see R&D as part of their core business, the processes by which one secures the necessary institutional support for this work remain time-consuming and idiosyncratic. Moreover, even when productive arrangements are eventually put in place, changes in district leadership or state policy can easily derail even longstanding partnerships. Ultimately, extant mechanisms are too cumbersome, slow, and unpredictable to support a vital DED infrastructure. It was precisely such concerns that led us to develop our own charter school at the Center for Urban School Improvement, to have a more stable and supportive environment for the alpha-level technology development work of IIS. Similarly, charter management organizations could prove to be an effective base for large-scale beta-level inquiries.

Building Capacity for Innovation Travel

After innovations have been prototyped successfully and field-tested across a number of sites, one might normally think about the next stage as focusing on diffusion at scale. The capabilities required to accomplish this vary as a function of innovation complexity and draw differentially on several key resources for scaling. First, successful scaling requires an *articulation of the core ideas and principles that undergird the innovation.* Inevitably, the innovation is adapted to some degree as it moves out to new sites, and a clear articulation of these core principles is critical to reducing the likelihood of flawed local adaptations. Second are the *new tools, materials, and procedures* that constitute the technical core of the innovation. When well designed, the core principles underlying the innovation are highly visible in this technology layer. As a result, use of these tools, materials, and procedures provides multiple opportunities to come to understand the core principles as well. Third, effective diffusion for some innovations also requires *developing expert human resources.* More complex innovations travel through individuals who have already developed expertise in this domain and can help guide its acquisition by others.[26] Fourth, many innovations are themselves dynamic entities and need to develop and maintain *social networks* that support their continued evolution and distribution.

Knowledge about simple innovations, such as benchmark assessment systems, is largely carried through tools, materials, and procedures. Because these elements have been subjected to practical testing and refinement over time and across many contexts, fidelity in their implementation is important. Such reforms make fewer demands on human resources and social network development. As a result, they may travel with relative ease.

In contrast, more complex innovations, such as the District 2 literacy initiative, are only partially defined through tool, material, and procedural specification. Their effective travel from one site to another draws significantly on the other resources discussed above. To the point, innovation diffusion in these situations is contingent on the available number of individuals, and networks of individuals, who have already established expertise in this domain.[27] In that sense, the maximum rate of travel at any given time depends on the current density of this expertise network surrounding the innovation. Moreover, since acquiring expertise in an ambitious instructional initiative may take several years, how rapidly such an innovation can spread is further limited.

This view about innovation complexity also necessitates rethinking of traditional notions about implementing programs with fidelity. The traditional conception of fidelity assumes a delivery standard to which local agents can be held accountable by external agents (for example, program managers) who are readily able to characterize local agents' observable behavior as consistent or inconsistent with the innovation. While this view may work adequately with artifact-centric innovations (for example, the introduction of ten-week multiple-choice benchmark assessments), more complex innovations, as noted above, make substantial demands on individual and organization-wide learning and change. These are better conceived as problems of expertise development than of fidelity implementation.[28]

For instance, IIS is developing a multimedia resource base and social network tools to enhance professional development in comprehensive literacy. This group is in the process of field testing and validating a Developing Language and Literacy Teaching (DLLT) observation system for charting teacher-practice improvement.[29] Within the DLLT, procedural fidelity in enacting various instructional components represents only a first stage in teachers' development toward pedagogical expertise. The high end of the spectrum focuses on teachers' in-class decisionmaking, how it draws on evidence of students' development as readers and writers, and the classroom strategies offered within a comprehensive literacy framework to advance student learning.

Creating More Supportive Policy Conditions

Improving the R&D infrastructure also requires focusing attention on the demand side for innovation among schools and districts. This depends in significant ways on public policy and the larger political environment in which schools operate. Sizeable public resources must be captured for innovations to go to scale. Districts will not typically engage in major reallocations of general education funds for this purpose, since their spending is highly constrained by statute, collective bargaining agreements, and community expectations. Some innovations, such as the purchase of a new textbook series, can be accomplished within these constraints. In contrast, more ambitious projects, even those with documented effectiveness, may not be adopted unless new resources are specifically targeted for these purposes.

Federal efforts over the last several years to use financial incentives and more generally the persuasive power of government (the bully pulpit) to press school districts to become more results-driven represent a constructive development in this regard. Even so, we should not underestimate the efforts entailed in making such changes in the structure and operating norms of schools and districts. Absent further new funding mechanisms that directly target the development and take-up of innovations, DED may well produce good products but still have to confront the troublesome question: "If we build it, will they really come?"[30]

ESTABLISHING THE DED AGENDA

Effective DED must take its roots in a deep understanding of the day-to-day problems of practice in ordinary schools trying to advance more ambitious teaching and learning for every child.[31] A critical act for DED involves identifying the high leverage problems embedded in this work. Essentially, this is a value-added question: How and where might introducing new tools and social practices advance the work of teachers and other school professionals in improving student engagement and learning?

A core consideration involves working on problems that come from practice rather than those we wished practitioners had. This distinction, however, cannot be made by simply asking practitioners what problems they want fixed. DED must also focus on problematizing practice (that is, identifying taken-for-granted aspects of schooling that may need to be challenged if meaningful improvements in student learning are to occur). For example, in many Chicago schools, it was taken for granted that supplemental academic, social, and psychological services did not work well for children and their families. No one, however, seemed to own the underlying problem of how to manage more effectively this vast and highly fragmented array of support activities. IIS identified this as a high leverage problem and sought to engage school practitioners in understanding the underlying issue and then developing new tools and practices that might resolve it.

In short, an ongoing dialogue needs to be established between the critical perspective that academics bring to practice and the day-to-day problems as understood by practitioners. Moreover, undergirding all of this is one large orienting concern for DED: Can we make schooling *more efficient* while simultaneously pressing toward *more ambitious academic achievement* for all children?

MANAGING A LIKELY TENSION

If a significant DED effort emerges in education, it will quickly confront its own resource allocation problem—that is, where should we focus our attention?

Improving Schooling: Working within the Horizon of Current Practice

This perspective takes a shorter-term view (approximately five years) and focuses on changes to the current operations of schools that might affect significant increases in students' basic learning skills. For example, today we are experiencing major change in the professional workforce as many new teachers are being hired. Anything DED could do to advance their initial entry into teaching and enhance the quality of their early professional learning should have a direct payoff for students. So one likely "low-hanging fruit" would be to enhance supports for teacher learning and the management of such learning systems. Some possible places to invest might include:

- New designs that integrate preservice, induction, and ongoing professional development aiming to increase the productivity of new teachers and retain the best of them. The innovative residency program in the Boston Public Schools represents one example of such a venture. It places apprenticeship in clinical practice at the heart of teacher preparation, brings master teachers into their work in a central rather than auxiliary capacity, and focuses attention on how schools must be redesigned to support new teachers. Understanding the operations of such a program, systematically evaluating its effectiveness, and learning how to accomplish efforts like this at scale could be one important DED focus;

- Developing hybrid face-to-face and web-based environments to support teacher learning and professional community formation. Such strategies can make more efficient use of professional time by reducing the amount of travel needed and enhancing the efficacy of coaching. For example, Doug Powell and colleagues at Purdue University are experimenting with coaching support for Head Start whereby a teacher sends videos of her own teaching to a coaching center, and a personal coach at the center reviews the video and sends back detailed commentary and suggestions. Rather than spending several hours a day commuting out to Head Start sites, coaches can now give more time to analysis and providing teachers with formative feedback. Moreover, emerging findings suggest professional feedback provided in this manner could ultimately be more effective.

- Taking on the core question in adult learning: "What is it that we want teachers to know, and how can we assure that they know it?" Explicating clear, measurable standards is key to building a professional performance assessment system. The DLLT observation system described earlier is an example of such instrumentation. It is anchored in careful specification of the instructional competency expected of teachers (for example, what does guided reading or a writers' workshop look like when well done, and how do we know if this is actually occurring?) coupled with rigorous scientific study of its reliability and validity. Absent such developments, districts will continue to make significant human resource investments without any microlevel data to inform the continued development of these professional education programs.[32]

Reinventing Education: Looking at and beyond the Horizon

A contrasting perspective for a DED agenda would focus on more fundamental, long-term changes in the basic organization and conduct of schooling. In the near future, all students will likely live in a ubiquitous, nonstop digital environment. How can this transform learning for adults and students? Can we use this, for example, to break out of the egg-crate structure of schooling, in which a teacher and a classroom of twenty-four to thirty students is considered the only way to organize instruction. Might we envision ways in which technology can enable more dynamic, flexible, and individualized environments for this activity? What might the new literacies in multimedia education for a global economy actually look like, and how might we accomplish this at scale? Can the engaging aspect of gaming be harnessed as a tool for advancing more traditional forms of academic learning? These are just a few examples of the problems of practice that might anchor an over-the-horizon agenda. While on such questions DED would not likely move the bottom line on test scores right away, such efforts could eventually transform the overall technology of schooling.[33]

THE SOCIAL ORGANIZATION OF DED ACTIVITY

We have already described how a DED infrastructure might form as a three-legged institutional stool where academic expertise engages in participatory design with clinical and commercial partners. Each sector—the academic, clinical, and commercial—brings distinctive resources and expertise, and a more effective melding of these resources is key to taking innovations to scale. In addition, two other core elements are needed to frame a viable social organization:

- An evolving theory of school practice improvement to guide action within this colleagueship of expertise; and
- A work organization that recognizes the distinctive multiple demands entailed in moving from rapid small-scale prototyping through larger efficacy studies to efforts aimed at continued learning.

Grounded in a Working Theory of Practice

While diversity of backgrounds and expertise is an essential resource for DED, this can also create its own tensions.[34] Lacking a common language for conceptualizing the problems embedded in school practice and thinking about effective innovation design can quickly create a tower of Babel within a DED group.

The activity framework summarized here was created in the context of IIS to address precisely this problem. It has proven valuable for two reasons. First, it focuses on day-to-day school activity and efforts to change this activity. In this regard, it constantly presses on the clinical validity of our efforts. Specifically, it offers a viable frame for conceptualizing key problems in school practice where new technologies and social practices might well add value. Second, from an academic perspective, it provides a language in which the efforts of learning scientists' thinking about problems of cognition and motivation and technologists' thinking about the design of new tools might constructively join with organizational sociologists thinking about problems of innovation diffusion.[35]

Our framework is organized around four key observations:

- A deep understanding of specific school practices and the intentional activity that each represents;
- A recognition of the different knowledge, skills, and dispositions that individual staff bring to these practices and the demands that this variation places on the design of a new innovation;
- An appreciation of how adult and student work in schools is shaped by local context and larger institutional features; and
- The effective mechanisms available to external agents to catalyze the take-up, use, and diffusion of innovations within schools and across districts.

School practice is broken down into work activity segments. Each represents some specific work problem embedded in some individual roles within a school. For instance, primary school teachers regularly group and regroup students for reading instruction. They use some tools to assist in this activity and carry it out in accord with certain standard operating procedures within the school. This process can be as simple as each teacher using her informal observations (the tool) to inform assigning students to a group as she thinks best (the standard operating procedure of relying on individual teacher judgment). In contrast, in a more specified instructional system like Success for All, standard benchmark assessments are administered every five weeks (the tool), and explicit guidance is afforded on how to use these data for regrouping students (a more bureaucratic standard operating procedure governs this process). In general, DED would focus on specific work activity segments of this sort and ask how they might be more effectively mediated by introducing new technologies.

It is important also to recognize that different individuals bring their own ensemble of beliefs, role conceptions, and expertise to their work. The perceived self-interests and competencies of these individuals influence how any new innovation enters the school and shapes whether and how engagement occurs. Moreover, this individual agency can operate quite differently

FIGURE 8.2: Design as a Technical Act of Developing New Tools and Social Practices

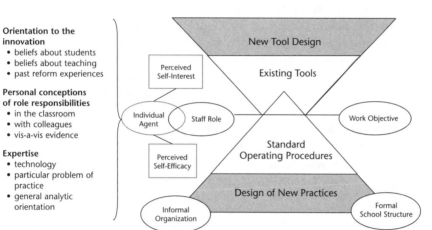

depending on the particularities of school context. Structural features, such as leadership priorities, availability of discretionary resources (for example, time and money), and the nature of the prevailing accountability system are obvious factors.[36] Similarly, the opinions of informal leaders within the schools and the basic work norms among faculty are significant.[37] These organizational features undergird the base state standard operating procedures and play a key role in determining whether an innovation may successfully enter a school and influence its pattern of local adaptation.[38]

This framing suggests that any efforts to design new tools and social practices for school improvement must be anchored in specific work problems engaged by particular individuals who work within a school organization. Each element represents a potentially critical consideration in DED work. In this respect, inadequate accounting for any one of these elements in the process of innovation design could precipitate failure. Figure 8.2 represents our attempts to characterize these interrelationships.

Going one step further, in addition to good tool and social practice design, effective DED also requires consideration of how best to support the significant individual and organizational learning that adoption of these tools and practices may entail. In this regard, as highlighted in figure 8.3, one also must attend to, first, the extant resources and mechanisms that can, and often must, be appropriated within a school's ecology to catalyze the introduction of innovations; and, second, any new resources that must be deliberately developed to support this take-up, learning, and use.

The resources on which DED draws include the will and skill of formal and informal leaders who can exert pressure to champion the innovation and accelerate its internal diffusion. It also includes the strategic efforts by principals and other leaders to buffer the innovation and create the necessary slack for agent experimentation and learning. Complementing these activities to capture and focus internal resources, DED programs may need to design structured opportunities to support agent learning and deliberately nurture their relationships with individual school actors. Taken together with the more technical aspects of design, these considerations constitute the active zone for DED efforts. These are shown in figure 8.3 highlighted in gray.

Finally, one needs a framework for conceptualizing the types of outcomes that might accrue. Broadly, these fall into three categories:

1. *Activity-level outcomes* relevant to each specific work problem, which we seek to mediate with new tools and social practices. For example and most basically: Do teachers use the new procedure? Do they find it helpful? Has any increased efficiency been realized? Is there any evidence of change in professional activity and student learning?

2. *Individual-level outcomes,* where the aspects of individual agents, which influence their initial engagements with an innovation, may in turn be reshaped as these activity cycles proceed over time. For example: If the innovation requires use of new technology, do teachers gradually come to feel more comfortable with the use of technology generally in their work?

3. *Organizational-level outcomes,* which are also often the deep long-term target of reform. For example, current reforms typically aim for a more tightly coupled professional environment characterized by a shared language about the technical core, enhanced communication across the organization, and greater reliance and use of information in instructional practice and guiding internal accountabilities. Is there any evidence that these changes, which other research has linked to major improvements in student learning, are occurring as well?[39]

Grounded in a Distinctive Work Plan

If one looks broadly across applied R&D in education (including activity in the commercial sector), one can see that our field has actually acquired considerable experience in such matters as product design, intensive qualitative field studies, and large-scale implementation and efficacy trials. How these tools are effectively interwoven into coherent programs of sustained DED,

FIGURE 8.3: Design from the Perspective of a Change Agent Problem

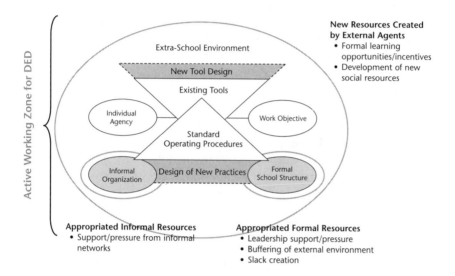

however, from prototyping, to multiple stages of redesign, to large-scale take-up is less well understood. We see three overlapping phases here, each with its own purpose and appropriate methods.

Phase 1: Alpha-Level Innovation Development

The design objective here is to develop a working prototype of some new tool or social practice. This phase of activity typically makes heavy demands on school practitioners who carry considerable responsibilities. Because the nature of the activity involves rapid prototyping (trying something out, modifying it based on field experience, followed by more field testing, etc.), it places a premium on developing and maintaining a strong number of alpha codevelopment sites where it is simply taken for granted that "this is part of what we do here." These sites need to be typical in terms of student populations, reform problems being confronted, and general resources available to address them, but they must also be carefully selected and supported to be high in the human and social resources necessary to sustain alpha-level codevelopment. Depending on the nature of the DED, this activity may also make demands on the technology infrastructure, require broad work-rule waivers with regard to use of time and ability to experiment with other core resource allocation processes (for example, class sizes and composition).

As noted, such DED will likely require authority relationships akin to charter school agreements. While such DED site conditions are necessary to support innovation development, these alpha sites also represent a critical first test. Basically, if one cannot make the innovation work under these conditions, it is unlikely to work anywhere. Depending on the particular innovation, alpha sites could be classrooms, schools, networks of schools, or whole communities.

The primary research objective during this phase of activity involves informing rapid prototyping and developing the first small-scale evidence of effects at the work activity level. The research tools used in this phase will rely heavily on participatory observations, interviews, and focus-group discussions, possibly supplemented with some more structured analyses (for example, examination of possible data use created by the technology itself).

Phase 2: Beta-Level Field Trials

At this point, the design task expands to consider how diversity among individual participants and contexts shapes the take-up of an innovation and how the innovation itself may need to be modified to enhance fit. This process of making the innovation field-ready is complemented with design activity focusing on developing structured learning processes and expanding the base of expertise available to assist others in using these new tools and social practices.

During this phase, DED needs access to a standing network of schools to support these innovation robustness trials, develop some multisite evidence on efficacy, and expand the human resource base that has some working expertise with these new tools and social practices. (The latter is a key development objective in preparation for working at scale in phase 3.) To facilitate this, preexisting arrangements need to be established with districts, CMOs, and other networks of schools so that such beta-level field trials can efficiently proceed. One might imagine state or federal funding that provides incentives to districts or CMOs to partner in this process. The participating schools might receive supplemental funding to cover the additional time and staffing needed to educate children and support the DED programs.

From a research perspective, efforts focus on understanding the sources of variability in innovation implementation and effectiveness, not just assessing the average treatment effect. These efforts, for example, seek to clarify the normative and structural prerequisites for a successful take-up, including identifying specific operating procedures that may need to be challenged and learning how to catalyze the necessary creative conflict for productive change to occur. During this phase, DED typically involves large-scale field trials using structured inquiry protocols. This latter instrumentation is itself an important design task, as increasing attention shifts toward building the necessary instrumentation for managing work at scale (that is, the toolkit for gamma-level efforts.)

Phase 3: Large-Scale Field Adoption

The gamma-level activity involves more than just marketing an effective practice. DED focuses on generative learning about the innovation through large-scale use. Efforts are made to amass and mine emerging new data bases, develop practice-improvement networks around new data and tools, and reflect on what has been learned that might help to inform the next round of activity. In addition, the spillover effects from the early engagement of commercial partners into the DED are likely to manifest at this stage. Through their participation in alpha and beta activity, processes of individual and organizational learning are being stimulated within these firms. As a result, when partnering firms move to bring innovations to scale, they are more likely to design appropriate strategies and organizational capabilities based on their evolving learning, rather than attempting to put the innovation into the box they have always known.

WHO IS GOING TO SUPPORT ALL THIS?
CATALYSTS, SHEPHERDS, AND SUGAR DADDIES

Finally, there is the broad question of who might actually catalyze developments of the type described. Given the problems already discussed, it seems unlikely that a new DED infrastructure will arise spontaneously out of the academy, public schools, or the commercial sector. Similarly, it is not probable that individual states will take this on, as a free-rider problem is embedded here.

While it is logical to conceive of this as a federal responsibility, especially for funding DED efforts at scale, federal history in education research is not especially promising. Political ideology has deeply intruded into agenda-setting processes. Moreover, institutional expertise and governmental capacity to lead a novel and ambitious effort of this sort are thin. In addition, such an admittedly entrepreneurial enterprise places a high premium on institutional trust (which is not currently in great supply), as many DED initiatives will likely fail in the course of developing a few true successes.

In contrast, the launch role seems like a high leverage investment for private philanthropy. With greater flexibility to operate and an environment where failure entails lower risk, the odds for a successful launch of a DED enterprise should be much better. Moreover, if this does succeed, one could easily envision the federal government eventually becoming a more central partner. In fact, accessing federal resources would be critical once a viable organizational design and expertise base have been established. Whether the initial institution-building task can be directed centrally, however, is far less clear.

CHAPTER 9

Breaking Regulatory Barriers to Reform

Ed Kirby

> *It is not only the regulatory environment that founders must directly challenge, but the entire sweep of policies, practices, and pedagogies, from federal law to local union contracts, from teacher preparation programs to the design of mainstream textbooks, that together define how most public schools today function. . . . Whether through calculation, timidity, or a failure of imagination, education entrepreneurs have generally failed to challenge such dictates. . . . Going along to get along locked them into enormously costly and ineffective practices little different from their district competitors.*
>
> *—Steven Wilson, charter school developer*

> *We have to be willing to break the rules. I am really thankful for organizations that are going to help push the politicians, especially the ones who have been on the side of protecting the status quo.*
>
> *—Michelle Rhee, Schools Chancellor, Washington, D.C.*

Regulatory barriers, erected and sustained over decades, constrain the work of supply-side entrepreneurs in education reform. Investors and operators on the supply side of reform dramatically improve their chances at success by reforming or removing these barriers. Such regulatory reform requires a level of will, resources, and skill at least equal to the intensity of investment that entrepreneurs already dedicate to building supply itself. Such regulatory reform requires advocacy both in its milder forms of policy guidance and its more aggressive forms of legislative lobbying and political action.

This chapter does not address the operational side of supply-side reform. Such analyses are presented in other chapters of this book as well as in several excellent recent essays.[1] Instead, I examine the opportunity entrepreneurs have—and must take—to build a parallel wing of reform, one that cultivates and applies political power to advance and protect supply-side initiatives and removes the formidable regulatory barriers standing in their way.

Additionally, this chapter is not an attempt to advocate for (or against) any particular supply-side reforms. While I am an enthusiastic proponent of much of the work happening in the current wave of supply-side education reform (and a harsh critic of just as much of it), my observations about advocacy address how the regulatory environment is shaped and reshaped by advocates, regardless of the educational reforms in question. Advocacy is an absolutely necessary component of any reform agenda.

Like any other wing of public-policy reform, K–12 supply-side reformers must develop skilled advocacy operations or they will see their work stall or altogether perish in short order. While the examples I use in this chapter illustrate the relationship between advocacy activities and regulatory conditions in and around supply-side initiatives, *they are not used to promote or reject certain reforms.* I could just as easily have written this chapter citing other examples, illustrating the dynamics between advocacy and regulatory conditions within No Child Left Behind (NCLB), teacher certification, special education, school finance, school lunch programs, or even athletic programs. But I am indeed using this chapter to advocate for something: I hope to persuade supply-side reformers that their work will remain marginal and unsustainable without aggressive and long-term advocacy operations.

INTEREST GROUPS MAKE THE RULES

I learned much of what I know about the dynamics of American schooling from Terry Moe. Moe, a Stanford-based political scientist, is widely known for *Politics, Marketplace, and America's Schools,* his 1990 call with coauthor John Chubb for a universal system of publicly funded school choice.[2] But a much lesser known work Moe wrote in 1989 lays the foundation for what investors and entrepreneurs most need to understand to support and protect their work on the supply side of school reform. His chapter, "The Politics of Bureaucratic Structure," has served as a fundamental basis of my perspectives on school reform since the 1990s.[3]

After reading his chapter in 1996, I called Moe and interviewed him about his analysis. During the discussion, I began to understand the fundamental influence of interest groups on the political creation and implementation of reforms. Boiled down, his analysis runs as follows:

- Public policies and regulations, as well as the bureaucratic entities and bureaucrats that implement and enforce them, are to a large degree defined and controlled by interest groups rather than a reflection of rational design;
- Interest groups wield influence over the regulatory environment not simply in the legislative process but at every level of rule-making and enforcement, from the drafting of regulations specifying a given statute to regulatory structures imposed by bureaucratic agencies at an operational level.

Implicit in Moe's analysis is the notion that if you want to change the regulatory environment to favor your own entrepreneurial agenda, you need to acquire and exercise the same kind of influence that your opponents have been wielding to block your advancement. Moe explains the essence of interest group influence: "Legislators [and, by extension, rule makers at lower levels of the bureaucratic environment] by and large, can be expected either to respond to group demands in structural politics or to take entrepreneurial action in trying to please them. They will not be given to flights of autonomous action or statesmanship."[4]

Moe was not writing specifically about education reform, but his analysis applies squarely to the reform of K–12 schooling, from entrepreneurial supply-side initiatives to NCLB. And, while his chapter is written from a federal perspective, it usefully translates to any regulatory environment that implicates schooling. Replace "president" with "governor," and "congressman" with "state legislator," and it provides a blueprint for understanding politics and policy at the state and local levels, where, despite the current overwhelming din of NCLB, most regulation of K–12 schooling actually takes place. Though I did not know it at the time, one year after getting off the phone with Terry Moe I would begin to experience firsthand the politics of bureaucratic structure in its full force.

A CAUTIONARY TALE: THE MASSACHUSETTS CHARTER SCHOOL STORY

In 1997, I joined the team responsible for implementing the Massachusetts Charter School Initiative on behalf of the state's single charter authorizer, the Massachusetts Board of Education. At the time, ours was one of the first charter school initiatives in the nation, and Massachusetts had fourteen charter schools in operation. The political and regulatory conditions for early implementation of this entrepreneurial initiative were quite favorable.

During its start-up years, the Massachusetts charter school initiative had a well-written law, with the only major flaw being a statewide cap of 25 schools. We enjoyed strong support from Governor William Weld and his senior staff as well as the leadership of both houses in the legislature. Our small four-person authorizer team reported to a remarkably atypical state board of education chaired by a maverick education reformer—Boston University chancellor John Silber—and led by smart, reform-oriented board members like James Peyser and Abigail Thernstrom. We also had an aggressive non-governmental ally—the Massachusetts Charter School Resource Center—which provided the early charter founders with technical assistance, fundraising support, and good human resource networks. Lastly, we had a highly effective legislative advocacy team consisting of two seasoned lobbyists who were well-funded and utterly mission-oriented.

Each of these leaders and resources served to temporarily protect our initiative from the ever-intensifying assault by interest groups working to restrict and decimate the entire charter initiative. In a state like Massachusetts, the interest groups protecting established education practices—from labor unions to professional associations to niche advocacy groups—are as strong and skillful as any in the nation. Remarkably, in the face of such opposition, we had unusually strong defenses. At least for a time. But our early good fortune soon lulled us into a sense of complacency.

The first mistake, one of the few made by Governor Weld's leadership team, was to shift management of the charter initiative from the governor's office to the Massachusetts Department of Education (DOE), a roughly 400-person staff tasked with administering the myriad obligations of a state education bureau. The Weld team's first instinct was right on: Move the management of the charter school initiative out of the governor's office to protect it from the potential threat of subsequent governors inimical to charter schools. However, their next instinct could not have been more wrong. By shifting us into the DOE, the governor's office placed us in an agency dominated by career bureaucrats generally opposed to charter schools and, in many cases, influenced heavily by the very interest groups who were determined to kill our work. It was a bit like sending the hen to live in the fox den and hoping for the best. Given the anti–charter school sentiment among so many of its employees, plus its historical deference to establishment interest groups, the Massachusetts DOE soon became a forceful anti-charter interest group in itself, quietly undermining the work of our initiative with its considerable and multifaceted regulatory powers.

Here is a quick picture of how something initially so right went so wrong in the course of five quick years. When management of the charter school initiative was shifted to the Department of Education in 1996, our charter school authorizer team still enjoyed relative autonomy. We had a small array of powerful political patrons protecting our interests despite our new landlords. Our authorizer team was small and philosophically aligned, and it represented a good mix of public policy and school oversight skills. We were led by a tenacious team leader, Scott Hamilton, who defended the initiative from incessant political and bureaucratic encroachment, thereby allowing the rest of us to get core work done.

Though we were housed in a generally hostile agency, we had control over the design and implementation of the most important regulatory aspects of the initiative. Our office reported directly to the commissioner of education and had open lines of communication with both the board of education and the governor's office. We handled our own media and external relations. We advised legislators and legislative staffers on the evolution and needs of the initiative. We even had our own office space in Boston, seven miles south of the DOE's cubicle-packed mothership in Malden. For a time, we were able to operate in a relatively safe and autonomous environment because we had political patrons who routinely fought for us when charter opponents exercised their significant political capital within the state's bureaucracy. By 2000, however, the opposition interest groups had caught up with us. The Massachusetts charter initiative, in part because of some strong school start-ups and good media coverage, was no longer on opponents' back burners. Our opponents, and the politicians and bureaucrats in their sway, began to wield influence to hamstring the initiative.

By seeing to it that public watchdog groups invasively and indefinitely investigated *every* single charter school in the state and our office's management of the policy, opponent interest groups successfully chewed up tens of thousands of hours of time that we and our initiative's school principals would otherwise have spent on worthy operational challenges. At one point, the state's charter schools and our authorizer team were subject to exhaustive and simultaneous reviews by no fewer than four public oversight entities: the Office of the State Auditor, the Office of the Inspector General, the U.S. Department of Education's Office of Civil Rights, and the Massachusetts Education Reform Review Commission. This is not to mention the thousands of hours that we and charter school principals spent responding to "investigative journalists" and the dozens of ideologically (and antagonistically) motivated education-school researchers hoping to uncover a conspiracy to privatize the public education system.

True, we still had a fairly good statute, a fair share of political patrons, and some very strong school operators beginning to produce good academic results. But the intensity of the opposition's well-orchestrated use of bureaucratic structures to slow us down, coupled with the inherent slog of any start-up operation, ensured that good days felt like being under siege and bad days felt like an all-out street fight. As much as our authorizer team and charter school leaders hoped to faithfully execute our entrepreneurial ambitions, the opposition ultimately owned the terrain.

Today, charter opponents have killed any near-term hope that the charter school initiative will provoke broader systemic reform of public schooling in Massachusetts. A statutory cap prevents charter schools from drawing more than 9 percent of any municipality's public education funding. The initiative's growth has slowed dramatically—now at only 61 schools in its thirteenth year of operation—and accounts for fewer than 3 percent of the state's K–12 public school students. The state's authorizer team, on which I served, is now buried deep within the DOE's now 500-person staff and no longer has power to provide practical or symbolic leadership for the initiative.

Most important from the perspective of students, families, and charter school operators, Massachusetts charter schools have suffered from damaging regulatory burdens. In the start-up years, our authorizer team developed a school accountability process that, compared to conventional school districts, was lean and focused intensely on each charter school's academic performance. Only a short time later, the state's charter schools were being additionally reviewed by the DOE's Title I teams, special education teams, and other longstanding oversight entities within the bureaucracy. Such additional reviews focused almost exclusively on regulatory compliance and almost never on whether charter students were actually learning anything. The regulatory reporting requirements for charter schools grew increasingly burdensome. In response, savvy Massachusetts charter schools have, by necessity (and at great cost), created year-round compliance positions to respond to the overwhelming reporting load, thus freeing up the school principal to actually run the school. If I had been a motivated school founder anywhere in the country in 1995, I would have hustled to Massachusetts, given the clarity of the state's charter statute and the relative simplicity of its regulatory burden. In 2008, I would look elsewhere.

Political support for charter schools has decreased dramatically in the last 10 years in Massachusetts. Simply put, charter proponents, from state leaders to school operators to parents, have not sufficiently recognized or acted on the need to represent their interests and exercise influence with public officials holding power. Wholesale turnover of once–charter-friendly leadership in the legislature, governor's office, and state board of education has yielded an environment where anti-charter bills and regulatory initiatives now have significant viability. The state's promotion and protection of charter schools as an education reform has largely gone by the wayside. Some of the best charter operators in the nation who got their start in Massachusetts have now relocated to charter states providing better start-up opportunities.

During the start-up years of the Massachusetts charter school initiative, we did a fair job of helping support the founding of some strong charter schools. In terms of helping to change the fundamental business of schooling in Massachusetts, we failed completely.

WHY DID WE FAIL?

While our political power was sufficient for early protection of the charter initiative, it was far too fragile to sustain. We benefited at the start from a rare confluence of political leaders with the courage to do the right thing for charters in the face of stiff opposition. But we should have known that we were in a quickly closing window of opportunity. To perpetuate the political power necessary to maintain favorable rules at the legislative and bureaucratic levels, we should have focused as much energy on building a base of political power and advocacy expertise as on implementing the initiative itself. Instead, we let ourselves get overly caught up in day-to-day operational challenges. By not building sufficient political power early on, we ensured that Massachusetts charter schools would stand little chance of becoming a large-scale reform mechanism that could actually influence the state's broader K–12 landscape.

Strong new charter school operators do not come to Massachusetts these days. The venture philanthropy funds do not look there for opportunity. The highly effective Massachusetts Charter School Resource Center, which once helped to start some of the best charters in Massachusetts (and the nation), has closed shop and reopened as a national charter school incubator—still located in Boston but doing all of its work outside Massachusetts.

NOT JUST A MASSACHUSETTS STORY

This story about Massachusetts is not just a story about Massachusetts. The interrelationships among interest groups, politics, and regulatory structures that either allow or impede reform are intensely alive and well across the country. Consider this sample of news stories and reform analyses from the daily influx of news clips I received in a two month period in summer 2007:

- Journalist Daniel Weintraub and Claremont Graduate University research-er Charles Taylor Kerchner assess the political history and interest group dynamics that have defined and undermined the recent restructuring of governance of the Los Angeles Unified School District;[5]
- Journalist Joe Williams tells the Oakland education reform story and examines the interest groups and political influences that undermined efforts to transform the school district into a service organization support-ing quasi-autonomous public schools;[6]
- Hundreds of national, regional, and local media outlets across the country document political campaigns in Utah by pro and con interest groups to rally the public to vote for or against the implementation of a statewide voucher program in a statewide referendum;[7]
- The *Columbus Dispatch* exposes email communications between anti-char-ter school interest groups and the Ohio attorney general's office regarding the design of methods to hold Ohio charter schools accountable using charitable trust law;[8]
- (and coming full circle back to Massachusetts) The *Wall Street Journal's* op-ed page examines the influence of education interest groups on Massa-chusetts governor Deval Patrick's efforts to review and revise the Massachu-setts Comprehensive Assessment System, the state's school accountability regime.[9]

Additional recent scholarly analyses provide more methodical evidence of the ways regulatory constraints and the interest groups behind them slow the growth and performance of supply-side reforms:

- A 2005 Fordham Institute study concludes that the average disparity in funding between a charter school and its host district counterpart is about $1,800 per student, a gap that results invariably from the political com-promises that produce the enactment and regulatory architecture of state charter statutes;
- The National Charter School Research Project's 2007 analysis of char-ter management organizations reports that political and regulatory environments dramatically frustrate the operations and scale of charter networks;[10]
- Journalist Joe Williams's 2006 article, "Games Charter Opponents Play," illustrates how municipal actors opposed to charter schools are some

of the savviest manipulators of the regulatory environment, using their influence over facility zoning, school transportation systems, and school funding mechanisms to stall a charter school's momentum.[11]

But there is also good news of late for supply-side reformers. Interest group influence over the regulatory environment is as much an opportunity as it is a threat. Education reform interest groups have won a small but important share of recent policy victories. Consider the 2007 decision by the State of Maryland to provide more equitable per-student public funding to its charter schools. Consider the new market opportunity produced as a result of the successful five-year campaign by Milwaukee school-choice advocates to persuade Wisconsin's legislature and governor in 2006 to raise the cap on the Milwaukee voucher program by more than 7,000 students. And consider the far larger market opportunity created in New York's charter school initiative after charter advocates secured a 100-school cap raise in 2007. The opportunities are present, it seems, when supply-side reformers invest the resources and talent necessary to meet, and eventually overpower, the interest groups that currently oppose their efforts.

WHY ARE SO MANY BARRIERS STILL STANDING?

Scholars Frederick M. Hess of the American Enterprise Institute and Chester Finn of the Thomas B. Fordham Foundation pointed out in a 2007 analysis that the new generation of supply-side reformers is successful at a small scale because they avoid direct conflict with their regulatory overseers. These operators accommodate, compromise, and cut deals with established rule makers to maintain operational momentum.[12] Impressive exceptions like The New Teacher Project combine direct service to catalyze new-teacher supply with explicit advocacy efforts designed to change the rules slowing that supply. I agree with Hess and Finn's view that we cannot fairly expect entrepreneurial operators to build the supply and simultaneously do all the work required to develop the political power. School builders need to stick to their knitting, focus on doing one or two things well, and produce powerful academic results. At the same time, supply-side operators must at least appreciate and support the need for somebody—even if it is not them—to fight the advocacy fight.

Regrettably, too many supply-side entrepreneurs underestimate the need to build the political power that will change the rules constraining their work. Some are content to accommodate and compromise. Others are overly optimistic that the regulatory environment will somehow reform itself after seeing good results from early supply-side work. The premise of such entrepreneurs seems to be that rule makers—politicians, policymakers, and agency bureaucrats—will respond and change when inspired by enlightened example or guidance. I call this "reform by enlightenment," the belief that if you build a high performing [*insert your favorite supply side initiative here*], policymakers will flock to it, take notes, and duly change the rules and incentives so that the rest of the sector can follow suit. In theory the concept sounds great. In reality it consistently fails.

There have always been highly effective examples of K–12 school supply in the United States. But recent (and not so recent) history has shown little deconstruction of regulatory constraints that would provide freedom for such supply to grow and prosper at a significant scale. "Reform by enlightenment" is dangerously devoid of a true appreciation of how the regulatory environment gets built and rebuilt—and who calls the shots in the process.

Overly confident adherents to "reform by enlightenment" miss a fundamental truth: Elected and appointed rule makers do not have much interest in, or time for, enlightenment. Despite the groundbreaking choice- and accountability-oriented education reforms enacted over the last two decades by Superintendent Angus McBeath's team in Edmonton, Alberta, not a single school system in Canada has attempted replication of those reforms.[13] A state legislator will occasionally vote his or her conscience but will more often vote in alignment with the interests of those who will determine the outcome of the next election. Rule makers with power will act to perpetuate their power: The best chance of getting a rule maker to change course for a certain set of policy conditions is to demonstrate the capacity to enhance or diminish that power. It is not that reform by enlightenment is wrong. It is just not enough. If it is to actually produce fundamental changes in the operating conditions of public schooling, any entrepreneurial reform must be executed in the context of an aggressive application of political power that compels rule makers to actually change the way business gets done in a given jurisdiction.

Consider recent reform initiatives pushed by maverick and courageous big-city superintendents and mayors. I am thinking of Mayor Michael Bloomberg and Chancellor Joel Klein in New York City, Mayor Bart Peterson in Indianapolis, Mayor Cory Booker in Newark, Chancellor Michelle Rhee in Washington, D.C., former superintendent Alan Bersin in San Diego, and former state-appointed manager of Oakland Schools Randy Ward. It is unfair and naive to expect that these truly strong leaders can possibly attain large-scale, long-lasting reforms without aggressive political support that will ensure faithful reform follow-through by their successors and regulatory protection of their reform gains. These leaders need aggressive political advocates standing with them and behind them and, as importantly, ensuring that their successors are the right successors.

Fortunately, recent calls for greater advocacy have come not just from Frederick M. Hess and Chester Finn but from other leading education policy analysts like University of Arkansas researcher Jay Greene, Education Sector founder Andrew Rotherham, and independent analysts Steven Wilson and Bryan Hassel.[14] I subscribe to their recommendations enthusiastically but also note that they fall short. While they all argue for advocacy activities far more aggressively than most supply-side reformers, they are still not sufficiently clear, forceful, and direct about the glaring need to politically challenge the status quo.

Here is a good recent example of how otherwise excellent policy analysis simply does not go far enough in calling attention to the need to get political. The University of Washington's National Charter School Research Project's accurate and insightful study of charter management organizations is followed by prescriptions for fighting regulatory burdens that are so vague and soft as to be unworthy of execution:

> Anticipating political risk. MOs [management organizations] need to do on-the-ground work with local community groups as well as savvy politicking at the state level

[and later in the report]

> Policymakers should:
>
> Convene panels of MOs to suggest ways to create growth-friendly regulatory structures at the federal, state, and local levels.[15]

Recent analyses of the barriers to supply-side reform are a healthy and necessary first step to dealing with the problem, but in and of themselves, they have little capacity to influence change unless they are taken up by advocates who have the power to actually get things done.

BREAK THE RULES

Supply-side investors and entrepreneurs have a clear opportunity—and imperative—to develop the advocacy power that will yield necessary changes in regulatory environments that, in turn, will allow their efforts to prosper and grow. In fact, such work is already well underway in a number of school-reform initiatives. However, given the many current regulatory battles being lost in such areas as charter schools, school choice, and teacher-licensure reform, these promising early advocacy efforts require dramatic improvement and expansion.

Relative to the supply side of school reform, current advocacy operations are found mainly in the charter school and school-choice movements. Strictly speaking, school choice—in the form of publicly funded voucher and tax-credit scholarship programs—may not qualify as a supply-side reform. The school-choice movement is focused on serving families (demand) rather than building schools (supply). Yet I include it because school-choice programs, when effectively designed and implemented, provide one of the biggest and least regulated market opportunities for supply-side reformers hoping to provide new high-quality schools to low-income families.

Given the relative youth of the current wave of supply-side reform work, nobody has yet produced a comprehensive or thorough overview of advocacy efforts in and around supply-side reform initiatives. A comprehensive how-to summary of public policy advocacy has been written in a parallel realm of public policy: tort reform. Texans for Lawsuit Reform (TLR), an advocacy team responsible for dramatically overhauling tort practices in Texas in the last decade, has documented its approach to high-intensity, long-term advocacy campaigns in its "Template for Reform."[16] While TLR's approach may not translate fully to education reform, it provides a provocative picture of the massive level of resources, will, and perseverance that its authors needed in a decade-long campaign to fundamentally restructure how tort law gets practiced in Texas. For now, in the absence of any thorough study of advocacy operations in the current wave of school reform, a crude taxonomy will have to do.

Three Types of Advocacy

Public policy advocacy—education-related or otherwise—falls roughly into three types, with the first two focused on informing and persuading the public and public officials regarding a certain policy direction, and the third focused directly on supporting or opposing candidates for elected office who are for or against a certain policy direction.

Type 1: Evidence Building, Education, and Going on the Offensive. Here, advocates employ assessment and documentation of K–12 education reforms and, conversely, evidence of failures or gaps in conventional schooling that need to be addressed. Advocates use such evidence to educate and mobilize citizens, community leaders, business leaders, public officials, and the media about the need for change and the efficacy of their proposed reforms. They also work with legal teams to defend their interests from legal assault and sue for revision of unfair rules. In addition to dedicated interest-group advocates (for example, the California Charter Schools Association or School Choice Wisconsin), such work is frequently conducted by advocacy-oriented think tanks and, on rare occasions, by supply-side entrepreneurs themselves (for example, The New Teacher Project). Work that falls within type 1 advocacy is conducted by "nonprofit public charities" organized under Section 501(c)(3) of the Internal Revenue code and, as such, is tax exempt.

Type 2: Legislative Advocacy. Here, advocates make direct attempts to influence—or lobby—for or against specific legislation and rules at the federal, state, and local levels. Lobbying can happen in Congress, in state legislatures, in municipal governing bodies, and in the context of public voter referenda or initiatives. Current charter school and school-choice advocacy is most often directed at state legislative action. Legislative advocacy may only be done minimally by 501(c)(3) organizations and is more aggressively practiced by 501(c)(4) organizations that are not permitted tax-exempt status by the Internal Revenue code.

Type 3: Political Action. Using taxable donations from individual donors, political action operations work to support the election or reelection of public officials sympathetic to their interests and, conversely, defeat candidates who oppose their interests. Reform-oriented political donors helped, for example, to elect the pro-charter school Governor Eliot Spitzer in New York's most recent gubernatorial election. Political action is the least developed arm of advocacy in the current wave of school reform, yet one of the strongest weapons employed by interest groups opposing charter schools, school choice, teacher-licensure reform, and state testing and accountability systems.

Advocacy within supply-side educational reform is (currently) mostly limited to advocacy types 1 and 2, although some early initiatives in type 3 are paving the way for how education reformers might develop and sustain powerful political action. Here is an initial glimpse of advocacy operations that are already in business to support the work of education reform. This list is illustrative rather than comprehensive but does provide a starting point for readers who wish to begin learning more about the "who" and the "what" of this work.

Working at a national level and across multiple states in the charter school movement are organizations like the National Association of Charter School

Authorizers and the National Alliance for Public Charter Schools. The school choice movement has parallel organizations, such as the Alliance for School Choice, the Friedman Foundation, and the Institute for Justice. Some national organizations, like the Center for Education Reform and the Black Alliance for Educational Options, work as advocates across the charter school and school choice movements, seeing both of them under one broad umbrella of "parental options." The respective missions of these several organizations vary, but all work in type 1 advocacy and some work directly or through partner organizations in type 2 advocacy. Leaders of a small number of these are beginning to help develop affiliated type 3 advocacy organizations.

Working within specific states are charter- or choice-specific organizations designed to initiate and sustain charter school and school choice programs in their states. Like their national counterparts, most of these state-based organizations work in type 1 advocacy, and some operate directly or through partner organizations in type 2 advocacy. On the charter side, the Colorado League of Charter Schools and the Michigan Association of Public School Academies are examples of advocates who have been leading effective and sustained campaigns for their member charter schools for more than a decade. Organizations like the California Charter School Association (CCSA) and the New York Charter Schools Association are newer to the work but have brought a mix of advocacy expertise and powerful allies to help protect and improve their respective charter initiatives. In parallel, state school choice advocacy organizations work to advocate for enactment and expansion of voucher and tax-credit scholarship programs. Organizations like School Choice Wisconsin, School Choice Ohio, and the Florida Education Freedom Foundation are the primary coordinators of advocacy for school choice in their states. Some states are beginning to develop dedicated political action efforts for both charters and choice, although such work has until recently been attempted in largely uncoordinated efforts by individual political donors.

Significant reform victories—such as New York's recent expansion of its charter cap or Wisconsin's expansion of the Milwaukee Parental Choice Voucher Program—most often happen when all three types of advocacy merge with intensity and skill for sustained periods of time. The Milwaukee voucher program cap raise and the New York charter school cap raise were both results of several years of effort across all three types of advocacy. While the various advocates in the New York campaign to lift the charter cap did not always (or even frequently) work in effective partnership with one another, that they were collectively invested for a period of years across all three advocacy types helped secure their collective success. The Milwaukee story is similar. Reform advocates in the city and statewide worked for several years across all three advocacy types to secure a cap raise: After three successive annual vetoes by the governor's office, an intensified advocacy campaign in the fourth year finally convinced Governor Jim Doyle to sign a cap raise into law in early 2006.

In general, advocacy in the charter school and school choice movements is increasingly well developed in type 1 advocacy, significantly less well developed in type 2 advocacy, and minimally developed in type 3 advocacy. Because education reformers are generally more familiar with (and comfortable with) advocacy types 1 and 2 than they are with type 3—political action—I will profile two recent entrants into K–12 education reform that are aggressively building type 3 capacity. Through trial, error, and perseverance, both are prototypical models for what political action on the supply side of school reform could (and should) look like.

All Children Matter

All Children Matter (ACM) was founded by school choice and charter school advocates in 2003.[17] ACM's founders realized that the school choice and charter school movements lacked the political action needed to ensure that elected officials—particularly state legislators—would support such programs. In targeted states, ACM seeks to complement existing type 1 and type 2 advocacy efforts with political action that provides a forceful counterweight to the enormous influence of interest groups that oppose school choice and charters.

Technically, ACM is a "527" political action committee dedicated to electing public officials to the legislative, executive, and judicial branches of state government who are committed to supporting school choice and charter school programs. ACM also works to oppose public officials who do not support such programs. While ACM neither endorses specific school choice nor charter school legislation, it supports or opposes candidates by judging them on criteria that include support for charter schools, tax-credit scholarship programs, and school vouchers.

ACM works across the country, most aggressively in states that either have existing large-scale school choice and charter school programs—such as Florida, Ohio, and Wisconsin—or states where significant proposed school choice and/or charter school programs have a likely chance of enactment. ACM typically targets ten states for political involvement for each two-year election cycle. Its most prominent recent successes came in the 2007 Louisiana elections, when it aggressively and effectively focused expenditures on candidates in the gubernatorial, legislative, and state board of education races.

Democrats for Education Reform

Democrats for Education Reform (DFER) began operation in 2006 to address a void in the political influence of education reformers within the Democratic Party.[18] Its founders—a small group of like-minded and politically active Democrats from New York City's investment community—were motivated to spur debate about education reform within a political party that they considered too monolithic and risk-averse in its views on K–12 schooling. Given that motivation, DFER is in a sense more focused on political reform than education reform, operating on the assumption that making the Democratic Party more willing to engage and debate controversial K–12 reforms will enhance the political viability of those reforms.

Technically, DFER is a federal political-action committee and a New York State political-action committee, a structure that allows it to raise money for candidates at the federal and state levels. DFER's founders have also started a separate 501(c)(4) organization, Education Reform Now Advocacy, and a separate 501(c)(3) organization, Education Reform Now. The 501(c)(4) is used to advocate for specific issues like charter schools. The 501(c)(3) is deployed only for non-political education and research purposes. As a result, DFER's founders can use their three distinct organizations to work across advocacy types 1, 2, and 3.

DFER works at both the federal and state levels and supports education reform candidates within the Democratic Party by "giving them a political reason to do the right thing."[19] DFER also spends significant resources attempting to expand the base of Democrats who support substantive education reform by bringing people together in frequent social and professional gatherings. It also aims to provide political cover for reform-oriented politicians by "making noise, organizing supporters, and getting different perspectives into the media." DFER's most prominent early successes came in the most recent New York governor's race and the subsequent (successful) advocacy effort to lift the charter school cap in New York.

INVESTING IN MORE ENTREPRENEURS OF POLITICAL POWER

As University of Arkansas professor Jay Greene advises, the best use of philanthropic investment in K–12 schooling is to redirect the spending of future public dollars. Private investors—philanthropic and otherwise—are already heavily invested in the operational aspects of the supply side of education reform. I assume (or at least hope) that, consistent with Greene's view, such investors intend to have their initiatives taken up by good public policy, financed fully (if not immediately) by public revenues, and sustained for the long haul.

To protect those investments and maximize the chances that supply-side initiatives will expand and prosper, supply-side investors and entrepreneurs must make additional, parallel expenditures to launch and sustain advocacy initiatives. The education policy environment at state and local levels is awash with advocacy interest groups protecting established structures of public schooling. This is a given, and it will remain so as long as we maintain our current systems of state and federal government. In contrast, supply-side investors and entrepreneurs have yet to build the counterbalancing interest groups that will ensure them competitive advantages in the regulatory wars that their initiatives inevitably provoke.

Essentially, the supply-side reform movement should build advocacy capacity to exert influence wherever public rules that implicate such work are defined and revised. Advocates should aim to enact changes that facilitate their work and revise or eliminate impediments. Here are some immediate supply-side advocacy opportunities:

- Suspending teacher and principal licensing requirements in jurisdictions where supply-side reformers are aiming to support "new schools" strategies that require a large number of highly skilled candidates from outside the traditional system;
- Raising or eliminating statutory caps on the number of charter schools in a given state or municipality;
- Making statutory revisions that would allow for multiple, high-quality charter school authorizers in states where current authorization has stifled new school start-ups or permitted low-quality schools;
- Enacting statutory changes, or seeking legal remedy, to address inequitable funding of charter school students;
- Securing allowance for charter schools (or any good new public schools) to use federal and/or state revenues to retroactively pay the costs of training programs (for example, KIPP, Building Excellent Schools, New Leaders for New Schools) that have invested heavily in a school's start-up.

Ultimately, investing in the political advocacy necessary to sustain reform requires the same long-haul view that should dominate the operational strategies of all supply-side reformers. What I learned in my Massachusetts experience is that the powerful interest groups that were determined to stall and weaken our charter school initiative had been building and honing their skills for decades. They remain active today and will continue to operate for decades to come. Any effort to build and exercise power in the interest of reform must understand that this is a perpetual fight.

CHAPTER 10

Schools, Tools, and Rules

Creating an Entrepreneurial Future

Frederick M. Hess

School reform takes place in an ecosystem, with webs of rules, relationships, and policies. These webs, the product of both public and private activity—of policy and statute as well as social networks and philanthropy—help determine the success of promising reforms and new ventures. This is especially the case when dealing with entrepreneurial efforts that take root outside the traditional frameworks of districts, schools, and state agencies. Still, most reform efforts, whether focused on improving familiar districts and schools or promoting choice-based solutions, have suffered from the tendency to regard this ecosystem as a given. Would-be reformers have concentrated on promoting their particular remedies without recognizing how the larger K–12 ecosystem will ultimately decide the fate of their handiwork.

Supply-side reform approaches the challenges we face from the opposite direction. Rather than centering on isolated strategies to fix schools or promote school choice, it focuses on making the ecosystem more hospitable to the emergence and expansion of effective problem-solvers. As we have seen in the preceding chapters, such a tack requires attention to both public policy and private action, to the roles of money, talent, and knowledge. It focuses on creating conditions that enable problem-solvers and does not presume that elected officials, district leaders, professors, or funders can systematically identify and implement workable solutions.

As I note in the introduction, there is a reason that IBM did not simply become Microsoft and that Microsoft did not simply become Google. It was not for lack of brains, effort, or resources—which these firms had in abundance—but because the price of stability, success, and size is a reduction in agility and adaptability. Breakthrough advances are not as straightforward or predictable as we would wish; they are often the handiwork of new entrants plowing fresh fields alongside or in competition with established providers. As Alfred E. Kahn, economics professor at Cornell University, explained in the early 1980s in reference to airline deregulation, "Defense of the status quo missed the point of deregulation. The pertinent question was not whether the performance of the airline industry as of the middle 1970s was 'satisfactory,' [but] . . . how that performance . . . compared with the results that might have been or would be achieved if the industry were instead opened to competition." He concluded, "Neither the government nor industry planners are capable of envisioning the ideal, potential performance of an industry—how its costs will behave, what innovations it may make, what choices it will offer consumers."[1]

This admonition is counterintuitive for reformers eager to identify best practices or surefire policies. Public officials like to fix things and are expected to enact policies that solve problems. School officials and education professors are inclined, by training and incentives, to devise and adopt solutions. Philanthropists naturally like to fund schools, scholarships, and programs that work. The understandable desire for orderly progress has, unfortunately, yielded a profusion of accumulated rules, regulations, and routines that impede the emergence or scaling of creative solutions to stubborn problems.

While we should not pretend that we can identify possible answers absent experimentation and false starts, this does not mean that random gyrations are the key to improvement or that sensible quality control should be an afterthought. Successful markets are not vacuums but arrangements that attract, nurture, and channel ingenuity and effort. The defining characteristic of entrepreneurial hotbeds is not lawlessness but dense networks of talent, capital, mentoring, technical and legal expertise, and investors searching for promising ventures. As AnnaLee Saxenian, dean of the School of Information at the University of California–Berkeley, has explained, "Students of regional development . . . view Silicon Valley and Route 128 as classic examples of the external economies that derive from industrial localization: as cumulatively self-reinforcing agglomerations of technical skills, venture capital, specialized suppliers and services, infrastructure, and spillovers of knowledge. . . . Far from being isolated from what lies outside them, firms are embedded in a social and institutional setting."[2] Investing in the supply side means building an ecosystem that will foster dynamic problem-solving—and that means attending to human capital and venture capital, to research and development, and to quality control.

We must look beyond today's most familiar successes to unlock the full potential of entrepreneurship in education. To date, there has been a decided emphasis on school models (like KIPP or Green Dot Public Schools), reflecting our ongoing fascination with best practices. In recent years, this focus has been complemented by increased attention to human capital providers like Teach For America, The New Teacher Project, and New Leaders for New Schools. Going forward, however, this focus on people and schools must increasingly be coupled with equal attention to tools and rules. By "tools," I mean the products and services that can instruct children; make teachers and schools more effective; or provide valuable support to teachers, schools, or systems. By "rules," I am referring to the statutes and regulations that can inhibit or facilitate the entrance and expansion of new ventures.

Today, the most successful school builders are increasingly trying to scale rapidly from a handful of campuses to many times that number. As they do so, they recognize that tools and rules are necessary complements to the zealous employees, determined philanthropic support, and pioneering excitement that have gotten them where they are. Models dependent on the extraordinary energy and ability of pioneers have found themselves tackling the same challenge of getting to scale that has humbled so many initially promising reforms. Helping today's generation of reformers do better will require far more than good models, passion, and a commitment to data; it will require a supply-side strategy.

THE CONSEQUENCES OF NEGLECT: THE CASE OF MILWAUKEE CHOICE

This discussion can seem fairly abstract, so it may be useful to consider briefly what inattention to the supply side has meant on the ground. In 1990, after a series of heated political struggles, Wisconsin enacted the nation's first modern public school voucher program.[3] Today, there are nearly twenty thousand students enrolled in the politically resilient program. Initially serving fewer than one thousand low-income Milwaukee students, the program proved popular with eligible parents. Proponents hailed its transformative possibilities—especially as the program grew tenfold in the ensuing decade—while critics fretted about possible adverse consequences. Both sides have cited research and test results in making their cases. Whatever one makes of the competing studies regarding the program's effects, however, even sympathetic observers acknowledge that the program has not done much to spur the emergence of high-quality new schools. Indeed, the concerns mirror those voiced by ardent charter supporters who have acknowledged the uneven quality of many charter schools. Advocates of Milwaukee's program and of charter schooling appropriately trace this state of affairs, at least in part, to issues with per-pupil funding and program design—though they speak also to the larger questions of supply-side reform.

Given these disappointments, some supporters of choice-based reform have asked whether school vouchers and charter schooling may be fundamentally flawed. A supply-side perspective, however, suggests that after nearly two decades we have little insight into the real potential of choice-based reform because we have never taken the actions necessary to support it. A brief thought experiment can illustrate how the Milwaukee story, for instance, might have played out very differently.

In 1994, two Teach For America corps members teaching in the Houston Independent School District set out to launch a new program for fifth-graders on the second floor of Garcia Elementary. Needless to say, the district had little to offer by way of facilities, mentoring, funds, or logistical support. Undaunted, the two young men, Mike Feinberg and David Levin, hunted down seed capital, books, and supplies—a process that included writing more than a hundred letters to potential funders to scrape together the few thousand requisite dollars. The program proved both popular and successful, even though the following year the reward for its success and rapid growth was being shuffled to three modular classrooms behind Askew Elementary. The next year, the popular program had again outgrown its space, and the district decreed that the children could not remain in the program and would have to attend their zoned middle schools. Unwilling to see their students forced to leave, the founders contacted the Houston Independent School District central office to see what they could arrange. They hit a wall, finding themselves unable to even obtain an appointment with the superintendent. Finally, Feinberg settled in on the hood of Superintendent Rod Paige's pickup, waiting for him to emerge from the district's downtown offices at 4400 West 18th Street. With the help of Paige, a hard-charging future U.S. secretary of education, they overrode district protocols and secured the needed space. This is how Feinberg and Levin launched the first KIPP Academy. The effort has gone on to attract national attention, encompass nearly sixty schools across the nation, and become the signature success of the charter school movement and perhaps the most powerful brand in American education today.

What if market proponents in Milwaukee had invested in the supply side—had erected a neon sign indicating that they would provide seed money, facilities, legal support, potential mentors, supportive infrastructure, and a friendly hand? Levin and Feinberg, or peers looking to launch similar ventures, ranging from the YesPrep public schools to the SEED public boarding schools, might well have sought the welcoming Milwaukee market rather than slogging through local political and practical challenges on their own. After all, high-tech talent flows to Silicon Valley because, as Stanford University's Chong-Moon Lee and colleagues have observed, "The habitat of Silicon Valley is one in which all the resources high tech entrepreneurial firms need to survive and thrive have grown organically . . . [to promote] openness, learning, sharing of information, the co-evolution of ideas, flexibility, mutual feedback, and fast responses to opportunities and challenges."[4]

Milwaukee's reformers could have embraced such a model and sought to become the launchpad for ventures like KIPP. A couple of one- and two-person organizations operating on a shoestring, primarily the Institute for the Transformation of Learning and Partners Advancing Values in Education, scrambled to offer a bit of assistance. While laudable, in context this was like seeking to terraform an expanse of Siberian wasteland by sending two men equipped with a shovel, a map, and a bucket of water.

More extensive efforts to nurture a supply-side ecosystem would also have provided a powerful lever for policing quality. Silicon Valley, for instance, ruthlessly (if invisibly) screens claimants for quality. After all, venture capitalists do not fund every starry-eyed dreamer. In fact, they fund only a minuscule percentage of pitches, ensuring that many ill-considered proposals die on the vine while capital, mentoring, advice, and support are directed to the most promising ventures. A disciplined approach of that ilk—akin to what The Mind Trust is attempting in Indianapolis, as Bryan Hassel discusses in chapter 2, or New Schools for New Orleans is seeking to provide, as Matt Candler talks about in chapter 6—could well have made a substantial difference. It might have made starting programs like KIPP a less excruciating process; permitted founders to focus more on program quality and less on overcoming political, logistical, and institutional hurdles; and enabled more rapid expansion of effective providers. Along the way, Milwaukee could have provided the nation with an engine for educational entrepreneurship and possibly cast the lessons of its voucher program in a far different light.

In retrospect, Milwaukee's voucher program is very much the story of a half-baked cake—a revolutionary development on the demand side without an equivalent response on the supply side. Entrepreneurship and vibrant markets require far more than choice; they need a stable and hospitable policy environment, self-interested actors seeking to identify and nurture promising ventures, networks of technical and logistical support, human capital, financial capital, a research and development base, and incentives that recognize and foster quality. Cultivating a welcoming space for new ventures in a sector long marked by the absence of initiative and the heavy footprint of public bureaucracy will require thoughtful attention to promoting a habitat that has had little opportunity to evolve naturally.

TOWARD A MORE ENTREPRENEURIAL SECTOR

K–12 schooling is no place for wild-eyed schemes, quick-buck artists, or romantics willing to excuse dismal results. Elementary and secondary education is entrusted with our children's welfare, vast amounts of public spending, and a crucial role in shaping our common future. This makes it imperative that supply-side ventures be purposeful and complemented by both public oversight and sensible quality control. Efforts to foster entrepreneurial energy should be conceived in ways that enhance the likelihood of success and coupled with research and development that can help ensure that advances are not one-hit wonders but part of a flourishing enterprise characterized by a growing base of knowledge.

Human Capital

What promising practices might education import from other sectors to attract, develop, and retain talented individuals? Making education a magnet for talent requires taking advantage of the intrinsic appeal of K–12 education. As Christopher Gergen and Gregg Vanourek note in chapter 1, "Education organizations begin with an inherent advantage: the mission of education is closely aligned with the values of rising generations of professionals and emerging leaders eager to engage in meaningful work and make a difference. In that sense, talent recruitment teams in education are beginning on the fifty-yard line." Relative affluence in twenty-first century America has produced a large pool of college graduates with an appetite for work that is engaging and empowering.

With sensible school reform, we would make far better use of that opportunity than we currently do—rethinking assumptions about hiring, training, work roles, and career trajectories. Intriguing examples are provided by Citizen Schools and the Big Picture Company, both of which have devised school-based programs for engaging local professionals as volunteer mentors or instructors.

This is not to deny that financial incentives are important, but to recognize the enormous advantage of K–12 schooling in attracting both profit-seeking and nonprofit "social entrepreneurs." Most critically, identifying powerful ways to exploit new trends in recruiting, nurturing, and retaining talent in K–12 is essential work that entities like Teach For America, The New Teacher Project, and New Leaders for New Schools have only just begun. Heated debates over merit pay and alternative teacher licensure consume our energies, yet these broad-gauge efforts mostly entail modest alterations to firmly etched practices of recruiting and retaining school personnel. Rethinking who we want to pull into the sector, how to attract them, how long they might stay, what services they will provide, and how their jobs might be designed will require the kind of ingenuity that Bryan Hassel suggests in chapter 2.

There are straightforward and substantial opportunities to improve our approach to human capital. First, networks allow enterprising individuals to recruit talented team members, collaborate with mentors, discover business opportunities, and share information. While much work must still be done, over the past decade, the NewSchools Venture Fund's annual summit has become an important gathering place for participants from various quarters of the new sector. Providers like Teach For America and KIPP are now large enough that their alumni networks and annual gatherings serve to connect their members with each other and with the broader supply community. The challenge is to expand these efforts and nurture more of them, especially in particular locations and with an eye toward particular kinds of talent.

Second, there is a need to be more conscious about opportunities for career advancement and how their absence in the education sector influences the supply of entrepreneurs. We take for granted the existence of varied opportunities in vibrant sectors, but there are few opportunities for classroom educators to develop managerial skills, exploit new instructional tools, or wrestle with questions of school and system design. This is one reason why so many "choice" schools tend to resemble existing schools. One remedy would be to craft hybrid positions that allow classroom teachers to remain in their classrooms while building skill sets and gaining experience in non-classroom settings. This would reduce the pressure on energetic and highly capable young teachers to decide by their mid-twenties whether to pursue leadership or leave the sector for graduate school or other work. Moreover, such positions would allow educators to gain seasoning, connect with like-minded peers and potential mentors, and get a taste of an alternate career path within K–12—all standard-issue opportunities in thriving sectors.

Third, many visible initiatives, like New Leaders for New Schools or The New Teacher Project, are designed to improve the flow of talent into K–12 education in spite of the considerable policy barriers that exist. Industrial-era compensation, benefit, and retirement systems that discourage mobility and reward educators who stay in one state or district for decades are a hindrance when it comes to competing for talent in today's workforce. In addition, they make it even more difficult to entice veteran teachers or principals to take a chance on a new venture, limiting their prospects and impeding the ability of new entrants to recruit the optimal mix of talent. There is a need to address and alter those barriers by reducing the hurdles and disincentives posed by professional licensure, bureaucratic compensation systems, and balky human resource operations that lack sensitivity to talent.

Venture Capital

The case of "clean technology" provides an inspiring and instructive example for boosting venture capital in education ("clean technology" includes alternative fuels, water purification, renewable energy, and recycling). Both clean tech and education reform are issues of public concern, have broad societal impacts, and attract attention from policymakers and philanthropists. While clean tech has been around for a much shorter period of time than have contemporary school-reform efforts, it has nonetheless quickly and massively outstripped K–12 in attracting private investment and generating investor enthusiasm.

For instance, the trade group CleanTech Network has reported that North American and European venture capitalists invested $1.9 billion in clean-tech companies in the first half of 2007, up 10 percent from that period in 2006. In 2006, Silicon Valley's most prestigious venture capital firm, Kleiner Perkins Caufield & Byers reserved $100 million of its $600 million investment fund for start-ups seeking to reduce carbon dioxide emissions—and expects to dedicate one-third of new funding to clean tech by 2009.[5] In its entirety, 2006 private investment in the $500 billion K–12 sector was a fraction of what Kleiner Perkins Caufield & Byers alone devoted to clean tech.

The question of investment capital is not simply about money. Equally vital may be the ability and inclination of investors to bundle investment dollars with ancillary support. Vanessa Kirsch, founder of the venture philanthropy fund New Profit, Inc., has tellingly noted that organizations in which

New Profit invests often find the strategic and technical assistance at least as important as the infusion of funds. More broadly, whether the issue is public, nonprofit, or profit-seeking investment, Kim Smith and Julie Petersen explain in chapter 4 that smoothly functioning capital markets require crucial supports, including appropriate regulation and established ground rules; security and banking standards that offer accountability and information; and the existence of networks and tools that permit various parties to identify likely investments and provide services. When these elements are absent, investment markets can yield inferior, or even disastrous, results.

One tactic for jump-starting investment in the education sector would entail the targeted use of public dollars. A step that Joseph Keeney and Daniel Pianko propose in chapter 3 would involve the U.S. Department of Education, or a consortium of states or school districts, creating an EduFund to mimic In-Q-Tel, a state-sponsored venture-capital firm that invests alongside private venture-capital firms in enhancing national security. In-Q-Tel's ten-person staff in Silicon Valley and fifty Washington, D.C., employees work to identify promising start-ups and other mid-size firms that have the potential to equip the CIA with transformative intelligence technology. In-Q-Tel invests through debt, equity, and pay-for-development of specific initiatives and then provides the strategic expertise and management support that targeted firms will eventually need to expand. Currently, nothing like this exists in education, and not even the largest school districts have procurement budgets large enough to make this feasible on their own.

Keeney and Pianko suggest several modifications that would help make the In-Q-Tel model fit K–12 education. One would encourage EduFund to foster investment funds targeted at particular services, such as enabling technologies (like curricula and software) or delivering effective reading instruction for disadvantaged students. A second would require public or private action to create a network of ten or twenty large school districts to "fast-track" purchases from EduFund companies, thereby achieving bulk savings, providing critical mass for demonstrably effective products, and overcoming research and development hurdles. A third would encourage the development of a network of venture and private equity firms so EduFund would be able to coinvest alongside an experienced partner. Ultimately, what the EduFund notion makes clear is that how educational capital is made available may matter as much as the mere availability of funds.

When investors perceive that effective new ventures have a plausible path to success, when they see a viable market and supportive statutory and regulatory environment, both for-profit and nonprofit givers are far more likely to put dollars to work. One of the benefits of this kind of investment is the quality control imposed by funders sorting through dozens of possible ventures to support. Such screening is highly imperfect and still yields armfuls of lemons, but it offers a powerful way to put self-interest to work in culling out all but the most promising ventures.

While the late 1990s saw a spurt of private-sector investment interest in K–12 schooling, this dissipated when it became evident that existing regulations, funding systems, technology, and norms made it difficult or impossible to identify profitable ventures. Indeed, Kleiner Perkins Caufield & Byers partner John Doerr has long been an avid champion of school reform—serving on the board of the NewSchools Venture Fund—yet the firm has made no effort in education comparable to clean tech. As the clean-tech example makes clear, the personal interest of investors and the existence of capital are not enough.

Barriers

A variety of formal and less visible barriers stifle supply-side ventures. These obstacles may include political and formal policy as well as more informal and organizational factors kinking the supply-side hose. A comprehensive supply-side strategy will explore and seek to address both kinds of hurdles.

In chapter 9, Ed Kirby argues that lowering the political barriers to supply-side activity requires reformers to confront established interests. Regarding the deregulation that transformed the American economy in the 1980s and 1990s and unleashed entrepreneurial energy, former Clinton administration official Paul London has observed, "Key industries like transportation, communications, and energy were fundamentally changed by legal, regulatory, legislative decisions that increased competition. These industries would never have changed if political battles had not been won by the advocates of greater competition."[6] Educational entrepreneurs who succeed in the generally inhospitable environment of K–12 typically do so, however, not by fighting political battles but by winning allies, pacifying local critics, and steering clear of conflict. As a result, they are poorly situated to press for systemic change. Kirby suggests, therefore, that it is imperative for advocates and funders to step into the breach. The ability of deep-pocketed foundations to set up advocacy organizations and engage in political fights is a critical piece of the puzzle. One compelling example is the well-funded EdVoice, a California outfit that seeks to influence state officials on legislation related to district budgeting, school choice, teacher training and recruitment, and academic accountability.[7] Funded primarily by wealthy power players like business developer Eli Broad, Silicon Valley entrepreneur John Doerr, and Netflix founder and former president of the California Board of Education Reed Hastings, the nonprofit has become a force for educational change in Sacramento.[8]

In a less political vein, Larry Berger and David Stevenson discuss in chapter 5 a number of ways reformers can lower organizational barriers. First, they observe that the tendency to regard staff and salaries as sunk costs is an enormous obstacle to the ability of school systems to radically improve efficiency. For reasons that can be traced to habit, training, and policy, district officials generally assume their expenditures on salaries and benefits are a given and therefore underestimate the value of new services that make faculty or staff more efficient. Rather than asking whether a tutoring provider would allow a reduction in the number of paraprofessionals or whether more sophisticated diagnostic tools would allow an elementary teacher to work more effectively with more children in the same amount of time, district and state officials imagine that technology and service providers should supplement but not supplant personnel. Lowering this barrier will require devising metrics that make costs and benefits of various staff-service combinations more transparent; coaching district officials to evaluate alternatives with this in mind; and revising state statutes, district policies, and bargaining agreements that hamper flexibility in personnel.

Second, Berger and Stevenson point out that most big-ticket items in education are purchased through competitive bidding in which a product needs to be largely finished before the contract is even awarded (for instance, for a textbook to be adopted, it first has to be written). As a consequence, big firms with lots of cash have an enormous advantage. In more R&D-friendly sectors, procurement works quite differently. When NASA wants a new spacecraft, it does not expect Boeing to build one at its own expense; instead, it invites competing proposals and may even fund the early development of competing designs before selecting a team with which to work. The merits of using the cooperative research and development model, when appropriate, deserve serious consideration.

Third, successful entrepreneurship is often driven by disruptive technologies and business models (that is, those that represent not incremental improvements but goods or services that are cheaper, simpler, more convenient and upend established expectations). It is, to say the least, difficult to determine how to encourage or support these, but a modest first step would be to ask for them—to identify the demands that might inspire entrepreneurs to create a supply. Launching an education X-Prize, in which outsized rewards are offered for game-changing accomplishments, would be a good way to whet the entrepreneurial appetite and spur public interest. The X-Prize model has leveraged enormous private investment in other sectors, and X-Prize Foundation president Tom Vander Ark has estimated that a $10 million X-Prize for education would spur twenty or thirty times that amount in private investment.

Finally, district and state procurement systems are designed to buy products, such as books, computers, tests, and training workshops—items easily counted and monitored. They have much more trouble with services. In many cases, the services are expected to be "free with order" (for example, the textbook comes with a consultant and a handful of training sessions, or the test comes with perfunctory data analysis). However, the innovative solutions being designed for schools are complex combinations of products and services, requiring first that educators have more discretion to make purchasing decisions and then that they be able to procure products and services that best meet their needs. This requires rethinking state policies, procurement guidelines, and management practices. The New York City Department of Education, for instance, has been a pioneer on this front, devolving substantial funding and decisionmaking authority to "empowerment schools" in areas such as professional development. In turn, the district has allowed principals to purchase services from both district collectives and authorized external organizations. A small market-maker office within the New York City Department of Education supports these arrangements, helps collect data on outcomes and customer satisfaction, and provides essential quality control through a competitive process in which would-be vendors are vetted.

There is a pressing need for advocates and reformers to illuminate the various obstacles that impede the emergence and growth of promising efforts. Charter school caps and teacher licensure systems are obvious examples, but there also exists a wealth of more subtle measures. These include the effects of zoning and liability laws on new schools, the lack of professional support for nontraditional ventures, and the reluctance of district officials to outsource services. Between reformers seeking to make charter schooling work and the opposition of traditional interests to the expansion of new providers, little attention is devoted to these challenges. One potentially powerful response would be to publicly and determinedly catalog the existing challenges, illuminate them, and start encouraging legislators and district officials to address them. Currently, with almost no awareness that they even exist, it is impossible to generate solutions or get public officials to focus on them. Convening various local, state, and federal commissions to examine and document these factors could prove enormously beneficial.

Quality Control and R&D

While we have embraced the importance of simple metrics like student performance in math and reading in this era of NCLB accountability, this development has been marked by an unfortunate blind eye to the limits of such measures. Standardized assessments are a valuable measure of student learning and offer a crucial basis for comparing providers. But ensuring the high-quality provision of services requires operational measures and data well beyond that of student achievement. To date, accountability efforts—and particularly the eight-hundred-pound gorilla of No Child Left Behind–style testing—have created an opportunity and appetite for schools seeking to teach the specified material more effectively. Yet these particular achievement measures can be largely irrelevant to motivating and managing many important school employees. It does not make sense, for instance, to hold a payroll processor responsible for student achievement rather than the speed and accuracy of his or her work. The criteria appropriate to appraising providers of professional development or data analysis are likely to be quite distinct from those that should be used to determine what Web-based foreign language course a school ought to offer or which local school a parent should select. In short, quality-control metrics need to focus on outcomes rather than inputs, but the understanding of outcomes needs to be much more nuanced than has been the norm.

In chapter 6, Matt Candler offers some hard-earned lessons regarding school-level quality control in the charter sector. Drawing on his experience opening and policing charter schools in New York and New Orleans, he emphasizes the importance of employing sensible metrics and providing honest assessments of school performance. For the worst schools, he says that it is critical to focus on quick and clear diagnoses of problems and establish measures to speed school closure when appropriate. Although Candler suggests that stronger oversight and monetary rewards have a role to play, he notes the challenges posed by a striking lack of knowledge about how to assist failing schools or drive breakthrough performances.

In chapter 7, Chester Finn observes, "Oversimplifying, we might label yesterday's quality-control model 'Regulating Inputs and Process,' or RIP, and we might term the one we need today 'Producing Academic Results Efficiently and Safely,' or PARES. Both are concerned with the welfare of children and the integrity of public resources, but RIP paid scant attention to effectiveness." In the case of charter schooling, Finn notes that parental information offices routinely invest in providing pamphlets and materials to parents and promoting awareness of choices, but that these efforts have not been matched by broader moves to develop reliable quality-control metrics. What is required is something more sensitive to diverse challenges and opportunities.

For example, *Consumer Reports* often suggests best buys in several price ranges; whether the $4,000 or the $1,500 flat-screen TV is a best buy for a given family will depend on their budget, preferences, and desired features. This is not dissimilar to the plight of superintendents trying to choose between alternative math curricula or Title I tutoring firms, although it is quite different from the case of parents selecting public school options, as their out-of-pocket costs will be identical—zero in every case. The bottom line is that some quality-control strategies work better for some goods and services, in some contexts, and for some users—yet we have focused in the past decade on generating one set of metrics while devoting insufficient attention to others.

Finn suggests some underutilized alternatives, each useful for certain purposes but each with its own limitations. Like the Food and Drug Administration, education's What Works Clearinghouse reviews reading or math programs with an eye toward hard evidence of effectiveness. Yet it is not a regulatory agency, and its approval is not mandatory; indeed, it is closer to a *Consumer Reports* model than to a formal system of drug approval. Inspectors, however, seek to determine whether providers are following rules and doing what they promised. This can yield constructive feedback (as with the British system of school inspections) or immediate policing (as when the health inspector shuts down an unclean restaurant). Wiki methods allow inexpert consumers to provide feedback on their experiences with particular providers or services. As with Amazon or eBay, one cannot regard ratings as "scientific," but, for a variety of consumers, they can aggregate and synthesize a wealth of data points that cannot otherwise be accessed or understood. There are enormous potential benefits in new models attuned to the needs of institutional purchasers like schools and districts as well as families.

It is not clear how to devise such quality-control mechanisms. There is a need for rethinking and experimentation on the quality-control and rules-of-the-entrepreneurial-road fronts. Tackling the quality-control challenges may, however, prove even more daunting. The rule-makers, enforcers, and data collectors tend to be creatures of government, subject to the caution, sluggishness, and political constraints we associate with public entities. While entrepreneurs will almost certainly outpace our ability to construct the appropriate metrics and measures, Finn concludes, "It would surely be good for American education if the quality-control systems could be made to keep pace with rather than left to retard—or ignore—the entrepreneurs. Public policy works best with tidy distinctions between what is and is not acceptable, between black and white, yes and no, permissible and intolerable. Yet education quality control is full of grays, maybes, and subtle balancing acts."

Finally, the sine qua non of any vibrant sector is research and development. Unfortunately, most education research is heavily reliant on either qualitative measures of various school environments or econometric analyses that attempt to find causal relationships between certain practices and test scores. The ability to advance teaching, learning, or service delivery by focusing on practical problems, devising effective solutions, and then subjecting them to rigorous evidence-based scrutiny is lacking. In chapter 8, Anthony Bryk and Louis Gomez provide a blueprint for an aggressive and expansive rethinking of our approach to research and development in schooling. They suggest a need for a tiered system that draws on the lessons from such knowledge-fueled sectors as aerospace and biotechnology, with collaboration among practitioners, researchers, and the commercial sector in R&D and product development. This research and design work would then be married to networks of school sites where advances could be systematically tested, refined, and evaluated.

Doing this at all—much less doing it right—is currently beyond the capability of any school district, commercial education venture, or university. Establishing the necessary infrastructure will require partnerships among schools, the academy, and commercial firms. These arrangements need not be geographically constrained but might utilize either school districts or chains of charter schools. Such a collective venture could include districts in Chicago and New Orleans, charter school management organizations like KIPP and Edison Schools, a handful of universities or research organizations, and a select group of for-profit and nonprofit providers. Commercial partners would be expected to contribute funding and expertise, but—as in biotechnology or aerospace—there is a vital role for public dollars to play in underwriting the basic research component of the R&D process.

PEEKING AROUND THE CORNER

A comprehensive strategy for fostering the supply side in schooling requires thinking beyond even cutting-edge approaches to human capital, investment capital, barriers to entry, and quality control, and embracing far-reaching efforts to rethink the fundamental assumptions that govern the shape of teaching and learning. Taking the next step requires that we emancipate ourselves from once-sensible but now confining assumptions regarding how schooling should be organized and funded and begin to construct policies and arrangements that take full advantage of twenty-first-century opportunities.

Thinking beyond Geography

Historically, we have thought of schools and school districts as being constrained by local geographies. Schools served the children in a given locale, and districts managed the schools in a designated community. Given the constraints on transportation, communication, and importability of support services, this approach made sense. However, in recent decades, school busing, magnet schooling, local choice programs, charter schooling, and voucher programs have gradually eroded those assumptions. Meanwhile, charter management organizations like National Heritage Academies, Aspire, and High Tech High now manage schools in multiple locales. Taken in its entirety, however, education is belatedly beginning to mirror developments in other sectors where advances in communication and transportation have yielded new and dramatic efficiencies.

There is no reason for operators, much less service providers like The New Teacher Project or SchoolNet, to confine their service to a particular locale. Indeed, expecting providers to serve the individual needs of every child in a given area introduces serious challenges. It requires the local district to figure out how to effectively and equitably address the various needs of all its students, whether gifted or in need of remediation or other specialized care. This is an enormous and potentially insuperable task and one that few districts do well.

Current arrangements essentially expect each district and school to reinvent the wheel when it comes to serving any particular segment of students. Rather than expecting a single school district to meet this array of needs, a variety of specialized providers operating alongside one another would allow targeted services to be provided to distinct clienteles in any given community. If experience in other sectors is any guide, such a collective effort of specialists would have enormous potential advantages over stand-alone districts in serving the various needs of the entire student population.

Promising examples of this approach abound. The SEED school in Washington, D.C., a public charter school, provides a boarding school experience for more than three hundred local low-income children in grades 7–12 whose parents believe they will benefit from its intensive environment. SEED does not seek to serve students desiring a conventional high school education, and the D.C. Public Schools would have a difficult time staffing, operating, or managing the SEED program alongside its other schools. Instead, this is a case of a specialized provider exercising a valuable role and complementing other available services. Some have described the vision of various schools coexisting in a community as a "portfolio" approach, though it may be more useful to think of as a "jigsaw" approach—with various schools and providers cooperating and competing alongside one another, collectively covering the spectrum of student needs.

Thinking beyond "Whole-School" Approaches

One advantage of the jigsaw metaphor is that it shifts the system from one in which successful providers need to duplicate the services of a school or district to one in which providers are encouraged to serve discrete needs for particular clients. In each case, the purpose of the innovation is not to replace the entirety of a school or school system but to provide a particular service that benefits students, schools, or school systems. In other words, the hunt should not be for the elusive 100 percent solution but for one hundred different 1 percent solutions.

The roles played by The New Teacher Project, in identifying promising teachers and supporting human resources; New Leaders for New Schools, in identifying and preparing principals; Wireless Generation, in supporting literacy instruction; Spectrum K12, in providing special education; Presidium Learning, in providing back-office support; Standard and Poor's, in supporting state-level data analysis; or ProActive School, in providing information technology solutions, are all examples of how this can work.

One advantage of this approach is that it allows providers to specialize and then slowly expand their reach. Michael Dell was able to start small merely by selling hand-assembled personal computers. Amazon started by just selling books. Microsoft provided software but never sought to provide the hardware that existing competitors did. If Amazon had only been taken seriously if it had been able to displace all the services provided by Barnes & Noble or Borders, or if Microsoft had been expected to sell computers and software, neither would have gotten off the ground. Yet, there is a clear bias in education toward whole-school replacement, an expectation that entrepreneurs should open whole new schools and not just deliver single, important advances. This makes it more difficult for specialized providers to attract funding or support and distracts them from developing, refining, and delivering a particular service or product.

Efforts to promote school accountability, including the No Child Left Behind Act, have generally aggravated this tendency by embracing the "whole-school" mindset. On the one hand, these accountability systems have been beneficial for supply-side activity because they have illuminated areas of need and provided a measuring stick that policymakers and practitioners can use to gauge the effectiveness of traditional systems and new providers. On the other hand, new accountability systems are intended to evaluate student performance metrics almost exclusively on a schoolwide basis. While this is useful for whole-school competitors, it makes it difficult for niche providers to demonstrate their worth. More broadly, the focus on NCLB-style test results has not been accompanied by serious progress in determining how effective a provider is in areas like recruiting teachers, professional training, K–2 literacy coaching, foreign language instruction, and data analysis. The ability to measure the effectiveness of niche services and steer funds toward those most deserving is essential to making it possible for them to succeed.

Thinking beyond "Block-Child" Funding

Even the most entrepreneur-friendly plans for rethinking educational spending have thus far accepted the presumption that funding will follow students to their particular schools. For example, charter schooling involves redirecting a percentage of the public contribution to a parent's chosen school; voucher proposals entail the stipulated voucher amount doing the same; and weighted-student funding plans involve districts allocating dollars to schools according to enrollment and then adjusting per-pupil allotments on the basis of student need.

Unfortunately, distributing dollars in this fashion hinders the emergence of specialized or niche providers and encourages a continued focus solely on whole-school replacement. For instance, a provider of a niche service may not be equipped to open whole schools but may be positioned to provide highly effective programs in early literacy coaching, foreign language instruction, or remedial tutoring. As long as public dollars flow en masse to districts or schools, however, providers must negotiate with districts for service contracts. These arrangements encourage the focus on specific relationships and local geographies and augur against the development of solutions that might help a certain percentage of children in every community.

This is an unnecessary and potentially stifling state of affairs. It would be analogous to Medicare prohibiting patients seeking health care from visiting a podiatrist, dermatologist, or general practitioner—and instead requiring them to visit a hospital, which would then assign staff or—if the hospital were so inclined—bring in an outside specialist. In the case of medicine, insurers and government programs are instead equipped to disburse dollars to a variety of approved providers in accord with quality-control mechanisms and safeguards. Patients may be required to first visit a primary care physician, but funding can flow to an array of providers as they seek to find appropriate care.

In schooling, a similar model might build on the intuition embedded in weighted-student funding, charter schooling, or the NCLB supplemental services program and truly allow families to direct dollars toward educational services as they see fit. Rather than having the money merely flow to the school or school system that a family chooses, a state government or school district could deposit a child's adjusted per-pupil expenditure into a virtual spending account and allow parents to direct those dollars to approved providers for tutoring, specialized instruction, pedagogical tools, or similar services. A parent might decide to send his or her child to a given school and then, if some dollars in the account were left over, use them to pay for additional reading or music instruction. This would create an incentive for schools to become more cost-conscious and could encourage them, in turn, to more aggressively seek out efficient niche providers. Of course, there are numerous complications here—ranging from quality control to the mechanisms used to determine an approved provider—but the idea suggests a promising avenue for exploration.

Another intriguing approach would entail refashioning funding systems to pay providers based on results rather than inputs. While even "radical" choice-based reforms have continued to allocate resources based on enrollment, providers might instead be compensated based on how many of their students achieve state-determined criteria. For instance, if Boston were to pay a provider $20,000 per year for every at-risk high school student that it got on course to achieve proficiency and graduate on time, the district would encourage a burst of activity among teachers, community activists, for-profit providers, and others to devise approaches geared to help particular students. One such model, conceived by MATCH charter school founder Michael Goldstein, involved the formation of teacher co-ops that established classes of seven students, met in a coffee shop, contracted with specialized providers for support services, and paid teachers upward of $90,000 or $100,000 a year if students achieved given benchmarks. An alternative course would entail states redesigning per-pupil funding formulas so as to incorporate student learning as reflected by state assessments rather than just relying on attendance—introducing new rigor to the charter school sector and freeing up district funds for potentially more effective providers. The potential of all such approaches currently remains unexplored and uncertain.

IT IS NOT ABOUT BUILDING GARAGES, IT IS ABOUT WHAT HAPPENS INSIDE THEM

Bill Gates and Paul Allen famously launched Microsoft by developing their software in the Gates family garage. An investor looking for the smart bet in American technology in the late 1970s would not have invested in these two kids. Such an investor would have been more likely to bet on IBM, the firm that dismissed the potential of Microsoft's new software, saw it as peripheral to its business, and passed on the opportunity to purchase the brand. This is the peril for those inclined to dismiss educational entrepreneurs and instead focus relentlessly on identifying and mimicking best practices.

After all, at one time, TWA and Sears, Roebuck, and Co. were giant and admired firms. The new entrants that challenged and ultimately displaced them—including Southwest Airlines and Wal-Mart—were initially regarded as tangential or regional curiosities. The challenge in a sector like K–12 schooling, where the government funds and operates dominant systems, is to ensure that it is possible for such ventures to emerge from under the bulk of the status quo.

Entrepreneurs in vibrant sectors are able to plug into ecosystems characterized by talent, expertise, research and development, capital, potential investors and mentors sensitive to quality and performance, and social networks. The lesson of Gates and Allen is not that the government should have funded any aspiring techie, much less that experts should have surveyed the land and determined that resources should be showered on two kids from suburban Washington. Rather, it is to demonstrate the value of an environment where it is possible to test new ideas, attract support, and reap rewards for devising a successful innovation and delivering it at scale.

Instead of waiting for this capacity to gradually evolve in the coming decades, a comprehensive supply-side response entails thoughtful public, private, and philanthropic efforts to nurture a solution-friendly ecosystem. The contributions of The New Teacher Project, Teach For America, Wireless Generation, New Schools for New Orleans, New Leaders for New Schools, Edison Schools, the SEED Foundation, Uncommon Schools, Achievement First, The Mind Trust, High Tech High, SchoolNet, Green Dot Public Schools, Aspire, KIPP, and other organizations are a powerful illustration of how these efforts can work on a micro scale—even while the uneven track record of systemic reform initiatives, charter schooling, and choice-based programs suggest the perils of inattention to the supply side on a macro scale.

Finally, a look at the names in the preceding paragraph should be enough to show that the supply side is not solely, or even predominantly, about charter schooling or school choice. Supplying effective new providers of various stripes is essential for those seeking to retool troubled schools and for those focused on choice-based reform. In reality, of course, these two approaches can and do operate in tandem. In New York and Chicago, for instance, charter management organizations are opening or operating dozens of schools, New Leaders for New Schools is recruiting and training principals, and The New Teacher Project is helping to hire hundreds of first-time teachers. Meanwhile, the districts have taken steps to provide some principals with charter-like authority and more aggressively recruit teachers. In fact, it is hard to say with precision the degree to which these new developments are happening inside or outside the district. The most promising initiatives skirt those boundaries, drawing on district infrastructure and political leadership while relying on the fruits of new personnel, tools, schools, and rules.

There should be no vapid expectations or slick pledges that entrepreneurial ventures will deliver happy results. Supply-side reform promises nothing more than opportunity, coupled with substantial doses of failure and frustration. We might like to determine the shape of the future, through research or best practices, and get there as rapidly and with as few diversions as possible—but that is not the way of the world. We are feeling our way toward a new and hopefully more fruitful era of teaching and learning. In getting there, we have been slowed by habits of mind that imagine a future for schools and school districts that embody today's familiar assumptions and romanticize the most promising of today's successes. While we must recognize that institutions change slowly and should celebrate incremental advances, we should not allow such thoughts to obscure the issue. We might wish for a simpler or neater path, but our choice is ultimately between trusting the authorities to fix aged and troubled bureaucracies in deliberate and incremental steps or trusting in the ability of a rising generation to seize on new tools, new opportunities, and human ingenuity to answer new challenges in unforeseen ways. If history teaches us anything, it is that this is really no choice at all.

Notes

INTRODUCTION. THE SUPPLY SIDE OF SCHOOL REFORM

1. National Center for Education Statistics, *The Nation's Report Card: Reading 2007* (Washington, D.C.: U.S. Department of Education, 2007), 16, 34; National Center for Education Statistics, *The Nation's Report Card: Mathematics 2007* (Washington, D.C.: U.S. Department of Education, 2007), 16, 34.

2. *The Programme for International Student Assessment 2006* (Organization for Economic Cooperation and Development, 2007), 16, 32.

3. Virginia B. Edwards, *Diplomas Count: An Essential Guide to Graduation Policy and Rates* (Bethesda, Md.: Editorial Projects in Education, 2006).

4. George Miller, "Commentary," *Forbes.com*, January 23, 2008, http://www.forbes.com/2008/01/22/solutions-education-miller-oped-cx_gmi_0123miller.html (accessed January 31, 2008).

5. Margaret Spellings, "Commentary," *Forbes.com*, January 23, 2008, http://www.forbes.com/2008/01/22/solutions-education-spellings-oped-cx_dor_0123spellings.html (accessed January 31, 2008).

6. Michelle Rhee, "Commentary," *Forbes.com*, January 23, 2008, http://www.forbes.com/2008/01/22/solutions-education-rhee-oped-cx_dor_0123rhee.html (accessed January 31, 2008).

7. Bill Gates, speech, National Education Summit on High Schools, Washington, D.C., February 26, 2005, http://www.nga.org/cda/files/ES05GATES.pdf (accessed December 7, 2007).

8. This disappointment has been severe enough that some who once ardently touted the promise of school choice have changed their minds. See, for example, Sol Stern, "School Choice Isn't Enough," *City Journal* 18, no. 1 (Winter 2008).

9. Richard F. Elmore, *School Reform from the Inside Out: Policy, Practice and Performance* (Cambridge, Mass.: Harvard Education Press, 2004).

10. See, for example, Harvard University, "PELP Coherence Framework," n.d., http://www.hbs.edu/pelp/framework.html (accessed January 22, 2008).

11. Bruce Fuller and Richard F. Elmore, *Who Chooses? Who Loses?* (New York: Teachers College, Columbia University, 1996), 9; Richard F. Elmore, *Building a New Structure for School Leadership* (Washington, D.C.: Albert Shanker Institute, 2000), 14.

12. For an example of how accountability results in small-minded micro-management rather than flexibility, see Daniel L. Duke, Margaret Grogan, Pamela D. Tucker, and Walter F. Heinecke, eds. *Educational Leadership in an Age of Accountability: The Virginia Experience* (Albany, N.Y.: SUNY Press, 2003) and Terry M. Moe, "Politics, Control, and the Future of School Accountability," in *No Child Left Behind? The Politics and Practice of*

School Accountability, ed. Paul E. Petersen and Martin R. West (Washington, D.C.: Brookings Institution Press, 2003); for an example of how school boards and superintendents do not challenge contract provisions, see Frederick M. Hess and Andrew P. Kelly, "Scapegoat, Albatross, or What? The Status Quo in Teacher Collective Bargaining," in *Collective Bargaining in Education: Negotiating Change in Today's Schools,* ed. Jane Hannaway and Andrew J. Rotherham (Cambridge, Mass.: Harvard Education Press, 2006) and Frederick M. Hess and Martin R. West, "Strike Phobia," *Education Next* 6, no. 3 (Summer 2006); for evidence that charter schools pay teachers roughly the same way as traditional district schools, see Julie Kowal, Emily Ayscue Hassel, and Bryan C. Hassel, *Teacher Compensation in Charter and Private Schools: Snapshots and Lessons for District Public Schools* (Washington, D.C.: Center for American Progress, 2002), 6; for an example in which district leaders with even high levels of flexibility and discretion still struggle with bottlenecks like human resources and technology, see Frederick M. Hess, ed., *Urban School Reform: Lessons from San Diego* (Cambridge, Mass.: Harvard Education Press, 2005) and Christine Campbell, Michael DeArmond, and Abigail Schumwinger, *From Bystander to Ally: Transforming the District Human Resources Department* (Seattle, Wash.: Center on Reinventing Public Education, 2004).

13. *The Economist,* April 18, 1992, quoted in Peter Senge et al., *Dance of Change: The Challenges of Sustaining Momentum in Learning Organizations* (New York: Doubleday, 1999), 5–6.

14. Paul Strebel, "Why Do Employees Resist Change?" *Harvard Business Review* (May–June 1996): 86.

15. Peter Senge et al., *Dance of Change,* 6.

16. Clayton M. Christensen, *The Innovator's Dilemma: When New Technologies Cause Great Firms to Fail* (Cambridge, Mass.: Harvard Business School Press, 1997).

17. Arthur L. Stinchcombe, "Social Structure and Organizations," in *Handbook of Organizations,* ed. James G. March (Chicago: Rand McNally, 1965), 153.

18. Arye L. Hillman, *Public Finance and Public Policy: Responsibilities and Limitations of Government* (Cambridge, U.K.: Cambridge University Press, 2003).

19. John E. Chubb and Terry M. Moe, *Politics, Markets, and America's Schools* (Washington, D.C.: Brookings Institution Press, 1990), 217.

20. Herbert J. Walberg and Joseph L. Blast, *Education and Capitalism: How Overcoming Our Fear of Economics and Capitalism Can Improve America's Schools* (Stanford, Calif.: Hoover Institution Press, 2003).

21. Paul London, *The Competition Solution: The Bipartisan Solution behind American Prosperity* (Washington, D.C.: AEI Press, 2005), 179.

22. Inevitably, there are a few exceptions. Two volumes that have paid some attention to supply-side considerations are Paul T. Hill and James Harvey, eds., *Making School Reform Work: New Partnerships for Real Change* (Washington, D.C.: Brookings Institution Press, 2004) and Frederick M. Hess, ed., *Educational Entrepreneurship: Realities, Challenges, Possibilities* (Cambridge, Mass.: Harvard Education Press, 2006).

23. Milton Friedman, "Using the Market for Social Development," *Cato Journal* 8, no. 3 (Winter 1989): 568–69.

24. Robert Devlin, Antoni Estevadeordal, and Andrés Rodríguez-Clare, eds., *The Emergence of China: Opportunities and Challenges for Latin America and the Caribbean* (Cambridge, Mass.: Harvard University Press, 2006).

25. Devlin, Estevadeordal, and Rodríguez-Clare, *The Emergence of China*, 22–23.
26. Shahid Javed Burki, "China: The New Global Giant," in *Transforming Socialist Econo-mies: Lessons from Cuba and Beyond*, ed. Shahid Javed Burki and Daniel P. Erikson (New York: Palgrave Macmillan, 2005), 145.
27. Jeffrey Sachs, *Poland's Jump to the Market Economy* (Cambridge, Mass.: MIT Press, 1993), 46.
28. Christopher A. Hartwell, "Eastern Europe: Different Paths, Different Results," in *Trans-forming Socialist Economies: Lessons from Cuba and Beyond*, ed. Shahid Javed Burki and Daniel P. Erikson (New York: Palgrave Macmillan, 2005), 81.
29. Steven A. Morrison and Clifford Winston, "The Remaining Role for Government Policy in the Deregulated Airline Industry," in *Deregulation of Network Industries: What's Next*, ed. Sam Peltzman and Clifford Winston (Washington, D.C.: AEI-Brookings Joint Center for Regulatory Studies, 2000), 25.
30. For a discussion in the context of schooling, see Frederick M. Hess, *Revolution at the Margins: The Impact of Competition on Urban School Systems* (Washington, D.C.: Brook-ings Institution Press, 2002), 242.
31. William D. Bygrave, "The Entrepreneurial Process," in *The Portable MBA in Entrepre-neurship*, ed. William D. Bygrave and Andrew Zacharakis, 3rd ed. (Hoboken, N.J.: John Wiley and Sons, 2004), 1–27, 4.

CHAPTER 1. TALENT DEVELOPMENT

1. Ed Michaels, Helen Handfield-Jones, and Beth Axelrod, *The War for Talent* (Boston: Har-vard Business School Press, 2001), xxii.
2. Charles Fishman, "The War for Talent," *Fast Company*, no. 16 (July 1998): 104.
3. Elizabeth Chambers et al., "The War for Talent," *McKinsey Quarterly*, no. 3 (1998).
4. Elizabeth Axelrod, Helen Handfield-Jones, and Timothy Walsh, "The War for Talent, Part Two," *McKinsey Quarterly*, no. 2 (2001).
5. Keith Hammonds, "Grassroots Leadership: U.S. Military Academy," *Fast Company*, no. 47 (May 2001): 106.
6. Frederick M. Hess and Andrew P. Kelly, "The Accidental Principal," *Education Next* 5, no. 3. (Summer 2005).
7. Peter F. Drucker, *Concept of the Corporation* (New Brunswick, N.J.: Transaction Publish-ers, 1973), 26
8. Jim Collins, *Good to Great: Why Some Companies Make the Leap . . . and Others Don't* (New York: HarperBusiness, 2001), 20, 39.
9. Malcolm Gladwell, "The Talent Myth," *New Yorker*, July 22, 2002. He argues that "smart people" may be "overrated": "The talent myth assumes that people make organiza-tions smart. More often than not, it is the other way around," http://www.gladwell.com/2002/2002_07_22_a_talent.htm (accessed April 4, 2008). As evidence, he points to successful places with effective systems, such as Southwest Airlines, Wal-Mart, and Procter & Gamble, versus talent factories such as Enron (and McKinsey).
10. Vivek Agrawal, James Manyika, and John Richard, "Matching People and Jobs," *McKin-sey Quarterly*, special edition 2003; Allan Schweyer, "An Internal War for Talent," *Inc.* (April 2005).
11. Carl Schramm, *The Entrepreneurial Imperative: How America's Economic Miracle Will Reshape the World (and Change Your Life)* (New York: Collins, 2006), 11, 49, 78.

12. Robert Fairlie, *Kauffman Index of Entrepreneurial Activity, 1996–2006* (Kansas City, Mo.: Ewing Marion Kauffman Foundation, 2005), 1; Paul D. Reynolds et al., *The Entrepreneur Next Door: Characteristics of Individuals Starting Companies in America: An Executive Summary of the Panel Study of Entrepreneurial Dynamics* (Kansas City, Mo.: Ewing Marion Kauffman Foundation, 2002), 14; Michael Selz, "Survey Finds 37% of Households Involved in Small-Business Arena," *Wall Street Journal,* December 13, 1996.

13. Carolyn Martin and Bruce Tulgan, *Executive Summary: Managing the Generation Mix 2007* (New Haven, Conn.: Rainmakerthinking, 2006), 3, 25.

14. Richard Florida, "The Rise of the Creative Class," *Washington Monthly,* May 2002; Richard Florida, *The Rise of the Creative Class and How It's Transforming Work, Leisure, Community, and Everyday Life* (New York: Perseus, 2002).

15. Michaels, Handfield-Jones, and Axelrod, *The War for Talent,* 11.

16. Michaels, Handfield-Jones, and Axelrod, *The War for Talent,* 29, 11.

17. Michaels, Handfield-Jones, and Axelrod, *The War for Talent,* 4.

18. Emily Caverhill Manns, "Report Summary: Executive Recruiting—The State of the Industry 2007" (Peterborough, N.H.: Kennedy Information, 2007), 2.

19. Fabian Hieronimus, Katharina Schaefer, and Jurgen Schroder, "Using Branding to Attract Talent," *McKinsey Quarterly,* no. 3 (2005).

20. Tamara Erickson and Lynda Gratton, "What It Means to Work Here," *Harvard Business Review* (March 1, 2007).

21. Interview with Gary Erickson, Clif Bar; Gary Erickson with Lois Lorentzen, *Raising the Bar: Integrity and Passion in Life and Business* (San Francisco: Jossey-Bass, 2004).

22. Michaels, Handfield-Jones, and Axelrod, *The War for Talent.*

23. Elinor Mills, "Who's Who of Google Hires," CNet News.com, February 27, 2006, www. news.cnet.com/whos-who-of-Google-hires2100-1030-3-6043231.html (accessed April 24, 2008).

24. Gary Hamel, "Management à la Google," *Wall Street Journal,* April 26, 2006.

25. HR Management, "Generating Leaders GE Style," n.d., http://www.hrmreport/current-issue/article.asp?art=269158&issue=186 (accessed January 4, 2008).

26. Erickson and Gratton, "What It Means to Work Here."

27. Erickson and Gratton, "What It Means to Work Here."

28. James O'Toole and Edward Lawler III, "A Piece of Work," *Fast Company,* no. 106 (June 2006): 87.

29. Jim Bolt, "How Leaders Learn," *Fast Company,* (December 19, 2005); Jim Bolt, "Coaching: The Fad that Won't Go Away," *Fast Company,* (April 10, 2006).

30. Douglas Ready and Jay Conger, "Make Your Company a Talent Factory," *Harvard Business Review* (June 1, 2007).

31. Hamel, "Management à la Google."

32. John Koten, "A Conversation with Scott Cook," *Inc.* (September 2007): 214.

33. Erickson and Gratton, "What It Means to Work Here."

34. *The Hidden Cost of Attrition: Why Retaining Top Talent Remains Mission Critical* (Vancouver, B.C.: People First Solutions, n.d.) According to another estimate, "the true cost of an average performer leaving is 1.5 times salary." Allan Schweyer, "An Internal War for Talent," *Inc.* (April 2005).

35. Michaels, Handfield-Jones, and Axelrod, *The War for Talent,* 42.

36. Douglas MacMillan, "No Office Like a Home Office," *BusinessWeek* (November 15, 2006).

37. Kimberly Palmer, "The New Mommy Track," *U.S. News & World Report,* September 3, 2007, 42–43.

38. Michael Arndt, "Nice Work If You Can Get It," *BusinessWeek* (January 9, 2006).

39. Michael Lewis, *Moneyball: The Art of Winning an Unfair Game* (New York: Norton, 2003); Dan Ackman, "Book Review: Moneyball," *Forbes.com,* May 28, 2003, www.forbes.com/2003/05/28/cx_da_0528bookreview.html (accessed April 24, 2008).

40. Ready and Conger, "Make Your Company a Talent Factory."

41. Ready and Conger, "Make Your Company a Talent Factory."

42. Arthur Levine, *Educating School Leaders: The Rise and Decline of School Leadership Programs* (Washington, D.C.: Education Schools Project, 2005), 1.

43. *Leadership for Student Learning: Reinventing the Principalship* (Washington, D.C.: Institute for Educational Leadership, 2000), 9.

44. Lynn Olson, "Getting Serious about Preparation," *Education Week,* September 12, 2007.

45. Both of these reports are cited in Hess and Kelly, "The Accidental Principal."

46. Denise Hearn, "Education in the Workplace: An Examination of Corporate University Models," *New Foundations,* May 10, 2002, http://www.newfoundations.com/Org Theory/Hearn721.html (accessed January 4, 2008).

47. Lisa Tanner, "Corporate University Approach Taking Hold," *Dallas Business Journal,* July 25, 2003.

48. *Leadership for Student Learning,* 13.

49. Lynn Olson, "More Power to Schools," *Education Week,* November 28, 2007.

50. James Sherk, "An Upside to Inequality?" *BusinessWeek,* July 9 and 16, 2007.

51. Interview with the authors by Christopher Gergen and Gregg Vanourek, *Life Entrepreneurs: Ordinary People Creating Extraordinary Lives* (San Francisco: Jossey-Bass, 2008), 7.

CHAPTER 2. ATTRACTING ENTREPRENEURS TO K–12

1. The author acknowledges the contributions of many people in preparing this chapter. From Public Impact, Emily Ayscue Hassel helped develop some of the key framing ideas and Lucy Steiner compiled research on the qualities of successful entrepreneurs. The chapter draws on, and in some cases is adapted from, a working paper coauthored by Frederick M. Hess and Bryan C. Hassel entitled "Fueling Educational Entrepreneurship: Addressing the Human Capital Challenge," which can be found at www.ksg.harvard.edu/pepg/PDF/Papers/Hess-Hassel_Human_Capital_Policy_PEPG07–06.pdf.

2. Smith and Petersen refer to this collection of people as "a 'hybrid team,' with skills from across the education, business, nonprofit, and public sectors. Public education has as much operational and financial complexity as any business, the mission-driven character of a nonprofit, the content and social complexity inherent in education, and of course the need to be accountable to a diverse public. As such, educational entrepreneurs need to surround themselves with skills and expertise from across these fields." See Kim Smith and Julie Landry Petersen, "What Is Educational Entrepreneurship," in *Educational Entrepreneurship: Realities, Challenges, Possibilities,* ed. Frederick M. Hess (Cambridge, Mass.: Harvard Education Press, 2006), 37–39.

3. See, for example, D. R. Gnyawali and D. S. Fogel, "Environments for Entrepreneurship Development: Key Dimensions and Research Implications," *Entrepreneurship: Theory and Practice* 18, no. 4 (1994); Z. J. Acs and D. B. Audretsch, eds., *Handbook of Entrepreneurship Research: An Interdisciplinary Survey and Introduction* (New York: Springer, 2005);

and L. M. Spencer and S. M. Spencer, *Competence at Work: Models for Superior Performance* (Hoboken, N.J.: Wiley, 1993).

4. Smith and Petersen, "What Is Educational Entrepreneurship," 23.

5. The New Teacher Project, "Overview," n.d., http://www.tntp.org/whoweare/overview. html (accessed September 4, 2007).

6. Personal correspondence with Dena Blank, Teach For America, August 27, 2007.

7. John Chubb and Terry Moe, *Politics, Markets, and America's Schools* (Washington, D.C.: Brookings Institution Press, 1990).

8. Frederick M. Hess, *Spinning Wheels: The Politics of Urban School Reform* (Washington, D.C.: Brookings Institution Press, 2000).

9. Andrew J. Rotherham, *Smart Charter School Caps: A Third Way on Charter School Growth* (Washington, D.C.: Education Sector, 2007), 1.

10. Author's tabulation from information provided in Education Commission of the States, "Charter School Authorizers/Sponsors," n.d., http://mb2.ecs.org/reports/Report. aspx?id=81 (accessed January 11, 2008).

11. Elise Balboni et al., *2007 Charter School Facility Finance Landscape* (New York: Local Initiatives Support Corporation, 2007), 4.

12. Sheree Speakman and Bryan C. Hassel, *Charter School Funding: Inequity's Next Frontier* (Washington, D.C.: Thomas B. Fordham Institute, 2005).

13. J. T. Bond et al., *Highlights of the National Study of the Changing Workforce* (New York: Families and Work Institute, 2003).

14. Susan M. Gates et al., *Who Is Leading Our Schools? An Overview of School Administrators and Their Careers* (Santa Monica, Calif.: RAND, 2003).

15. Hess and Hassel, "Fueling Educational Entrepreneurship," 5.

16. In addition to the initiatives profiled here, there are also several venture-philanthropy firms.

17. Arthur Levine, *Educating School Leaders* (Washington, D.C.: Education Schools Project, 2005).

18. Frederick M. Hess and Andrew P. Kelly, "Learning to Lead: What Gets Taught in Principal-Preparation Programs," *Teachers College Record* 109, no. 1 (2007): 244–74.

19. Frederick M. Hess and Andrew P. Kelley, "An Innovative Look, a Recalcitrant Reality: The Politics of Principal Preparation Programs," *Education Policy* 19, no. 1 (January–March 2005) 155–180.

20. Broad Residency in Urban Education, "About the Residency," n.d., http://www.broad residency.org (accessed April 21, 2008).

21. New Leaders for New Schools, "History," n.d., http://www.nlns.org/NLWeb/History.jsp (accessed April 21, 2008).

22. Teach For America, "Teach For America places largest-ever corps, expanding its impact to 26 regions nationwide," August 15, 2007, www.teachforamerica.com/newsroom/ documents/081507_Largestcorps.htm (accessed January 11, 2008).

23. In addition to this direct teacher-pipeline work, TNTP also provides human resources consulting services to districts and engages in research and advocacy on issues related to the teacher pipeline.

24. The New Teacher Project, "Impact: New York City," n.d., http://www.tntp.org/ourimpact/ impact_nyc.html (accessed April 21, 2008).

25. See, for example, P. Dubini and H. Aldrich, "Personal and Extended Networks Are Central to the Entrepreneurial Process," *Journal of Business Venturing* 6, no. 5 (1991): 305–13; P. Adler and S. Kwon, "Social Capital: Prospects for a New Concept," *Academy of Management Review* 27, no. 1 (2002): 17–40; D. DeCarolis and P. Saparito, "Social Capital, Cognition, and Entrepreneurial Opportunities: A Theoretical Framework," *Entrepreneurship Theory and Practice* 30, no. 1 (2006): 41–56; D. Gnyawali and D. Fogel, "Environments for Entrepreneurship Development: Key Dimensions and Research Implications," *Entrepreneurship Theory and Practice* 18, no. 4 (1994): 43–62.

26. See, for example, Moot Corps Competition, "About," n.d., http://www.mootcorp.org/about.asp (accessed April 21, 2008).

27. Hess and Hassel, "Fueling Educational Entrepreneurship," 5–6.

CHAPTER 3. CATALYZING CAPITAL INVESTMENT

1. Janet Hickey, personal interview, March 6, 2007.

2. Susan Rosengrant and David R. Lampe, *Route 128: Lessons from Boston's High-Tech Community* (New York: Basic Books, 1992).

3. Paul A. Gompers, "A Note on the Venture Capital Industry," Harvard Business School Case 9-295-065 (July 12, 2001).

4. Gompers, "A Note on the Venture Capital Industry."

5. Gompers, "A Note on the Venture Capital Industry."

6. Pension funds are not subject to income tax and are therefore not sensitive to changes in the capital gains tax rate.

7. PricewaterhouseCoopers, "MoneyTree Report," n.d., https://www.pwcmoneytree.com/MTPublic/ns/nav.jsp?page=notice&iden=B (accessed August 4, 2007).

8. Note that each fund may have different investors and even different managers.

9. PricewaterhouseCoopers, "MoneyTree Report."

10. Jeffrey E. Sohl, "Angel Investing: A Market Perspective," in *State of the Art: An Executive Briefing on Cutting Edge Practices in American Angel Investing,* ed. J. May and E. O'Halloran (Charlottesville, Va.: Darden Business Publishing, 2003).

11. Lori Wright, "Angel Market Grows 10 Percent in 2006," press release from the University of New Hampshire, March 19, 2007.

12. Jeffrey E. Sohl, "The Angel Investor Market in 2006: The Angel Market Continues Steady Growth" (Durham, N.H.: University of New Hampshire, Center for Venture Research, 2007).

13. Jeffrey E. Sohl and Jill Areson-Perkins, "Current Trends in the Private Equity Financing of High Tech Ventures: An Analysis of Deal Structure," *Frontiers of Entrepreneurship Research: Proceedings of the Twenty-First Annual Entrepreneurship Research Conference,* ed. William D. Bygrave et al., 2001, http://www.babson.edu/entrep/fer/babson2001/toc/toc.html.

14. Sohl, "The Angel Investor Market in 2006."

15. Sohl and Areson-Perkins, "Current Trends in the Private Equity Financing of High Tech Ventures."

16. Frances M. Amatucci and Jeffrey E. Sohl, "Business Angels: Investment Processes, Outcomes and Current Trends," in *Entrepreneurship: The Engine of Growth,* Vol. 2: *The Process,* ed. A. Zacharakis and S. Spinelli (Westport, Conn., Praeger Perspectives, Greenwood Publishing Group, 2006).

17. Jeffrey E. Sohl, "Angel Investing: Changing Strategies During Volatile Times," *Journal of Entrepreneurial Finance and Business Ventures* 11, no. 2 (2006).

18. See, for example, Angel Capital Education Foundation, "Listing of Groups," n.d., http://www.angelcapitaleducation.org/dir_resources/directory.aspx (accessed January 8, 2008).

19. Jeffrey E. Sohl, "The Organization of the Informal Venture Capital Market," in *Handbook of Research on Venture Capital*, ed. Hans Landstrom (U.K.: Edward Elgar, 2007).

20. Jeffrey M. Silber, *Equity Research: Education and Training* (New York: BMO Capital Markets, 2006).

21. The Education Investor: 2005 Year-End Review and Outlook (Boston: Eduventures, LLC, 2006).

22. The Department of Education has outsourced the accreditation process to regional and national bodies that monitor education quality.

23. Silber, *Equity Research.*

24. Silber, *Equity Research.*

25. See, for example, X Prize Foundation, "Welcome," n.d., http://www.xprize.org/about/index.html (accessed January 8, 2008).

26. "All Shall Have Prizes," *Economist*, March 1, 2007, http://www.economist.com/world/international/displaystory.cfm?story_id=8779419.

27. Silber, *Equity Research.*

28. Carnegie Endowment, "Trade and Globalization," n.d., http://www.globalization101.0rg/index.php?file=issue&pass1=subs&id=8 (accessed October 5, 2007).

29. Jennifer Cheeseman Day and Eric C. Newburger, "The Big Payoff: Educational Attainment and Synthetic Estimates of Work-Life Earnings," U.S. Census Bureau, July 2002, http://www.census.gov/prod/2002pubs/p23–210.pdf (accessed October 5, 2007).

30. Henry Levin et al., "The Costs and Benefits of an Excellent Education for All of America's Children," January 2007, http://www.cbcse.org/media/download_gallery/Leeds_Report_Final_Jan2007.pdf (accessed January 8, 2008).

31. John M. Bridgeland, John J. DiIulio Jr., and Karen Burk Morison, *The Silent Epidemic: Perspectives of High School Dropouts* (Washington, D.C.: Bill & Melinda Gates Foundation, 2006).

32. Of the 65,000 students, there are an average of 5,417 students per grade. In each grade, there is about a 30 percent dropout rate. Thus 1,625 students would be eligible for the initiative, but only about half of those would graduate, at an average cost of $10,000 per student.

33. Defense Venture Catalyst Initiative, "An Overview of the Defense Venture Catalyst Initiative," n.d., http://devenci.dtic.mil/pdf/Overview.pdf (accessed January 10, 2008).

34. Matt Richtel, "Tech Investors Cull Start-Ups for Pentagon," *New York Times*, May 7, 2007.

35. Sohl, "The Organization of the Informal Venture Capital Market."

36. Gavin Don and Richard T. Harrison, *The Equity Risk Capital Market for Young Companies in Scotland, 2000–2004* (Glasgow, U.K.: Scottish Enterprises, January 2006).

37. Josh Lerner et al., "In-Q-Tel," Harvard Business School Case 9-804-146 (February 12, 2004).

38. Sarah Lacy, "Meet the CIA's Venture Capitalist," *BusinessWeek*, May 10, 2005, http://www.businessweek.com/technology/content/may2005/tc20050510_4072_tc_210.htm?chan=search (accessed January 8, 2008).

CHAPTER 4. SOCIAL PURPOSE CAPITAL MARKETS IN K–12

1. Although others may sometimes use the word "sector" to refer to an industry or area of common interest, such as the "education sector" or the "military sector," we have here used "sector" to refer to the economic divisions among sources of capital: the public sector (government), the private sector (business), and the nonprofit sector (philanthropy).

2. Federal Reserve Board, "Testimony of Alan Greenspan," July 17, 2002, http://www.federalreserve.gov/boarddocs/hh/2002/july/testimony.htm (accessed January 10, 2008).

3. *SROI Methodology: Analyzing the Value of Social Purpose Enterprise within a Social Return on Investment Framework* (San Francisco: Roberts Enterprise Development Fund, 2001), 6.

4. Lawrence J. Schweinhart, "How the High/Scope Perry Preschool Study Grew: A Researcher's Tale," *Phi Delta Kappa Center for Evaluation, Development, and Research*, no. 32 (June 2002).

5. Jay P. Greene, "Buckets into the Sea: Why Philanthropy Isn't Changing Schools, and How It Could," in *With the Best of Intentions: How Philanthropy Is Reshaping K–12 Public Education*, ed. Frederick M. Hess (Cambridge, Mass.: Harvard Education Press, 2005).

6. Personal communication with entrepreneur who prefers to remain anonymous, August 2007. Because the social purpose capital market for education is so small, several entrepreneurs with whom we spoke asked not to be identified so they could be as candid as possible.

7. William A. Sahlman et al., *The Entrepreneurial Venture* (Cambridge, Mass.: Harvard Business School Press, 1999).

8. George Overholser, *Patient Capital: The Next Step Forward?* (New York: Nonprofit Finance Fund, 2006), 12.

9. *MoneyTree Report* (New York: PricewaterhouseCoopers and the National Venture Capital Association, 2005); *Distribution of Foundation Grants by Subject Categories, circa 2005* (New York: Foundation Center, 2007).

10. Jed Emerson and Sheila Bonini, *The Blended Value Map: Tracking the Intersects and Opportunities of Economic, Social and Environmental Value Creation* (Menlo Park, Calif.: William and Flora Hewlett Foundation, 2003); Beth Sirull, "Private Equity, Public Good," *Stanford Social Innovation Review* 5, no. 4 (Fall 2007).

11. U.S. Census Bureau, *Federal Register* 72, no. 21 (February 1, 2007), http://www.census.gov/cac/www/pdf/cacnomination.aian.020107.pdf (accessed January 10, 2008).

12. U.S. Department of Education, "Department of Education Fiscal Year 2008 Congressional Action," December 19, 2007, http://www.ed.gov/about/overview/budget/budget08/08action.pdf (accessed January 10, 2008).

13. U.S. Department of Health and Human Services, "Budget," May 16, 2007, http://www.nih.gov/about/budget.htm, http://www.nih.gov/about/researchhighlights/index.htm (accessed January 10, 2008).

14. Sirull, "Private Equity, Public Good."

15. D. T. Conley, *Toward a More Comprehensive Conception of College Readiness* (Eugene, Ore.: Educational Policy Improvement Center, 2007).

16. Paul Brest, "Creating an Online Information Marketplace for Giving," The William and Flora Hewlett Foundation, n.d., http://annualreport.hewlett.org/statement/index.asp (accessed January 8, 2008).

17. Interview with Kat Rosqueta, Center for High Impact Philanthropy (August 2007).

18. Ben Gose, "Accounting Helps Charities Raise Growth Funds, for a Price," *Chronicle of Philanthropy* 19, no. 22 (September 6, 2007): 13.

19. See, for example, National Venture Capital Association, "The Venture Capital Industry," n.d., http://www.nvca.org/def.html (accessed January 10, 2008).

20. Virginia M. Esposito, ed. *Conscience and Community: The Legacy of Paul Ylvisaker* (New York: Peter Lang, 1999), 346.

21. Stephanie Strom, "Businesses Try to Make Money and Save the World," *New York Times,* May 6, 2007.

22. Keith Hammonds, "Now the Good News . . . ," *Fast Company*, no. 121 (December 2007).

23. William F. Meehan et al., "Investing in Society: Why We Need a More Efficient Social Capital Market—and How We Can Get There," *Stanford Social Innovation Review* 1, no. 4 (2004).

24. Overholser, *Patient Capital: The Next Step Forward?*, 3.

25. Interview with Tim Freundlich, Calvert Foundation, July 2007.

26. Jeffrey Bradach, "Going to Scale: The Challenge of Replicating Social Programs," *Stanford Social Innovation Review* 1, no. 1 (2003): 25.

CHAPTER 5. BARRIERS TO ENTRY

1. Chris Whittle, *Crash Course* (New York: Berkley Publishing Group, 2005).

2. Marcia Angell, *The Truth about the Drug Companies* (New York: Random House, 2005).

3. The total market of $15.5 billion includes basal, supplemental, reference, assessment, enterprise software/services, and professional development. J. Mark Jackson et al., *K–12 Solutions: Learning Markets & Opportunities* (Boston: Eduventures, 2004).

4. Jackson et al., *K–12 Solutions.* Hardware, software/services, and 50 percent of assessment totals $7.6 billion. National Center for Education Statistics, *Revenues and Expenditures for Public Elementary and Secondary Education: School Year 2004–2005 (Fiscal Year 2005) First Look* (Washington, D.C.: U.S. Department of Education, 2007). Current expenditures equal $424.6 billion.

5. "From Clipboards to Keyboards," *Economist,* May 17, 2007.

6. Kathleen Kennedy Manzo and Andrew Trotter, "Houghton-Harcourt Deal Seen as Yielding Big 3 of Textbooks," *Education Week,* July 16, 2007.

7. School Specialty also has revenue in the billions, but its focus on supplies leads us to exclude the organization from this analysis.

8. "2007 1st Half M&A Trends Report" (New York: Berkery Noyes Investment Bankers, 2007). This analysis carries us down through the $1.5 million bucket, but our experience on the ground tells us that there are many more small businesses below this revenue threshold that were not represented.

9. See, for example, Chester E. Finn Jr. and Diane Ravitch, *The Mad, Mad World of Textbook Adoption* (Washington, D.C.: Thomas B. Fordham Institute, 2004).

CHAPTER 7. QUALITY CONTROL IN A DYNAMIC SECTOR

1. There are, of course, many more causes of the paucity of inventiveness and enterprise in the traditional system, including collective bargaining contracts, school board poli-

tics, and personnel systems that do not exactly beckon innovators to work in public education.

2. See, for example, Children First, "Surveys," n.d., http://schools.nyc.gov/Offices/Children First/Accountability/Surveys/default.htm (accessed January 1, 2008).

CHAPTER 8. REINVENTING A RESEARCH AND DEVELOPMENT CAPACITY

1. The authors wish to thank Larry Berger for his detailed comments on an earlier draft.

2. The institutional and organizational structure for our current public education system came into existence early in the twentieth century and quickly became the dominant paradigm for educating America's youth. The history of the emergence of this system is detailed in David Tyack, *The One Best System* (Cambridge, Mass.: Harvard University Press, 1997).

3. Hugh Burkhardt and Alan H. Schoenfeld, "Improving Educational Research: Toward a More Useful, More Influential, and Better-Funded Enterprise," *Educational Researcher* 32, no. 9 (December 2003): 3–14.

4. Whittle estimates an even smaller amount, $260 million per year, spent currently in the United States on educational R&D. See Chris Whittle, *Crash Course: Imagining a Better Future for Public Education* (New York: Riverhead, 2005).

5. This chapter focuses on problem solving R&D in education. Professional schools of education are key institutions supporting this activity; while our remarks here can be interpreted as an implied criticism of these institutions, the concerns raised here can, and have, been raised more generally about professional schools. Warren G. Bennis and James O'Toole, for instance, offer a similar critique of graduate schools of business in "How Business Schools Lost Their Way," *Harvard Business Review* (May 1, 2005).

6. In further discussion of this point, Hiebert, Gallimore, and Stigler detail an attractive vision for developing a professional knowledge base out of and in conjunction with clinical practice. That these ideas are viewed as innovative, which they are, is quite telling about the state of this overall enterprise. See James Hiebert, Ronald Gallimore, and James W. Stigler, "A Knowledge Base for the Teaching Profession: What Would It Look Like and How Can We Get One?" *Educational Researcher* 31, no. 5 (June–July 2002): 3–15.

7. Tom Corcoran, Susan H. Fuhrman, and Carol L. Belcher, "The District Role in Instructional Improvement," *Phi Delta Kappan* 83, no. 1 (September 2001): 78–84. It is noteworthy that this phenomenon is not limited to education. For a similar account in the business context, see Jeffrey Pfeffer and Robert I. Sutton, *Hard Facts, Dangerous Half-Truths and Total Nonsense: Profiting from Evidence-Based Management* (Cambridge, Mass.: Harvard Business School Press, 2006).

8. Cohen, Moffitt, and Goldin explore the dilemmas embedded in effective policy actions for practice improvement. They argue that the more ambitious the policy intent, the less likely it is that a ready capability exists to advance these ends. In this context, districts make choices in an effort to manage these new demands that often have the consequence of subverting the ambitious intents of the policy. In the end, neither the necessary innovation development nor capacity building to advance use occurs. See David K. Cohen, Susan L. Moffit, and Simona Goldin, "Policy and Practice: The Dilemma," *American Journal of Education* 113, no. 4 (August 2007).

9. See research studies by Melissa Roderick and colleagues at www.consortium-chicago. org.

10. These remarkable developments have been documented by the High Performing Learning Communities Project at the Learning Research and Development Center (LRDC) at the University of Pittsburgh. Many of the lessons learned here proved formative for subsequent LRDC work in initiating its Institute for Learning.

11. Louis Gomez and Guilbert C. Hentschke, "K–12 Education: The Role of For-Profit Providers" in *Research and Practice in Education: Toward a Reconciliation,* ed. John Bransford et al. (Cambridge, Mass.: Harvard University Press, forthcoming).

12. For several years, Bryk served on the investment partners' board of the NewSchools Venture Fund, where occasionally he would review proposals for support from social entrepreneurs seeking to develop new tools and services for the educational marketplace. Products aimed at the home marketplace were regularly viewed as better financial bets than those aimed at schools.

13. Committee on a Strategic Education Research Partnership, *Strategic Education Research Partnership* (Washington, D.C.: National Academies Press, 2003).

14. Whittle, *Crash Course.*

15. Learning Federation, *Learning Science and Technology Roadmap* (Washington, D.C.: Federation of American Scientists, 2003).

16. We have deliberately chosen this title of design-engineering-development efforts to distinguish it from more conventional educational research that has historically been conducted under the umbrella of "research and development." Following arguments by Burkhardt and Schoenfeld, in "Improving Research," the emphasis in this applied research is on the acts of design, engineering (for example, rapid prototyping, field testing, revision, retesting, et cetera), and development of capacity for use at scale. While such work is ripe for also teasing out more basic conceptual understandings about practice (for example, general knowledge development), in a DED environment this is now viewed as a valuable byproduct. In this regard, DED stands in sharp contrast to design experiments where the primary intent is usually new knowledge development.

17. In extolling the virtues of new forms of partnership, we are also cognizant that many potentially serious pitfalls may also lie ahead. The design of the enterprise itself demands critical inquiry and may be best thought of as an evolutionary design problem where more formal institutional structures take final form through the actual conduct of the work.

18. We wish specifically to acknowledge the contributions of Diana Joseph, Nichole Pinkard, Lisa Walker, and Lisa Rosen, with whom we have collaborated on developing the overall framework for IIS. For a further discussion of current work activities of IIS, see Anthony S. Bryk and Louis Gomez, *The Research and Practice of Shaping Schools toward Evidence-Based Cultures* (a symposium presented at the AERA annual meeting in Chicago in 2007; papers available at www.iisrd.org). More generally, we wish to acknowledge the support of the Center for Urban School Improvement at the University of Chicago, which is the organizational hub for IIS and its affiliated charter school, North Kenwood Oakland, whose principal (Stacey Beardsley) and staff have collaborated in numerous alpha development activities of IIS. Similarly, we wish to acknowledge the contributions to this work by the Literacy Collaborative at Ohio State University (Gay Pinnell and Pat Scharer) and Lesley University (Irene Fountas). In addition

to bringing their literacy teaching and learning expertise to the group, they have been coinvestigators in our larger beta-level field trials. Finally, a special thanks to our commercial partners, Teachscape and Wireless Generation. Their respective leaders, Mark Atkinson and Larry Berger, have been very supportive of our R&D and brought the substantial technical expertise of their companies to bear on this work. Funds from the University of Chicago endowment helped establish a technology group within USI, out of which came IIS. Core funding for the work of IIS comes from multiyear general operating support from the MacArthur Foundation and the Hewlett Foundation. This is supplemented by additional federal grants for specific projects. Combined, IIS currently operates on a budget of about $1.5 million a year.

19. To be clear, we are referring here simply to the incorporation of these new tools for administration and collection of student data in regular classroom practice. In contrast, the ongoing analyses of these data and drawing out the implications for changing instruction can be much more complex. The degree of the latter, however, depends on the nature of the instructional system in which these data are embedded. For example, in a basal-driven reading curriculum, data integration may simply consist of something like: "If the score falls below some cut point, go back and reteach pages yy to zz." In contrast, in a comprehensive literacy curriculum, which seeks to integrate skill-development activities in the context of broader literacy activities, the prescription phase for differentiating instruction can be much more complex. As the complexity of the task increases, new demands are placed on teacher learning, the likelihood of teachers experiencing failure in these new tasks increases, and maladaptions that divert efforts away from the original ambitious reform objectives are likely. Again, see Cohen, Moffit, and Goldin, "Policy and Practice."

20. It is important to note that even at the simple end of the innovation continuum, practices like these are often undertaken in a superficial manner. In the case of ten-week formative assessments, for example, use of this data might mean simply going back and repeating previous lessons even though they did not work the first time.

21. The roots for this argument can be found in Thomas Friedman, *The World Is Flat: A Brief History of the Twenty-first Century* (New York: Farrar, Straus, and Giroux, 2005). The educational implications for this are teased out in Frank Levy and Richard J. Murnane, *The New Division of Labor: How Computers Are Creating the Next Job Market* (New York: Russell Sage Foundation, 2004) and Daniel H. Pink, *A Whole New Mind: Moving from the Information Age to the Conceptual Age* (New York: Riverhead, 2005).

22. We note that District 2 no longer exists within the New York City Public Schools. It disappeared as part of the larger district reorganization under Joel Klein.

23. This is a central argument in Cohen, Moffit, and Goldin, "Policy and Practice."

24. The Success for All Foundation and the National Writing Projects are two other good examples of very different intermediate organizations that have both been successful in sustained school-improvement DED work.

25. This is closely related to the idea of professional development schools that has had salience in education since the 1990s. The idea discussed here, however, entails a considerably more radical change than we have seen to date in most professional development schools. Basically, professional development schools accept as given most of the organizational constraints of public schools and schools of education and seek greater collaboration among these two parties, given these constraints. While signifi-

cant improvements have surely occurred, they still fall far short of the teaching-hospital image that originally inspired this movement.

26. Julian E. Orr, *Talking about Machines: An Ethnography of a Modern Job* (Ithaca, N.Y.: Cornell University Press, 1996).

27. Much of the initial expertise base for District 2 included consultants and staff developers from Australia and New Zealand, where many aspects of what we now term comprehensive literacy were first developed: District 2 was not an immaculate conception but rather drew on an extensive preexisting human, intellectual, and social resource base to catalyze its own subsequent developments.

28. For related work on this topic, see Coburn's analysis of changes in classroom practice in California that occurred as a consequence of a decade of policy efforts to enhance literacy instruction. Cynthia E. Coburn, "Beyond Decoupling: Rethinking the Relationship between the Institutional Environment and the Classroom," *Sociology of Education* 77, no. 3 (July 2004): 211–44.

29. The DLLT tool is designed both to provide scientific evidence about teacher development and to be used clinically by literacy coaches and teachers in charting out professional development plans. For a further discussion of DLLT, see David Kerbow et al., *Measuring Change in the Practice of Literacy Teachers* (under review, currently available online as a technical report at www.iisrd.org).

30. One interesting example in this regard is the technology development efforts in the Chicago Public Schools led by David Vitale. Even though technology has changed virtually every workplace, it has failed in many districts to gain a stable toehold in the general revenue budget. Vitale's strategy was to fund this as a capital improvement. Although some parts of the project, such as wiring buildings and network infrastructure, were truly capital items, they also folded in here staff training, human resource infrastructure, and leasing arrangements to replace technology on a regular basis. In other districts, providing for these latter aspects of a technology infrastructure might have to compete with textbook purchases and other instructional supplies. Through this fiscal strategy, Vitale guaranteed that an important district development would be buffered from other competing demands, even as the district went through several years of general budget retrenchment.

31. The ideas discussed in this section draw heavily from an ongoing collaboration within IIS, which comes largely from a larger working manuscript, written with Nichole Pinkard, Lisa Rosen, and Lisa Walker.

32. To the extent that evidence is brought to bear here at all, the natural tendency would be to look at student learning gains (value-added indicators) to evaluate program effectiveness. While this does provide overall summative evidence, it says little about where in the microlevel causal cascade improvements might be engineered.

33. For a further elaboration, see Ted Kolderie, *Education Evolving: Innovating with School and Schooling* (unpublished manuscript, 2007).

34. This section is a capsule summary of a separate working paper in progress.

35. While we posit that the core elements in the framework summarized here are essential for innovation, this set of propositions are and should be subject to empirical study. Inevitably, they will be modified, perhaps substantially, through formal study and practical experience. Thus, a significant aspect of the overall DED enterprise involves extending this conversation, thereby further detailing these key elements and how

they interrelate with one another to form a useful theory of practice improvement in education.

36. For a conceptual and empirical account on these points in the context of technology use in schools, see Yong Zhao and Kenneth A. Frank, "Factors Affecting Tech Use in Schools," *American Educational Research Journal* 40, no. 4 (Winter 2003).

37. For an account of school context effects on efforts to improve reading instruction, see Coburn, "Beyond Decoupling."

38. To complete the framework, we should also add that each school exists within an external institutional environment, fashioned by district, state, and federal policies that provide resources and constraints, as well as incentives and sanctions, which aim to delimit and control appropriate individual behavior. While reform efforts now seek to make this environment more coherent and aligned, nonetheless it continues to exert a largely entropic effect as schools remain highly open to its multiple, often competing influences.

39. For a summary of foundational work along these lines, see Fred M. Newmann and Associates, *Authentic Achievement: Restructuring Schools for Intellectual Quality* (San Francisco: Jossey-Bass, 1996). For a large-scale, longitudinal analysis of school organizational change and its effects on enhancing student learning, see Anthony S. Bryk et al., *Organizing Schools for Improvement* (Chicago: University of Chicago Press, in preparation).

CHAPTER 9. BREAKING REGULATORY BARRIERS TO REFORM

1. See Frederick M. Hess, ed. *With the Best of Intentions: How Philanthropy Is Reshaping K–12 Education* (Cambridge, Mass.: Harvard Education Press, 2005).

2. John E. Chubb and Terry M. Moe, *Politics, Markets, and America's Schools* (Washington, D.C.: Brookings Institution, 1990).

3. Terry M. Moe, "The Politics of Bureaucratic Structure," in *Can the Government Govern?*, ed. John E. Chubb and Paul E. Peterson (Washington, D.C.: Brookings Institution, 1989).

4. Moe, "The Politics Of Bureaucratic Structure."

5. Daniel Weintraub, "A Murky Picture: An Attempted Takeover Goes Awry," *Education Next* 7, no. 3 (Summer 2007); Charles Taylor Kerchner, "A Ray of Hope: Politics May Still Save L.A. Schools," *Education Next* 7, no. 3 (Summer 2007).

6. Joe Williams, *National Model or Temporary Opportunity: The Oakland Education Reform Story* (Washington, D.C.: Center for Education Reform, 2007).

7. See, for example, "Anti-Voucher Movement Donations Pour In," *Associated Press*, September 18, 2007.

8. Catherine Candisky, "Teachers behind Dann's Strategy?" *Columbus Dispatch*, October 2, 2007.

9. Guy Darst, "Mass Testing," *Wall Street Journal*, September 22, 2007.

10. Lydia Rainey et al., *Quantity Counts: The Growth of Charter School Management Organizations* (Seattle: University of Washington, National Charter School Research Project, 2007).

11. Joe Williams, "Games Charter Opponents Play: How Local School Boards—and Their Allies—Block the Competition," *Education Next* 7, no. 1 (Winter 2007).

12. Frederick M. Hess and Chester E. Finn Jr., "What Innovators Can, and Cannot, Do: Squeezing into Local Markets and Cutting Deals," *Education Next* 7, no. 2 (Spring 2007).

13. Angus McBeath, "Creating Successful Schools," Pioneer Institute for Public Policy Research: 2005 Lovett C. Peters Lecture in Public Policy 59 (February 2006).

14. Jay P. Greene, "Buckets into the Sea: Why Philanthropy Isn't Changing Schools, and How It Could," Andrew J. Rotherham, "Teaching Fishing or Giving Away Fish? Grantmaking for Research, Policy, and Advocacy"; and Bryan C. Hassel and Amy Way, "Choosing To Fund School Choice," all in Hess, *With the Best of Intentions*; and Steven F. Wilson, "Challenge the Status Quo," *Education Next* 7, no. 2 (Spring 2007).

15. Lydia Rainey et al., *Quantity Counts*.

16. Hugh Rice Kelly and Richard W. Weekley, *Template for Reform: How Texas Is Restoring Its Civil Justice System* (Austin: Texans for Lawsuit Reform, 2006).

17. Interview with Greg Brock, All Children Matter, September 2007.

18. Interview with Joe Williams, Democrats for Education Reform, September 2007.

19. Interview with Joe Williams, Democrats for Education Reform, September 2007.

CHAPTER 10. SCHOOLS, TOOLS, AND RULES

1. Alfred E. Kahn, "Deregulation and Vested Interests: The Case of Airlines," in *The Political Economy of Deregulation: Interest Groups in the Regulatory Process,* ed. Roger G. Noll and Bruce M. Owen (Washington, D.C.: AEI Press, 1983), 139–40.

2. AnnaLee Saxenian, *Regional Advantage: Culture and Competition in Silicon Valley and Route 128* (Cambridge, Mass.: Harvard University Press, 1994), 6–7.

3. For more extensive accounts of the Milwaukee Parental Choice Program, see Frederick M. Hess, *Revolution at the Margins: The Impact of Competition on Urban School Systems* (Washington, D.C.: Brookings Institution Press, 2002) or John F. Witte, *The Market Approach to Education: An Analysis of America's First Voucher Program* (Princeton, N.J.: Princeton University, 2001).

4. Chong-Moon Lee et al., "The Silicon Valley Habitat," in Chong-Moon Lee et al., *The Silicon Valley Edge: A Habit for Innovation and Entrepreneurship* (Stanford, Calif.: Stanford University Press, 2000), 3, 6.

5. Rachel Konrad, "Gore Joins Major Venture Capital Firm," *Associated Press,* November 12, 2007, http://hosted.ap.org/dynamic/stories/G/GORE_VENTURE_CAPITALIST (accessed November 13, 2007).

6. Paul London, *The Competition Solution: The Bipartisan Solution behind American Prosperity* (Washington, D.C.: AEI Press, 2005), 5.

7. EdVoice, "Welcome to EdVoice," n.d., http://www.edvoice.org/Home/tabid/36/Default.aspx (accessed January 31, 2008).

8. Robert Gammon, "Eli's Experiment," *East Bay Express News,* October 10, 2007.

About the Contributors

Larry Berger is CEO and cofounder of Wireless Generation, an education company with offices in New York, Atlanta, Dallas, and Washington, D.C., that pioneered the adaptation of mobile technologies for use in managing and improving teaching and learning in prekindergarten through sixth grade. Berger led the invention of Wireless Generation's mCLASS system, which enables educators to administer early reading and math formative assessments using handheld computers, then immediately receive easy-to-understand Web-based reports that help educators use data to make decisions about instruction. Prior to launching Wireless Generation, he helped launch a series of technology playgrounds for the Children's Aid Society.

Anthony S. Bryk is president of the Carnegie Foundation for the Advancement of Teaching. Formerly, he held the Spencer Chair in Organizational Studies in the School of Education and the Graduate School of Business at Stanford University. As the Marshall Field IV Professor of Urban Education and Sociology at the University of Chicago, he was founding director of the Center for Urban School Improvement and launched the university's professional development charter school in the North Kenwood/Oakland neighborhood of Chicago. Bryk is also the founding director of the Consortium on Chicago School Research, a federation of Chicago-area research organizations. In 2003, he was awarded the Thomas B. Fordham Foundation Prize for Distinguished Contributions to Educational Scholarship and the Distinguished Career Contributions Award from the American Educational Research Association.

Matt Candler is CEO of New Schools for New Orleans. He has taught and coached at the elementary, middle, and high school levels, and he helped build the main operations center for the 1996 Olympics in his hometown of Atlanta. He founded a consulting practice specializing in start-up support for new charter founders and cofounded a charter school in North Carolina. He then joined the KIPP Foundation in 2001 as vice president of school development, where his team established thirty-seven new schools. Candler served as the founding COO of the New York City Center for Charter School Excellence, which provides support to charter schools in New York.

Chester E. Finn Jr. is president of the Thomas B. Fordham Foundation and a senior fellow at Stanford's Hoover Institution. During his career, Finn has served as a professor of education policy at Vanderbilt University, counsel to the U.S. Ambassador to India, legislative director in the office of former senator Daniel Patrick Moynihan, and as an assistant secretary of education for research and improvement. He serves on the board of numerous organizations concerned with primary and secondary schooling and has authored fourteen books and over 350 articles. His work has appeared in the *Weekly Standard,* the *Christian Science Monitor,* the *Wall Street Journal,* the *Washington Post,* the *New York Times, Education Week, Harvard Business Review,* and the *Boston Globe.*

Christopher Gergen is a founding partner of New Mountain Ventures and cofounder and chairman of SMARTHINKING, the country's leading online tutoring provider. His other entrepreneurial ventures include helping launch Entrepreneur Corps, a national service initiative sponsored by AmeriCorps VISTA. Gergen is on the founding board of E. L. Haynes Public Charter School in Washington, D.C., and is founder and former director of Lead!, a nonprofit leadership and entrepreneurship program for local high school students. He served as vice president of new market development for K12 Inc., where he led efforts to introduce K12's multimedia curriculum and online learning platform into public schools. Prior to joining K12, Gergen was the COO and vice president of business development and strategy for New American Schools. He is currently director of the Entrepreneurial Leadership Initiative at the Terry Sanford Institute of Public Policy at Duke University. He is coauthor of *Life Entrepreneurs: Ordinary People Creating Extraordinary Lives* (Jossey-Bass, 2008).

Louis M. Gomez is the Aon Professor of Learning Sciences at Northwestern University and codirector of the Center for Learning Technologies in Urban Schools, a National Science Foundation–sponsored partnership of the Chicago Public Schools, the Detroit Public Schools, the University of Michigan, and Northwestern University. He has also served as codirector of Northwestern's Learning Through Collaborative Visualization Project. Before joining the faculty at Northwestern, Gomez was director of human-computer systems research at Bellcore in Morristown, New Jersey. He is chair of the Educational Testing Service Visiting Panel of Research and is a recipient of the Spencer Foundation Mentorship Award.

Bryan C. Hassel is codirector of Public Impact. He consults nationally on charter schools and many aspects of public school reform, including district restructuring, comprehensive school reform, and teaching quality. President George W. Bush appointed him to serve on the national Commission on Excellence in Special Education, which produced its report in July 2002. In addition to numerous articles, monographs, and how-to guides for practitioners, Hassel is coauthor of *Picky Parent Guide: Choose Your Child's School with Confidence* (Armchair Press, 2004), author of *The Charter School Challenge: Avoiding the Pitfalls, Fulfilling the Promise* (Brookings Institution Press, 1999), and coeditor of *Learning from School Choice* (Brookings Institution Press, 1998).

Frederick M. Hess is a resident scholar and the director of education policy studies at the American Enterprise Institute. His many books include *When Research Matters* (Harvard Education Press, 2008), *No Remedy Left Behind* (coedited with Chester E. Finn Jr.; AEI Press, 2007), *No Child Left Behind: A Primer* (Peter Lang, 2006), *Educational Entrepre-*

neurship (Harvard Education Press, 2006), and *Common Sense School Reform* (Palgrave Macmillan, 2004). His publications have appeared in numerous outlets including *Harvard Educational Review, Teachers College Record, Education Week, Phi Delta Kappan, Education Next,* the *Washington Post,* and the *Boston Globe.* Hess currently serves on the review board for the Broad Prize in Urban Education and as a member of the research advisory board for the National Center on Educational Accountability. He is a former high school social studies teacher and former professor of education and government at the University of Virginia.

Joseph Keeney is founder and CEO of 4th Sector Solutions, Inc., a consulting firm that provides organizational capacity building and business process management services to public and private educational organizations. Keeney has more than fifteen years of education industry and consulting experience. From 1997 to 2005, he was with Edison Schools, Inc., where he was president of Edison Charter Schools and was responsible for charter school operations, client development, finance, and real estate. He was previously a divisional president and COO of a Fortune 1000 global manufacturer and a corporate strategy consultant at LEK Consulting, Inc.

Ed Kirby manages the Walton Family Foundation's work in the U.S. school-choice movement. Previously he served on, and then directed, the team that launched the Massachusetts charter school initiative in the late 1990s. He began his career as a high school English teacher.

Julie Petersen is the communications director at NewSchools Venture Fund, where she oversees the firm's communications and publications strategy. Prior to joining New-Schools, Petersen spent three years as a writer at *Red Herring Magazine,* a business and technology publication, where she covered venture capital as well as a range of other beats, including education, entrepreneurs, and startups. In 2001, she was named one of the "30 Under 30" business journalists in the country by TJFR Group, for her online and print writing at *Red Herring.*

Daniel Pianko is a principal of Knowledge Investment Partners. He has extensive experience in investment management and education, and since 2000 has been advising, operating, and investing in education businesses, most recently as an associate at Ameriquest Capital Group. He began his career as an investment banker at Goldman Sachs and entered the education industry as director of strategy and planning at LearnNow, a for-profit charter management company later acquired by Edison Schools. Pianko then joined Edison, where he played a key role in the largest privatization of American public schools in Philadelphia.

Kim Smith cofounded NewSchools Venture Fund in 1998 to transform public education by supporting educational entrepreneurs. She served as CEO of NewSchools from 1998 to 2005, and she currently serves as a senior advisor and board member. Smith was a founding team member of Teach For America in 1989 and went on to become founding director of Bay Area Youth Agency Consortium AmeriCorps, a consortium of nonprofits in the San Francisco Bay area. Her background includes marketing experience with Silicon Graphics' Education Industry Group, where she focused on the online learning industry, and experience as the founding director of a trade-show venture. In 2001, she was featured in *Newsweek*'s report on "Women of the Twenty-first Century" as "the kind of woman who will shape America's new century."

David Stevenson is vice president of business development and government affairs for Wireless Generation. In that role, he is responsible for government policy, advocacy, and outreach activities for the company. Stevenson previously managed the product development group at Wireless Generation, where he led the software teams that developed the Texas Primary Reading Inventory, Tejas LEE, and other assessment products. He has developed partnerships with the University of Texas, the University of Chicago, and major publishers, including Pearson, McGraw-Hill, and Harcourt. Prior to joining Wireless Generation, Stevenson was a producer and product manager at Scholastic, where he developed online planning and communication tools for teachers and led an e-commerce development project.

Gregg Vanourek is a founding partner of New Mountain Ventures. Previously, he ran Vanourek Consulting Solutions, LLC, a Colorado-based company specializing in strategic planning, organizational alignment, and market research. He has also served as senior vice president of school development for K12, Inc., and vice president for programs at the Thomas B. Fordham Foundation, where he launched a private scholarship program for underserved youth in Dayton, Ohio. Previously, Vanourek was a research fellow at the Hudson Institute. He is coauthor of *Life Entrepreneurs: Ordinary People Creating Extraordinary Lives* (Jossey-Bass, 2008). He has also written a book on charter schools, *Charter Schools in Action: Renewing Public Education* (with Chester E. Finn Jr. and Bruno V. Manno, Princeton University Press, 2001), several research reports and book chapters, and dozens of articles.

Index